RELATIONSHIP ASTROLOGY

RELATIONSHIP ASTROLOGY

The Beginner's Guide to Charting and Predicting
Love, Romance, Chemistry, and Compatibility

FAIR WINDS

**SARAH
BARTLETT**

Quarto is the authority on a wide range of topics.

Quarto educates, entertains and enriches the lives of our readers—enthusiasts and lovers of hands-on living.

www.QuartoKnows.com

First published in the United States of America in 2016 by
Fair Winds Press, an imprint of
Quarto Publishing Group USA Inc.
100 Cummings Center
Suite 406-L
Beverly, Massachusetts 01915-6101
Telephone: (978) 282-9590
Fax: (978) 283-2742
QuartoKnows.com
Visit our blogs at QuartoKnows.com

20 19 18 17 16   1 2 3 4 5

ISBN: 978-1-59233-727-9

Digital edition published in 2016
eISBN: 978-1-63159-171-6

Library of Congress Cataloging-in-Publication Data

Names: Bartlett, Sarah, 1952- author.
Title: Relationship astrology / Sarah Bartlett.
Description: Beverly : Fair Winds Press, 2016. | Includes bibliographical
   references and index.
Identifiers: LCCN 2016022955 | ISBN 9781592337279 (pbk.)
Subjects: LCSH: Astrology. | Love--Miscellanea. | Mate
   selection--Miscellanea. | Interpersonal relations--Miscellanea.
Classification: LCC BF1729.L6 B37 2016 | DDC 133.5/64677--dc23
LC record available at https://lccn.loc.gov/2016022955

Design: Megan Jones Design
Cover Image: Megan Jones Design

Printed in China

To Jess and Damien.
I would also like to thank my family and friends for being who they are.

CONTENTS

Introduction

When it comes to relationships, why do we attract certain people to us, and why are we, in turn, attracted to them? What kind of chemistry or planetary influence is at work when we first meet our partners? Are we star-crossed lovers, "ill-met by moonlight," as the Bard wrote, or are we a match made in heaven?

I turn to synastry to help answer these questions. Synastry is, simply, a way of comparing and interpreting the natal charts of two people who are in a relationship. When the two charts are juxtaposed, they create an affinity chart that reveals the areas in which you naturally feel comfortable with your partner (or don't). It can also alert you to issues surrounding different emotional needs, as well as provocative energies around sex or power. It also points toward whether the relationship is purely physical (and there's nothing wrong with that!) or there's room for long-term love.

This is an introductory and intermediary guide to synastry for those who know a little about astrology and want to know more. But regardless of your astrological know-how—and of where you are in your search for love—you're sure to find within these pages all that you need to know about understanding (or, at the very least, attempting to understand) the power of relationships. And synastry won't just help you to gain insight into your relationships: It'll also help you to understand other people—and, most importantly, yourself.

To that end, we'll first look at rising signs to see how important they are in the initial "attraction factor" in a relationship and how our sun signs are not all what they seem. Then we'll see how Venus, Mars, and the asteroid Eros all describe our sexual compatibility—but we'll also discover how Pluto unconsciously provokes us to embrace unknown and dark passion. And we'll find out why Saturn is an indicator of long-term commitment, often binding us to our mates in obscure ways that have nothing to do with physical or romantic attraction.

WRITTEN FROM THE HEART

I've been hooked on astrology since I was about twenty-five, simply because it seemed to be a system that offered me a guiding light to help me understand why my relationships at the time were so messy, fraught with drama, and either totally empowering or excruciatingly painful. Idealistic, passionate, and, at the time, terrifyingly possessive, I married far too young (at nineteen) in the belief that it was what I had to do to "catch my man." But a month or so after the wedding, I discovered that my partner had been having an affair with someone since before he married me—and that he was still in the thick of it. Then, when I finally found the confidence to split from him a few years later, the men I met never stuck around for long. To make a long story short, my love life was far from ideal.

I worked in central London and spent my lunch hours in bookshops, where I came across Liz Greene's book, *Relating* (1977). I was hooked, and soon I realized I wasn't alone. That was the trigger I needed to embark on my astrological journey. During my training with the Faculty of Astrological Studies in London, I went to a weekend conference in Brighton where Liz was one of the speakers. Mesmerized by her charismatic style and profound words, I vowed to continue my studies—and nearly thirty years later, Liz became one of my mentors when I studied with the Center for Psychological Astrology in London and was awarded a diploma in their course.

For more than thirty years, I've been a professional consultant astrologer (among other things). I've heard a lot of stories of unrequited love, marriages made in heaven, or terrible, destructive relationships. I've seen them plotted out in affinity charts, and what seems to ring true time and again is that the chart never lies—although people often do. Astrology often mirrors the truths of our relationships and ourselves. I have written this book, then, with both a passion for astrology and a great deal of compassion for those who love from the heart and the soul and who want to learn more about themselves and their potential as they do so.

I truly hope this will book will help you on your own unique relationship journey.

1 The Mystery of Attraction:
Fate, Astrology, and Relationship

Falling in love is an experience that takes us outside of ourselves, so to speak. When we're in love, we feel as if we've been transported into another world or onto a different planet. Sometimes we're totally lost in it in the most wonderful way: We find ourselves caught up in a whirlwind of physical desire, self-indulgence, giving, taking, and fairy-tale romance. And it seems as if all our dreams have come true.

But then things change—for most of us, anyway. Of course, it's not that you or your beloved have changed as people; rather, the fantasy of perfect love we thrust upon each other with romantic gusto begins to wear off. So-called ideals, after all, aren't always compatible with the reality of human nature, and our heady illusions about the perfect lover can become tattered and torn. And when our illusions about our beloved lose their glow, so too do aspects of our own self-image since we're often unconsciously attracted to people very much like ourselves, and we may imbue them with the same qualities that we value in ourselves. So when the rose-colored glasses come off, suddenly we're not so confident in our ability to, say, give and receive pleasure, or in our capacity for dominance, power, or submission—or even in our financial stability. And that can be tough to accept.

FATE AND ENERGIES

But why do we get so worked up about someone in the first place? Is there something at work in the universe that sets us up to meet this special person, and if so, why? Some would call this idea "fate" or say that it's "written in the stars." And there are plenty of people who believe in fate as an external force that overrides free will and controls your life as if you were a marionette on a string. But I'm not one of those people. If you ask me, a viewpoint like this one prevents you from taking responsibility for your actions and choices—and then it's far too easy to blame everything on your circumstances. This is why many people fear astrology: They think astrology determines their future. But from my point of view, astrology is a marvelous reflection of each of us and all of us, at any one moment in time, and of that moment in time. Sure, you might hear astrologers chat about "solar influences" or say that "his Mars sits on my moon," but that's really just jargon. Essentially, we are as much a part of the stars as they are part of us, and the energy of the moment we were born is reflected in the patterns in the sky. So why does it seem as if we're "fated" to meet particular people? What does it all mean?

To my mind, there are two different "energies" at work here. First, what we are "inside" is also what is all around us; that is, what and who we attract to ourselves—and reject from ourselves—is who we are, too. And this quality of attraction and rejection is one way to know ourselves better since the beloved, the rival, or the enemy is as much a reflection of our inner landscapes as the stars are.

The second kind of energy—the one that seems omniscient and uncontrollable, also known as the strange thing called fate—is, to me, the "divine or universal oneness that permeates all." So when we get a sense of it or when we're touched by it, we feel we're being guided toward our purpose by some external force or god. I certainly don't have all the answers to the secrets of the universe here, but perhaps we are simply at one with the cosmos. Ultimately, the thing we call fate and the thing we call free will are, in a sense, that which is *out there* and that which is *in here*, respectively—and they're mysteriously working in tandem.

AS ABOVE, SO BELOW

"As above, so below" is a well-known maxim taken from the Emerald Tablet, an ancient Hermetic work. It is this "all is one" philosophy that weaves its way through astrology; it implies that the stars and planets are patterns in the sky that simply reflect the inner and outer world of the individual—as within, so without. But the planets don't actually "make" us fall in love; they simply reflect that experience. Nor are they responsible for the choices we make or how we act; those things are our responsibility. So there appears to be a kind of merger of "that which is out there" and "that which is inherent in us and is our potential." This can be read through interpreting astrology because astrology is a symbolic language that reads us well, too.

So if we keep thinking, "I blame fate for my terrible love affairs," then we're missing the vital point that *we are our fate*. The ancient Greek philosopher Heraclitus once said that our *daimon*, or "guiding light" or "soul spark," is our fate. This unique inner landscape, as revealed in our birth charts, is a reflection of the moment in time into which we were born—as mirrored in the sky "out there."

IDEALIZATION

Falling in love is when we project an ideal or imagined perfect form of love onto someone and they carry it well to begin with, simply because—in our eyes, at least—that's how they are: perfect. But as the relationship unfolds, we start to see cracks in the perfect work of art we've created. The beloved becomes "real" again, complete with character flaws, warts and all. Just as we projected our desires at their finest onto this person, so do we soon begin to see our shadows—often the dark side of ourselves—across the room, too, and our beloved, the "other," becomes less and less perfect, and eventually that fabulous façade is riddled with more holes than a moth-eaten dress.

So even though the person we love remains the same—after all, she didn't acquire warts, bad breath, and character flaws overnight—we withdraw our idealization and things fall apart. (The other person may be going through the same process with you, too, but not always; in fact, this kind of projection is often one-sided.) And this is where astrology can help. It can reveal to you the truth of a relationship and the way in which that truth is often twisted and ambiguous—but it's a necessity if we are ever to learn anything about ourselves, let alone accept and truly love the other person for who she or he is. That can be difficult: you may not want to learn, or you may just carry on falling in and out of love, or you may simply accept that this is your lot. But these common patterns prevent you from learning about yourself and from moving on.

This is precisely what I love about the "love affair": It teaches you to know yourself and to have more acceptance and tolerance of others. And what I love about astrology is that it's a system and a symbolic language from which you never stop learning. As you work with these symbols, you'll begin to understand the deeper workings of the universe within the individual, too.

BEING "IN" A PLANET

The Renaissance neoplatonist and astrologer Marsilo Ficino wrote extensively on esoteric subjects. In his infamous work (considered to be heretical by the Catholic Church) *The Planets*, published in 1489, Ficino wrote that "we have an entire sky within us," suggesting that the planetary archetypes represented by the signs of the zodiac are deeply rooted within us. Ficino also reminds us that we are "in" a planet when we are filled with, or consumed or overwhelmed by, the qualities of the planetary power or deity, such as passion, desire, or anger.

For example, some of us are so "in" our Neptune, dreaming of romantic love, that we miss the fact that relationships are about reality—dirty socks in the bathroom and sheets in the laundry bin. (There are as many idealistic Neptunian men as women who romance about love and yet can't bear the hard fact that women bleed.) Others of us are so "in" our Venus, Mars, or Eros that all we want is to indulge ourselves in the pleasures of the flesh, compete in the bedroom, or follow our erotic impulses—yet find doing the dishes or paying the bills pure drudgery.

When we are so "in" our suns, we give up our lunar needs to concentrate on our vocation or what matters to us. When we are so "in" our Jupiter, we cannot accept anyone else's point of view and would rather roam the world and fall in love with countless strangers than settle down and let someone else in on our faults. When we are so "in" our moon, we only think of our own needs and forget everyone else's.

As you can see, astrology is not just a symbolic language; it resonates with the power of the archetypal nature of the gods. Never forget that whatever turns you on may not always be what turns your partner on because you may not be "in" the same planet as the other person. (You'll learn more about this in the coming chapters.)

CAN YOU FIND LOVE IN THE BIRTH CHART?

Love itself has a mysterious energy, and it's hard for astrology to define or pin down that energy. Sure, we can say that Venus is about pleasure and the love of self and resting happily in the arms of another; or that Mars represents our physical desire and our instinct for penetrating the love of our partner; and so on. But the word *love* itself has as many different meanings as there are individual birth charts. It will mean one thing to you and something else to your partner—but trying to define it in one neat sentence, from the birth chart alone, is not what this book is about.

Instead, we'll look at the mystery of love from many different angles. We'll examine first attractions; the lofty heights of "fated" compelling attractions; the chemistry between two people; and the issues that arise when we get to know someone well. How do those issues develop? Well, when we first meet as strangers, we're off to a good start simply because we're a mystery to each other. Both people are free from inhibitions and don't have "the power of knowledge" of the other. Once we start to unconsciously hook into the behavior of the other or to react to his defense mechanisms, we drop our own guard and the battle commences. That's when a little knowledge becomes a dangerous thing indeed. We know how to justify our desires; we know how to hurt our partner; and we know how far we can push her. We start to defend our space and to test the conditions of love rather than return to the unconditional love of the stranger.

This is why working with synastry, or astrological compatibility, can give you a more objective viewpoint not only of other people's relationship "stuff," but of your own, too. First, though, chapter 2 will give you a quick refresher course in the basics of astrology.

THE IMPORTANCE OF THE ORDER OF PLANETS IN THIS BOOK

Most astrology books feature a conventional order for looking at aspects between planets. They start with the sun, followed by the moon, Mercury, Venus, Mars, Jupiter, Saturn, Uranus, Neptune, and Pluto—with each planet's contacts to the others in that order. However, in this book, we're going to do things a bit differently, not least since I believe that Saturn is one of the most important planets in the affinity chart. This revised order of planetary contacts is, according to my experience with synastry, the most effective way to observe what's going on in the affinity chart and to construct a complete picture of the relationship and its various dynamics.

For the purposes of this book, then, the planets are ordered as follows:

THE RISING SIGN: **The Attraction Factor**

THE SUN: **Sacred Light**

THE MOON: **Attachment and Need**

SUN/MOON: **Reflecting Each Other's Light**

VENUS: **The Heart's Desire**

MARS: **Excitement and Libido**

VENUS, MARS, AND EROS: **Sexual Attraction**

SATURN: **Binding Love**

MERCURY: **Meeting of Minds**

JUPITER: **Great Expectations**

THE OUTER PLANETS, URANUS, NEPTUNE, AND PLUTO: **A Twist of Fate, Illusion, and Power**

2 Astrology Basics

W hether you already know a lot about astrology or you're a complete beginner, you'll benefit from this simple but important introduction to the symbolic language of the planets according to the dynamics of relationships. Remember that *symbolic* is a key term here: I don't believe that the planets actually "do" anything to us, but that they reflect us, according to the concept of "as above, so below" I mentioned in chapter 1. That said, you'll notice that, throughout this book, I use phrases like "her Mars does this or that to his Venus," or "her Mars makes her partner uncomfortable." This is because verbal punches like these are helpful ways for us to understand how the mysterious symbolic imagery of an affinity chart works.

MAPPING YOUR BIRTH CHART

Here are two reliable websites where you can access your birth chart and find out your planetary placements. It only takes a few minutes, and both sites are free of charge.

- **Astrolabe (www.alabe.com).** This site is the easiest to use. All you need to do is fill in your time, date, and place of birth in the appropriate boxes. It also provides brief information on your natal chart.
- **Astrodienst (www.astro.com).** This comprehensive site is one of the best around, but it's a little trickier to navigate unless you know your stuff. But here's a shortcut. To get a quick view of your chart, do the following:
  Select "Free Horoscopes," and then scroll down and select "Natal Chart, Ascendant." Then you'll have the option to either become a registered user (which is invaluable if you want to store some charts for comparison later) or to create a chart as a guest right away. Fill in the information as required and select "continue."

HOW TO START

Luckily, almost everyone has Internet access these days, and going online is the easiest way to find out your birth chart. Most sites even give you a breakdown of what each planetary placement means. So the first thing you need to do is to map your and your partner's birth charts; you'll need them for the following chapters.

Here are the key features of each planet and its interpretation. You'll find plenty more detail on each of the planets in the relevant chapters of this book, but this quick guide will help you get started if you're new to astrology.

The Sun
What matters to us; our sense of identity; how we want to be recognized; our goals, will, sense of purpose, and potential

The Moon
Our sense of belonging; our habits, reactions, and feelings; how we feel nurtured and how we nurture others; where we feel safe; what we need to feel okay

Venus
Sharing, cooperation; sensual love; values of love, both unconditional and conditional; pleasure, exchange; making ourselves and others happy

Mars
The way in which we go out and get what we want; assertion, courage, competitive urge; physical lust, sexual libido, sexual excitement

Eros
Erotic connection, erotic triggers and fantasies; the wild abandon of sexuality

Saturn
Our Achilles' heel; vulnerability, fear, control, and denial; self-discipline; pretense; mastering the clumsy part of ourselves; turning psychological "lead" into "gold"

Mercury
Communication; the mind, opinions, and making connections; how we absorb and transmit information; our powers of logic and reason

Jupiter

Exaggeration, belief, inflation; finding a meaning in life; grandiosity, greedy desires, excessive lust

Uranus

The urge to rebel; freedom, independence; sudden awakening, revolutionary change, radical ideas, and reformation of the norm; sexual electricity

Neptune

Purification, deception, illusions, idealization, escapism, sacrifice, enchantment; dissolving boundaries; seduction

Pluto

Transformation, obsessive desires, compulsive power, violation, the dark side of love; plummeting to the depths; the taboo and the sacred

THE ELEMENTS: FIRE, EARTH, AIR, AND WATER

The four elements of astrology are four different principles or qualities that are archetypal in nature, and, according to the renowned psychologist Carl Jung, they are also functions of the human psyche. These principles can be applied symbolically not only to characteristics or types of people, but also to ideas, concepts, art, and music, to name a few. In astrology, the presence or absence of elements in an individual horoscope reveals fundamental aspects of the personality.

These principles vary in proportions, depending on the planets in the birth chart that occupy specific elements and manifest as part of our characters. We talk about very fiery people (Fire) or rational or airy types (Air); then there are moody or creative people (Water) and their down-to-earth colleagues (Earth) who are more interested in getting results than dreaming of what might be.

THE FOUR ELEMENTS

The signs for each element are as follows:
FIRE: **Aries, Leo, Sagittarius**
EARTH: **Taurus, Virgo, Capricorn**
AIR: **Gemini, Libra, Aquarius**
WATER: **Cancer, Scorpio, Pisces**

Elemental Balance

If most of your planets fall in any single element in your natal chart, then you can consider yourself to be a strong type of that element. Of course, your planets might also be spread throughout all the elements, which often means it's easier for you to navigate and relate to all the other types—as long as you are aware of these different qualities within yourself.

If you have an excess of one element, such as Fire, you may consider yourself to be a Fire person, so you might find it hard to interact and negotiate with those people whose elements aren't so compatible with Fire, like Water and Earth. (You'll find out which elements play well together—and which ones don't—a bit later in this chapter.)

Here are basic examples of the four different types.

Fire

Fire people are spontaneous, passionate, and active. They have powerful imaginations and look to the future rather than the past.

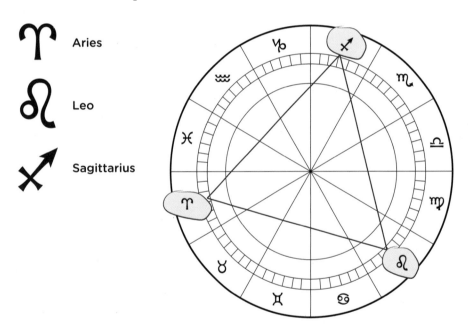

♈ Aries

♌ Leo

♐ Sagittarius

Earth

Earth people are aware of the environment and make use of their talents in the material world. They have an ability to stay grounded and focused.

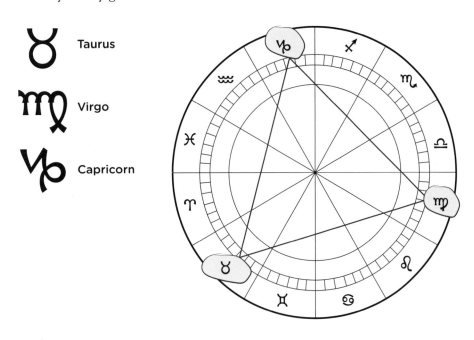

♉ Taurus

♍ Virgo

♑ Capricorn

Air

Air people are diverse and lively but often erratic. They think on their feet and tend to rationalize away their feelings and philosophize about their expectations.

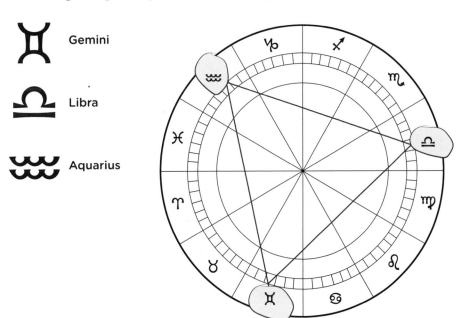

♊ Gemini

♎ Libra

♒ Aquarius

Water

Water people identify with their feelings and are very sensitive to the feelings of others, too. They often live very dramatic or emotional lives.

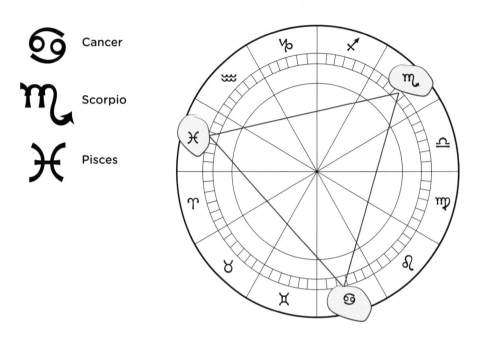

Cancer

Scorpio

Pisces

The Houses

The houses in your birth chart show you the areas of your life in which the experience or quality of the planet in that house (and the sign it's in) will manifest. For example, if you have Venus in the twelfth house, it's likely that you've had many clandestine love affairs (the twelfth house is about hidden places). Or, if you have Venus in the fourth house, you would enjoy love in homey surroundings (the fourth house is about your roots and your comfort zone).

There are various systems for interpreting houses, but the Placidus system is the one that's preferred among most astrologers (myself included). In it, the houses aren't equal slices of the 360-degree "pie" or circle. This is due to different approaches to measuring the rotational movement of the earth, the angle of ecliptic—the apparent pathway of the sun through the zodiac—and other factors that relate to the place and time of birth. But for the purpose of this book, I'll use a chart with the zodiac signs represented in equal segments of 30 degrees to make it easier to see the contacts between planets. The only houses we're going to use are the first and seventh since the cusps of the first and seventh houses are easy to plot on our simplified chart.

ANGLES

The angles in the chart are the Ascendant and Descendant and the M.C. and I.C. The M.C. stands for the Medium Coeli, also known as the Midheaven, and the I.C. stands for the Immum Coeli. The Midheaven is the highest point in the sky that the sun (or planet) can reach in the day's cycle, and the Immum Coeli is the lowest point in its daily cycle. These form the two most important axes in the chart. The Ascendant/Descendant axis is the horizontal axis that crosses your chart, and the I.C./M.C. axis is the vertical axis. These are, if you like, the most personal parts of ourselves that manifest in the tangible world.

Ascendant and Descendant

Basically, the Ascendant, which marks the beginning of the first house and therefore the beginning of the rising sign, is the impression we make on others and the way in which we see the world. The Descendant, which marks the beginning of the seventh house, symbolizes the people "out there" who give us a sense of the "me" in here. We are going to concentrate on this axis and its associated houses: the first and seventh houses.

I.C. and M.C.

The I.C. is the deepest anchor of the self: It is about what roots us and sustains us and how we connect to our source. The M.C. is the spirit in us that guides us and helps to bring to light our solar "sacredness" through our vocational goals. It is like Apollo's arrow: It points to what we are becoming. The M.C. describes our true calling and what we need to achieve in the world in order to fulfill our solar potential.

The M.C. and I.C. are useful in synastry in that if your partner's sun, for example, contacts your M.C., you might find yourself propelled into discovering what your true potential and calling actually is. Or if your partner's moon contacts your I.C., you might discover what a true sense of belonging really means to you. But at this level, I'm only going to work with the Ascendant and Descendant axis since it's the more important of the two axes when it comes to dealing with love relationships.

ASCENDANT/DESCENDANT AXIS

The angles of the birth chart show where and how we interact with the apparent outside world. The Ascendant and Descendant show what we "see" and what we "get" respectively, particularly regarding love relationships.

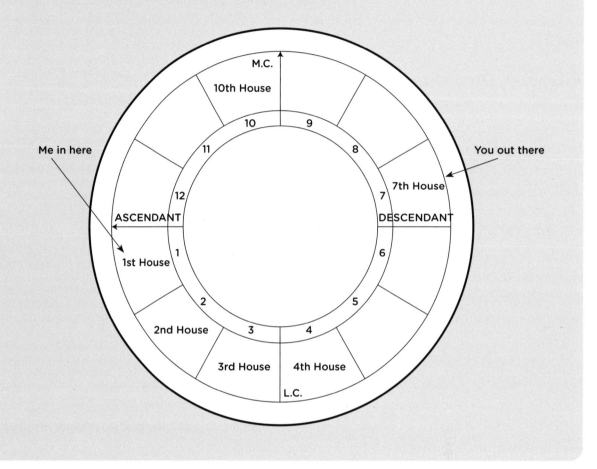

Aspects

In astrology, an aspect refers to the angular relationship, measured in degrees of longitude, between two planets or other celestial bodies (such as the Nodes—the invisible points in the sky where the orbit of the moon crosses the ecliptic—or asteroids) along the ecliptic, the apparent pathway the sun takes around the zodiac. In fact, all the planets in your chart are in aspect to one another.

Here's another way to look at it: The planets in your chart are like a group of dinner guests sitting around an elliptical dining-room table. Each guest can see or at least get a glimpse of all the others, but proximity—how close one guest is to another or the angle at which they're seated—will determine who's

THE ASPECTS

The most important aspects for relationship astrology are the opposition (180 degrees), the square, (90 degrees), the trine (120 degrees) and the conjunction, or same sign planetary position.

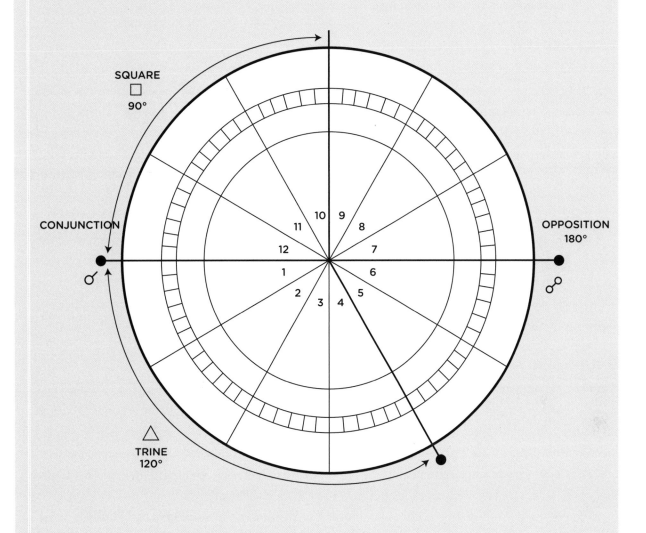

able to touch, chat with, or gaze at whom. Similarly, planetary aspects can be close, awkward, easy, or attractive, to name but a few possibilities. From our point of view across the dinner table, then, we're going to stick to the basic aspects:

- The main challenging ones—the opposition (180 degrees) and the square (90 degrees, or three signs apart)
- The harmonious trine (120 degrees) and therefore same element (or four signs apart)
- The focused conjunction, or the powerful, subjective energy of a same-sign planet

Close Aspects

Traditional astrology looks at contact between charts depending on how close in degree terms the aspects between the planets are. This is known as the orb of the aspect. And the closer the aspect, the more tense or harmonious the contact. For example, if your rising sign were 5 degrees Taurus, and your partner's sun were a conjunction of 5 degrees Taurus, this would be an extremely tight, exact aspect and a highly important one, too, since it would fuse the two of you in an alembic of mutual identification. If, however, your sun were at 18 degrees or more in Taurus, most astrologers would consider this orb to be too wide to make a powerful contact. Most astrologers allow an orb of about 10 degrees for a conjunction and up to 8 degrees for the other aspects.

Luckily, we won't have to worry about that for the purposes of this book since we're mostly working with the basics. I believe that if you do have a planet in the same sign as your partner, even if it's 28 degrees away, a mutual understanding is still present because of the quality of that sign's influence on the planet. This is why we're talking about same element, same signs as well as oppositions and squares as being "signs away" from one another rather than a specific number of degrees away from one another.

Out-of-Sign Aspects

There is one other point I need to note. If your moon is at 1 degree Aries and your partner's moon is at 29 degrees Cancer, then the planets are almost 120 degrees apart (29 degrees for Aries, plus 30 degrees for Taurus, plus 30 degrees for Gemini, plus 29 degrees for Cancer). Even though they are, by sign, in incompatible elements (or three signs apart), a 120-degree angle means they form a trine, the harmonious energy of same-element signs and planets. So if trines are like same-sign elements, how do we interpret this when we'd normally consider Aries to Cancer as a great challenge?

It does seem that any planets within one or even two degrees of the cusp often carry a flavor of the preceding sign or pick up an essence of the following sign. So the 1 degree Aries moon carries with it a little spark of Pisces (Water), and the 29 degrees Cancer moon is almost in Leo, which means it carries a whiff of Fire. Thus, we can say that these two moons would in fact form a supportive relationship with one another because they both "know" the element of the other and could therefore subtly pick up on the duality of the elemental nature of their own moons, too.

"OUT-OF-SIGN" TRINE ASPECT

This "out-of-sign" trine aspect shows that even though the moon in Aries is not normally compatible by sign with Cancer, the exact degree of the moon at 1 degree Aries is actually almost 120 degrees (a trine) away from the moon at 29 degrees of Cancer and therefore they are compatible by degree.

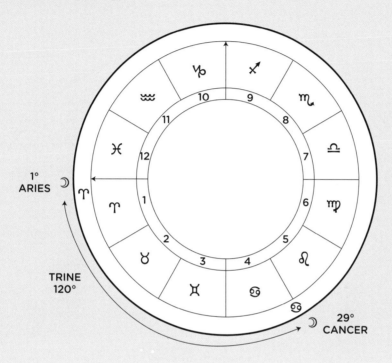

Counting Signs

To make it easier to understand the aspects and to work them out in the affinity chart, I'm going to use a simplified version by counting signs. Here's how it works:

Say, for example, you have the sun in Aries and your partner has the sun in Leo. These are in the same element (Fire) and are therefore harmonious. To count how many signs your partner is away from yours, count the next sign after Aries—Taurus as one, Gemini as two, Cancer as three, and Leo as four (four signs away). Working backward from Aries, the next sign is Pisces as one, Aquarius as two, Capricorn as three, and Sagittarius as four (the other Fire sign). These are harmonious aspects.

Three signs away from Aries is the tense, square aspect (90 degrees) of Cancer; counting back three signs, we arrive at the other square aspect to Aries from Capricorn. The opposition aspect is easy because it's the sign directly opposite the sign in question in the affinity chart—in this case, the opposite of Aries is Libra. These are all challenging aspects.

ELEMENTS OF THE ZODIAC

By counting round the signs of the zodiac you can generally find out which signs are compatible and which aren't. So starting with Aries, count the next sign in a counterclockwise direction, Taurus, as one, then Gemini as two and Cancer as three, which is the tense 90-degree aspect.

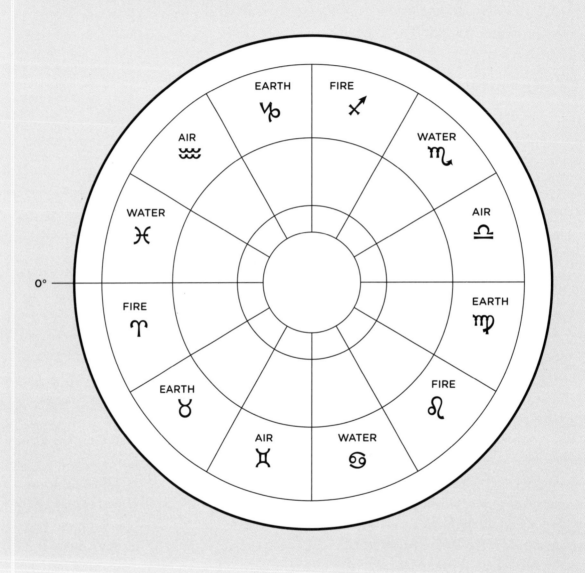

On the Cusp

When looking up your planetary placements in the ephemeris, please note that if you were born with a planet on the cusp (i.e., on the day you were born, the planet in question moved from one sign to the next), then it is essential to know your birth time for a calculation to be made to determine which sign the planet was in at the moment of your birth. Without a time of birth on a cusp day, you won't be able to find out your rising sign or work out which sign a planet is in. If you really can't find out your birth time, then you'll have to resort to asking yourself some questions related to the planet and signs involved—and you'll need to be really honest in your answers—in order to determine the likeliest sign the planet is in. For example, say you have Venus on the cusp of Aries and Taurus, and you can't really be sure which sign it's in. In that case, try this: Write down a few things that give you pleasure—since pleasure is Venus's territory—then see which of the two signs match or are most relevant to them. You may have written, "I take pleasure in slow, sensual massage and foreplay," which means you're more likely to have Venus in Taurus. Or you may have noted, "I take pleasure in spontaneous sex and being the first to suggest it," which means it's likely that your Venus is in Aries. You can do this exercise with your partner, too, if your partner doesn't know his or her birth time and has any planets on the cusp.

BIRTH-CHART CONFIGURATIONS AND CONVENTIONAL ASTROLOGY

The one big problem with most mass-market astrology books is that they can't take into consideration all the configurations going on in the affinity chart—nor can they consider the host of aspects and configurations that are at play in each individual's natal chart. This is where you'll have to work to put the pieces together and to make creative decisions about whether an aspect is helping, supporting, or reinforcing the relationship—or subduing, diminishing, or wrecking its potential.

By the time you've made notes, listed the aspects found, and worked out which are the most important configurations (and which ones aren't so important), you'll begin to see the affinity chart as a map that can help you to travel down the right road toward success within this particular relationship—if that's what you're looking for. Always remember, though, that every individual has her or his own very distinct, unique inner and outer landscapes, and traveling across unknown terrain always turns up a few obstacles. On your relationship journey, your most valuable assets are awareness, acceptance, and openness—so make sure to carry them with you as you travel.

3 Astrological Affinity:
Synastry and the Affinity Chart

You've taken a refresher course in the basics of astrology, so now it's time to create your own affinity chart. This chapter will show you how to do just that—and how to take the first steps in interpreting it.

All relationships—and people—have the potential to be creative, worthwhile, and loving, if we can open our minds to what's going on within them. In Latin, the word *relate* means "to carry back" or "bear again," and it seems to me that each individual is called again and again to bear the weight of who she is as she negotiates with the outer world and the people in it. So when that Neptunian guy can't "bear" the dirty dishes that are piled in the sink, then neither can he relate to the person who left them there. When the woman with the moon in Leo can't "bear" her husband's desire to go on a ski trip with his guy friends, then she cannot relate to the needs of his ego; and perhaps even more significantly, she cannot relate to herself. But if we take responsibility for our choices, our loves, our feelings, and our desires, then we can start to relate to, or "bear," others—and, most importantly, to "bear" ourselves. And that's where synastry comes in.

WORKING WITH SYNASTRY

Working with synastry can lead you to new discoveries about yourself and your partner's inner "light" as you travel along its extraordinary pathway. Synastry can help you to realize, understand, or accept what it is you need or want from a relationship, and it can also tune in to what your partner needs or wants. And while having similar needs and wants usually makes for a compatible long-term relationship, each person is unique in the kind of love relationship she desires or "attracts." So when faced with a challenging partner, for example, whose needs may conflict with yours (represented by moon contacts) or whose long-term goals (represented by the sun) conflict with your core beliefs (Jupiter), then you'll have to find ways to navigate and negotiate these differences.

When you're using synastry, always try to look objectively and separately at the two individual birth chart configurations first. (You may find that it's hardest to look at your own chart with objectivity.) Then, once you have a good understanding of the general themes or repeat patterns in each chart, you can begin to work with the charts together.

Many books on synastry lay emphasis on a points system for the planetary contacts. In other words, you score more points for positive contacts and less for negative ones; then you add it all up and figure out the level of compatibility for which the relationship is destined. I don't use a points system simply because I don't think it's possible to place a numerical value on something as mysterious and nuanced as the energy between the two people involved and on how they will work with the contact in question. As I've said before, an intimate love relationship is the union of what two people "bear" together, and one person may not bear the relationship as well as the other. Once you have a deeper understanding of the dynamics of synastry, you can take things a step further and work with something called the composite chart—but that'll have to be saved for another book!

HOW TO CREATE AN AFFINITY CHART

The affinity chart is a simple, effective way to compare and analyze your birth chart in relation to your partner's. It reveals the things you have in common and what can bring you joy, comfort, happiness, and togetherness, but it also shows the things that might cause rifts, tensions, and problems. It reveals both the harmony and the discord within a relationship, and it can help divine whether you have a chance for long-term happiness or if this relationship is likely to be a short, sexy fling. (The latter isn't necessarily a bad thing; it might be just what you need at the moment!) Yet, paradoxically, even the most challenging, apparently incompatible charts can be harbingers of long-term success. That's because the challenge presented by the incompatibility proves to be the very magnet that holds two people together.

From my experience, I believe there is still one unknown factor at work here: the mystery of love itself, a kind of divine essence that permeates all. As astrologers, we all try to "pin down" a quality in the chart that will show us this thing called love, but that mysterious element is like the soul itself—ineffable, numinous, beyond the grasp of astrology yet intertwined with the stars and the universe itself. So work well with your charts, but let the mysterious essence of love weave in and out of your life, too. It draws together the threads of a relationship like a new tapestry, but sometimes—inevitably—the precious work is unpicked by an unknown and invisible pair of hands.

What Is an Affinity Chart?

The affinity chart usually consists of an inner wheel showing your chart and an outer wheel showing your partner's chart, so that you can easily see where the planets make contact.

In synastry, the inter-aspects, or contacts, between the planets of both charts are analyzed, as well as house positions, elemental balances and signs, and the current transits relating to both charts. But we'll keep things simple in this book and will focus only on the first and seventh houses.

Creating the Chart

If you haven't already done so, use one of the websites mentioned on page 17 to work out your natal chart. Birth certificates for most people born in the United States list the time of birth, but for those born in England and in some other countries, there may be no official record of your time of birth on your birth certificate. If that's the case, ask a family member if she or he can recall the approximate time of your birth; having even a rough idea can be helpful. If, for instance, you feel that your personal characteristics don't at all correspond to the ones traditionally associated with your rising sign or if you were born on a cusp, then read the adjoining rising-sign description. If you really have no idea of the time of your birth, ask a friend to work out the rising sign he or she thinks you are—after all, your rising sign is about the impression you are giving to others, so an objective friend's opinion can be valuable here.

To draw up the affinity chart, copy the blank chart shown on page 34.

When plotting your affinity chart, start by placing the sigil for your own rising sign in the inner wheel and work round counterclockwise with all the following signs in the order shown. So if your rising sign is Cancer for example, place the symbol for Cancer in the first slice of the wheel beside 1, and then Leo in the second slice, at 2 and so on.

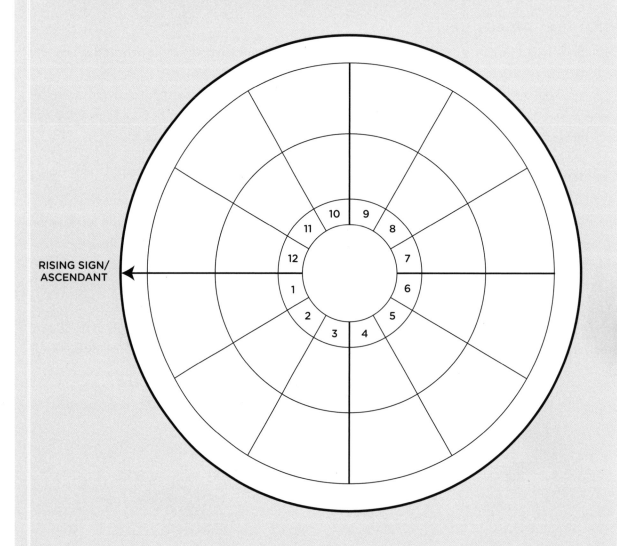

RISING SIGN/
ASCENDANT

First, you need to enter your rising sign in your wheel, starting from the arrow on the left of the chart. This is the sign that was rising over the eastern horizon at the moment of your birth. (Because it moves approximately one degree every four minutes, this can play havoc with people born on the cusp without exact birth times.) Write the glyph for the sign and/or the name of the sign in the wheel segment that is marked 1. Then note the first letter of the sign's element; this will help you later with elemental balance. So, for example, for Aries, you'd write the glyph for Aries, then F for Fire, and so on. Then place all the other zodiac signs in the order shown below, in a counterclockwise direction, following the numbers around the wheel. For example, if your rising sign is Cancer, then the sign that goes in the second segment (marked 2) will be Leo, and so on. Below is the order of the signs.

Aries: Fire
Taurus: Earth
Gemini: Air
Cancer: Water
Leo: Fire
Virgo: Earth
Libra: Air
Scorpio: Water
Sagittarius: Fire
Capricorn: Earth
Aquarius: Air
Pisces: Water

Next, place your own planets in the corresponding sections of each sign on the next ring moving outward. Use the glyphs or just write the name of the planets if you have the space.

Sun
Moon
Mercury
Venus
Mars
Jupiter
Saturn
Uranus
Neptune
Pluto
Eros

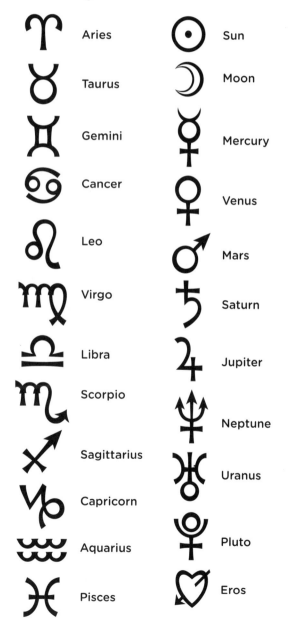

For example, if you have Aries rising, sun in Virgo, Moon in Aries, and Jupiter in Libra, then your chart would look something like this:

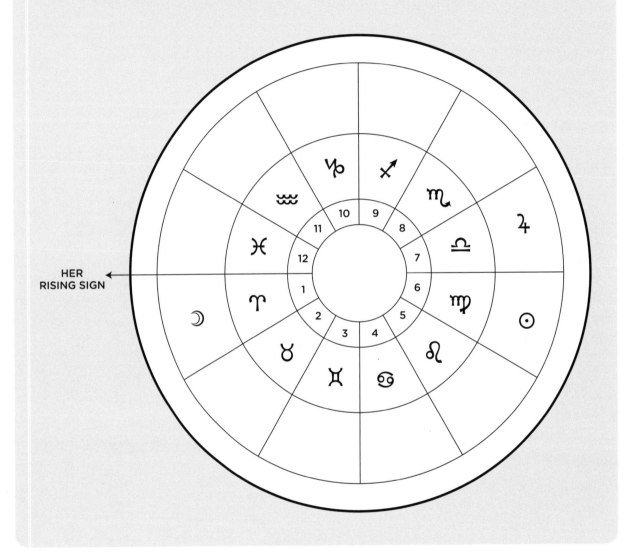

Now fill in the rest of the planets accordingly. Of course, this isn't a professionally finished chart, as you have neither degrees nor houses marked, but it is the quick and easy way to check your planets against your partner's.

Then fill in your partner's planets in the outer wheel. For his rising sign, draw a thick line through the outer band of the wheel where his rising sign starts, add an arrow, and mark it "his rising sign." In our example chart, he has Virgo rising (which starts on the outer ring at the beginning of her segment 6), the moon in Libra, sun and Venus in Cancer, Mars in Pisces, and Saturn in Taurus.

EXAMPLE: STEP 2

Once you have all the planets filled in, your affinity chart should look something like this:

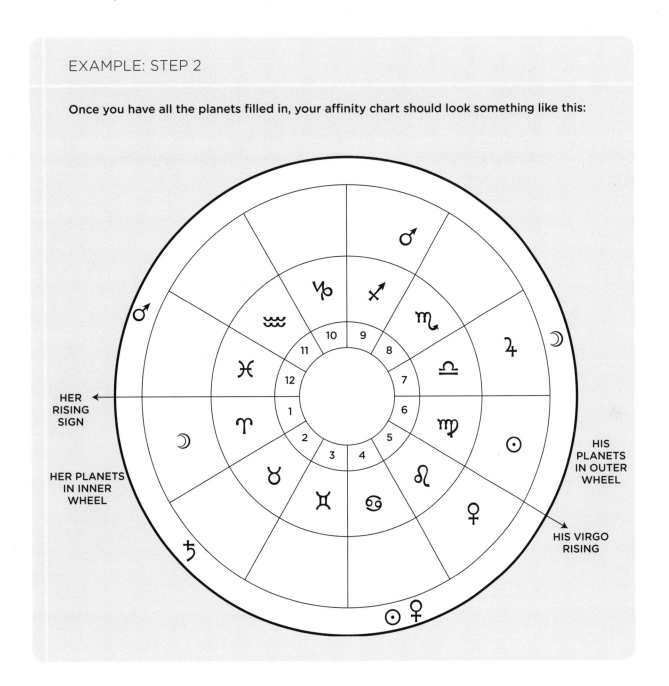

HER
RISING
SIGN

HER PLANETS
IN INNER
WHEEL

HIS
PLANETS
IN OUTER
WHEEL

HIS VIRGO
RISING

HOW TO USE THE CHART

We can see at a glance that her rising sign and moon are Aries, while her Jupiter is in her seventh house of Libra. His moon is in Libra, too, making a harmonious contact to her Jupiter, but opposite her rising sign and moon. (We'll see how this can be interpreted a little later on.)

If you'd like to use orbs for aspects, in order to "tighten up" the contacts, then of course you can do so. Checking whether aspects are within the maximum number of degrees apart may create a greater resonance. It is believed that the closer the aspect or an exact aspect, then the more the affinity or the challenge is felt between the two people. However, this book is a basic signpost to the main points of contact between you and your partner and is based on the elemental qualities that click into place and those that don't get along too well together.

I don't believe that any type of contact is ever negative, but pitfalls and conflicts can arise if you are unconscious of your potential or if you aren't living out certain aspects of your character. That's when we project our shadow sides onto other people, and these qualities can become exaggerated or distorted in ourselves—or we may "arrange" to distort them in our partners. (You'll understand this "projection" facet of relationships better as you read through the example contacts later in this book.)

WORKING WITH THE ELEMENTS

Before you start to work with the planets one by one, one way to check the overall compatibility of the affinity chart is to work out the elemental balance—that is, the total number of planets that fall in each of the four elements.

In the affinity chart, the more planets you and your partner have in the same element or generally spread around the elements, the more likely you're able to understand one another, make a success of your relationship, and feel comfortable with each other's behavior or outlook on life.

Take a look at your completed affinity chart, and by using the initial letters of each element marked in the inner wheel, you can quickly count up the number of planets in each element. First, count the planets that fall in Fire, then count the planets that fall in Earth, then Air, and finally Water. The total balance of elements in the chart will reveal to you the joint expression, or elemental nature, of the relationship.

Including the rising sign, sun, moon, Mercury, Venus, Mars, Jupiter, Saturn, Uranus, Neptune, Pluto, and Eros, you should have a total of twelve "planets" in the inner wheel of your chart and twelve (including the rising sign) in your partner's outer wheel. With a total of twenty-four planets in combination, work out how many planets fall in each of the four elements. Having approximately five or six planets in each of the four elements is a good balance.

A Good, Even Balance of Elements

If you and your partner have a good balance of planets spread through all of the elements, then it's likely that both of you are able to compromise and to work through any differences that arise. Also, if you find you mostly have planets in two elements that traditionally get along well together, such as Fire and Air, and a sprinkling of planets in the other two elements, then a harmonious dynamic is added to the other contacts in the chart; it suggests that you both express and relate well to the kind of energy represented by Fire and Air. The same would be true for an affinity chart with most planets in Earth and Water and a sprinkling of other planets in the other two elements.

Imbalance of Elements

There are two kinds of imbalances. The first occurs when the planets fall mostly in one element; the second is when planets fall balanced among three of the elements, with none in the fourth.

Where there's too much of a single element, you're likely to exaggerate the behavior and expression of that element at the expense of the other energies. This can create the kind of intense, highly claustrophobic relationship in which the two of you might well be found wearing matching sweatshirts—but you might not have a second to spare for anyone but each other!

When there's a balance among three elements but one element isn't represented at all, you'd both go all-out to import the qualities of that missing element into your lives because of a sense of inadequacy in that area of your relationship. What's wrong with that? Well, one of you just might discover that missing element in the arms of another person!

So when you're working with the elements in your own affinity chart, try to be as objective as you can about any imbalances. Instead of denying that imbalances exist, acknowledge them and work with them to add harmony, not discord, to your relationship.

Now that you've created an affinity chart and understand more about its elemental nature, chapter 4 will help you to work with the planetary contacts one by one.

4 Measuring Affinity:
Working with Contacts between

You're ready to look at your affinity chart in detail and to start to assemble the pieces. As with any jigsaw puzzle, when you first start, the myriad of possibilities seems daunting. But moving through each of the contacts step-by-step, in the order of the planets in the checklist on page 45, will quickly help things to make sense.

Obviously, if you have planets in the same sign or element as your partner (even if the planets don't fall close to one another), you're going to feel comfortable with whatever those planets represent. This is particularly true of the personal planets: the sun, moon, Mercury, Venus, Mars, Saturn, and Jupiter. Because the outer planets—Uranus, Neptune, and Pluto—move so slowly, they spend long periods of time in one sign, and so it's believed that the planet influences the generation of people who share that planetary placement. Again, these are usually harmonious on some level. However, in these cases, the affinity isn't experienced as something special or personal between the two people involved—it's more that the two of you just generally get along well together.

Before we go any further, it's important to remember that no contact is ever a sign of a doomed love affair, nor is it a sign of a perfect one. The contacts can manifest as harmonious, challenging, or provocative, but they can still be indicators of long-term relating because sometimes the very difficulties that challenge us in our relationships can actually hold us together.

FINDING THE PLANETARY CONTACTS BY COUNTING SIGNS

The easiest way to work out how many signs apart the planets are is to count the sign following the planet's sign as one and work forward from there. For example, with the sun in Aries, count Taurus as one, Gemini as two, and Cancer as three; so Cancer is the third sign away from Aries. Working backward the same way, Capricorn is three signs before Aries.

Harmonious Contacts

These harmonious contacts are usually between planets either in the same sign or of the same element (four signs away). Here, there is usually a mutual empathy, natural affinity, or attraction based on "understanding" and "feeling" the same way as the other person, meaning that it's "easy" to get along with him or her. However, even though too many "good" contacts in a chart might look like a marriage made in heaven on paper, such harmony can turn a relationship into a dull, inert affair, especially for those who thrive on a little challenge. That's when one or other of the partners may turn to someone else—or to their work or career—for a more adventurous love affair or a lifestyle with more excitement.

Challenging Contacts

These are also usually contacts between planets in the opposite sign or three signs away.

In this case, a first attraction can fizzle out quickly if there are no other beneficial contacts in the chart because the two partners have totally different ways of expressing the quality of the planets in question. However, these contacts don't always manifest in the early flurries of romance because other dynamics of the chart take over or disguise these differences. Then they surface much later in the relationship as resentment, deception, and other negative or "dark" behavior.

But challenging contacts aren't all bad news. Planets in opposite signs (and sometimes also three signs away from each other) can create different kinds of positive challenges. At first, they can spark attraction or desire, and later, the tension they present can keep both partners "hooked" and, depending on other factors in the chart, can contribute to highly creative, compelling relationships.

WORKING WITH THE CHART

Let's take our example chart, where Jill has sun in Virgo and Jack's rising sign is Virgo (see page 44). There's plenty of attraction and they click well since they have a great deal in common and Jill identifies with John's Virgoan outlook on life. (By the way, this is a good example of how to analyze and interpret the affinity chart as you go along. Try speaking it out loud to yourself as you go along; that way, you won't get lost in or distracted by your own thoughts!)

Jack has the moon in Libra, which is very sexy and has a physically exciting contact to Jill's Jupiter in Libra. He's looking for a romantic, coupled relationship, and her innate talent is to be the ultimate romantic and to show how she can seduce and attract a mate to her.

But notice that her moon in Aries is opposite his moon in Libra. This can mean that there is a conflict between what makes each of them feel comfortable in life; it also suggests a conflict between their natural responses and reactions, how they give and take, reach out or retreat, or where they feel at home. Jill's reactions are quick, impulsive, impatient, and self-willed, and she feels most comfortable when she's not relying on anyone else to make her decisions for her. Jack, however, wants to make decisions with his partner; he reacts to events by rationalizing them and feels at home when in a relationship where two people rely on each other. This can create a powerfully challenging relationship or a turbulent clash.

So with clashing moon signs and with very different emotional reactions, they may well get into arguments in which Jack will try to stay calm and rational and Jill will throw a few plates—which her Aries moon will probably quite enjoy, but his "anything for peace and quiet" Libran moon will actually loathe.

Meanwhile, if we count from Jill's Aries moon (fiery, driven, and impulsive), we come across Jack's sun in Cancer, three signs away and therefore in incompatible elements. Her moon will make Jack's sun in Cancer feel insecure because his whole core sense of identity is defined around attempting to find a sense of belonging and security in life. He is most comfortable doing the home cooking, while her reactionary moon would rather be out partying. Although her sun in Virgo adds a more stabilizing factor, sun in Virgo doesn't particularly want him slaving over a hot oven: She'd rather be taken out to a trendy restaurant!

Note how the most striking aspects are the oppositions between Jack and Jill's moons, and Jack's Mars and Jill's sun. This implies a certainly challenging, but spicy friction.

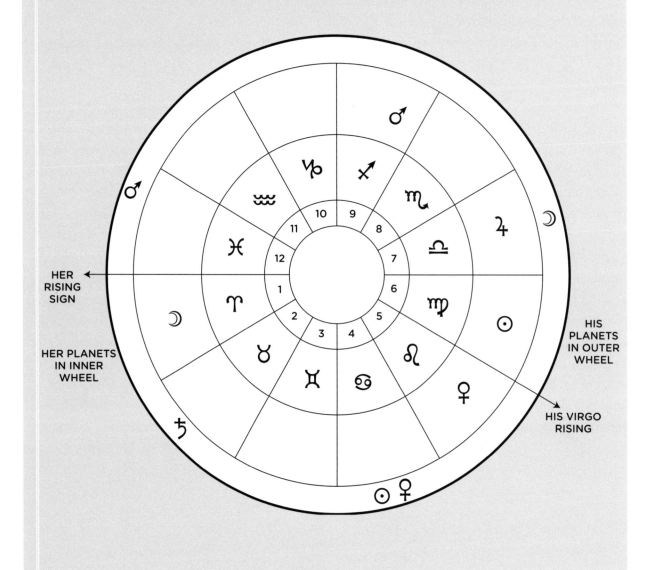

Checklist of Contacts

The easiest way to check all the contacts between your chart and your partner's is to make two columns, with your name at the top of the first column and your partner's at the top of the second, as shown below.

Then make a list under your name, starting with the rising sign, followed by the sun, moon, Venus, Mars, Saturn, Mercury, Jupiter, Uranus, Neptune, Pluto, and Eros. (This is the order of planets I have adapted for using with this book; I explain why on page 15.) Give yourself a few lines or a block of space beneath the name of each planet, as you may have more than one contact to note. Once you've made your list like the one below, the first thing to do is to look at the affinity chart and see if there are any contacts between your rising sign and any of his planets.

For each contact, write the planet under his name on the same line as your planet and place a check mark or an X beside it on the same line: The check mark represents harmonious contacts, and the X represents the challenging ones.

For instance, say you have Aries rising like Jill, and your partner has the moon in Libra like Jack. Write the glyph for the moon (or just write "moon") under your partner's column on the same line as your Aries rising and add an X (since it's a challenging contact). Next, look at your sun and see if there are any contacts between your sun and his planets. Then do the same thing with the moon, and so on.

Soon your list will look something like this:

JILL	JACK
RISING SIGN	☽ X
☉ SUN	♄ ✓ ♂ X
☽ MOON	☽ X
♀ VENUS	
♂ MARS	
♄ SATURN	
☿ MERCURY	
♃ JUPITER	☽ ✓
♅ URANUS	
♆ NEPTUNE	
♇ PLUTO	
♡ EROS	

PUTTING IT ALL TOGETHER

When you're putting all the information together, I suggest that you look for contacts that add weight or give a general overall flavor to the affinity chart. These can be either repeat themes or major contacts that seem to take over the affinity chart to give it a life and shape of its own.

First, look for any seventh-house planets in one chart that correspond to seventh-house planets in the other; then do the same for rising-sign contacts; and then check out his Venus and your Mars and vice versa. And remember that you've already assessed whether or not you have a great balance of elements. Your main contacts can also include powerful moon-to-sun and sun-to-moon contacts; or, on top of that, both of you might have a planet (it doesn't matter which one) conjunct the other's rising sign, sun, Saturn, or the outer planets.

When it comes to long-term love, I do think that Saturn is the glue that holds most relationships together because Saturn contacts are incredibly important binders between the two people involved. But other factors are at work, too. Is there enough belief (sun/Jupiter beneficial contacts) in the relationship? Is there sufficient compassion and understanding (moon/Venus) or desire and sexual compatibility (Venus/Mars/Eros), which can balance the chart if it's weighed down by heavier planets like Saturn and Pluto contacts?

Follow the order of planets in your checklist and move down through each of them. Look at Mercury and Jupiter as communication factors in relationships. And don't forget to check out what Uranus, Neptune, and Pluto are doing in your chart. Are you or your partner in a Neptunian fog of illusion and deception or a Plutonian cloud of explosive power? Remember that you need to look at your planets in relation to his and then his in relation to yours. Think about how all the planets operate as characters together and read through the examples to see how these energies might manifest and how you can work with them.

But before we move on to the dynamics of the planets and what they mean to you, chapter 5 will take a look at the first and seventh houses and how this mirroring effect between two people is often an indicator of what we call falling in love.

5 The Mirror of Love:
Hooks and Lures of the First
and Seventh Houses

When we're lacking love in our lives, we go fishing for it. We throw out a few lines in the form of spoken words or body language, in the hopes of catching and reeling in the kind of fish we think we need. In the affinity chart, one of the most important axes—the first to seventh house—can show us a lot about the type of fish we're attracted to and about the kind of bait we use to reel in our prize.

THE LAW OF OPPOSITES

Almost every esoteric, occult, or philosophical system—including astrology—is based on the ancient law of uniting opposites, or seeing duality as an illusion. Let's take a moment to explore what that might mean.

We're all familiar with the concept of opposites. There's dark and light, yin and yang, male and female, and sun and moon, to name a few. The list goes on and on; in fact, it's universal because everything has an apparent opposite. But we often forget that things that are in opposition to one another are actually alike: They are, as the saying goes, different sides of the same coin. Working with relationship astrology will help you realize that love is about finding a middle way between extremes or polarities, neither siding with one or the other, and this is where compromise (and sometimes struggle) comes in. It's why two partners juggle, clash, merge, reject, desire, blow hot, blow cold, and so on, as they strive toward love's universal Oneness. After all, a part of each one of us wants to be just like the proverbial coin: united and fused with her polar opposite into one.

Look at your first and seventh houses. They reflect one another; they are on the same axis. One looks at the other, the other looks back, and so on, infinitely. They seem to be separate and opposite. But this apparent separation is an illusion. When we say that people are "poles apart," we mean that they're disparate from one another. But the north and south poles are on the same axis and are therefore part of one energy.

Most ancient, esoteric or philosophical systems attempt to unite the opposites. For example, as we can see in Taoist thought, yin and yang are here arranged to be as One, but of course we still persist in living in a dualistic world. For example, we still see black and white in this diagram, as completely distinct from one another. We polarize our natal and affinity charts in the same way, so our seventh house is usually projected out and represented by the people who come into our lives.

It's a bit like standing in a foyer, between two doors, and suddenly hearing a knock on both doors simultaneously. Which do we answer? Since we can't be in two places at once, one door will take preference over the other. First, we may answer the door that we think conceals the safe option—yet we know we mustn't neglect the other door either because otherwise the stranger left outside in the cold will try to enter in some subversive way, whether we open the door to her or not. Similarly, with the first and seventh houses, you are more likely to side with the devil you know (your rising sign) than the devil you don't (the seventh house).

On the affinity chart, you marked your rising sign as beginning at the left-hand side of the circle, and the following twelve signs formed equal segments of 30 degrees each around the circle. Now we're going to use this method to help us understand how important the first and seventh houses are for understanding relationship astrology. When we first fall for someone or begin a new relationship, it is often the rising sign and any planets in this first house that are the lure or attraction between two people. So what is the first house, and why is it so powerful?

THE FIRST HOUSE

The Ascendant is the degree of the zodiac sign that was ascending, or rising, on the eastern horizon at the moment of your birth, and it marks the degree of the first house of your chart. The first house (what we're calling the rising sign throughout this book) describes not only the way you see the world and your general attitude toward it, but also the impression you make within it; the way you present yourself to the world; your image; and how you are noticed.

Some people may have a planet located in this first house, which adds extra "power" to the quality of that sign. Or they may have a planet in close conjunction to the actual degree of the Ascendant, either in the first or twelfth house within a 15-degree maximum orb. Any such planet conjunct the Ascendant will color and shape the viewpoint of the rising sign.

The first house is opposite the seventh house, but it's important to realize that we're dealing with an axis here. The Ascendant and Descendant axis forms the most personal point of the chart based on the actual moment and place of birth (apart from the I.C./M.C. axis, which we aren't using in this book).

So what is the attraction factor that draws us in or lures us to another? Usually, it's something do with our elusive seventh house, the bit of ourselves we don't easily own, accept, or believe. I call the seventh house elusive because we tend to side with the first-house part of ourselves, the "I" we identify with the moment we are born in order to survive. The Ascendant is often thought to describe the first moment we open our eyes and see the world, however frightening or beautiful it might have been in that instant. It is the first moment of "knowing" life, and so all we can do is trust that first moment, even if it's unreliable or unsafe. We peer out from the vantage point of the first house and see the seventh house as something "other," "out there," or "not me," in the belief that we haven't got it. Then we either resist it or desire it. And "it" usually appears in the form of another person.

The Mirror

According to well-known psychologists like Carl Jung and James Hillman, relationships are all about discovering oneself through the other.

Synastry is like looking in a mirror—especially if your seventh house is where you project a part of yourself as "you out there," or "the thing that I'm not," and someone comes along who fits the "role" of your seventh house (perhaps he or she has a sign or planet falling in that house). Now, from where you are in your first house, you see a new part of yourself for the first time. This wonderful creature may be delightful or dangerous, dark or luscious, desirable or fearful—regardless, somehow you know that you must have this person in your life. In fact, he represents and mirrors your own beauty. And even better, the person who fits the seventh-house role wakes you up to this dimension of yourself and can bring awareness and attention to who you truly are (although it's possible that you won't recognize it and will still go on projecting it onto the "other").

So when the first-house person meets her seventh house in the form of a partner's rising sign or in someone with loads of planets in that seventh-house sign (for example, if you're a Virgo rising and you meet a Pisces rising or someone with lots of planets in Pisces), it's as if each partner is looking at himself or herself in a mirror, reflecting each other's qualities. (Usually, they won't realize they're mirror images of each other, even though they feel a powerful affinity.) This kind of opposite attraction can create both wonderfully challenging relationships and disastrous clashes.

Put another way, your rising sign is, in a sense, "me in here," while your seventh house is projected as "you out there." But remember that your seventh house is still *your* house. If someone else has the same qualities by sign or planets as your seventh house, then what you're seeing and are attracted to "out there" are those qualities of your seventh house, which you have not yet realized are part of your character. This projection of your seventh-house quality is then imported back into your life through "the other." We then want, desire, or even cannot resist our opposite: We seem fated to lure them on or to be lured on by them.

Two Mirrors, Not One

In this case, Jill's Aries first-house moon and rising sign are opposite Jack's moon and her own Jupiter, which falls in her seventh house. But if we now look at his rising sign, Virgo, which is opposite the sign of Pisces, the only planet here is Jack's own Mars. Jill has no planets in his seventh house, so what he "sees" from his first house is a glimpse of the seductive yet elusive—and often highly manipulative—nature of others (Mars in Pisces), but he doesn't realize that is who he is, too.

Then along comes headstrong, Aries-moon-rising Jill. She may provide Jack with a battle of wills, a challenging and probably sexually exciting ride to passion, and will go some way to fitting that Martian image he has of the world in the mirror (by virtue of the fact she has a warring Aries rising). Yet his seventh house will never feel quite complete; in other words, she will fit that role on paper and in her attitude and moods, but with no planets herself in Pisces, it's unlikely that she will hook into his Mars

In our example chart, Jill has a moon in Aries (strong-willed and fiercely independent), while Jack has moon in Libra (laid back and eager to please), which is in her seventh house. Due to his lunar nature, In fact, Jack takes on the role of Jill's seventh house quite easily. However, because he has Mars in his own seventh house (he attracts feisty people into his life and looks for a fight from others), things can get tricky.

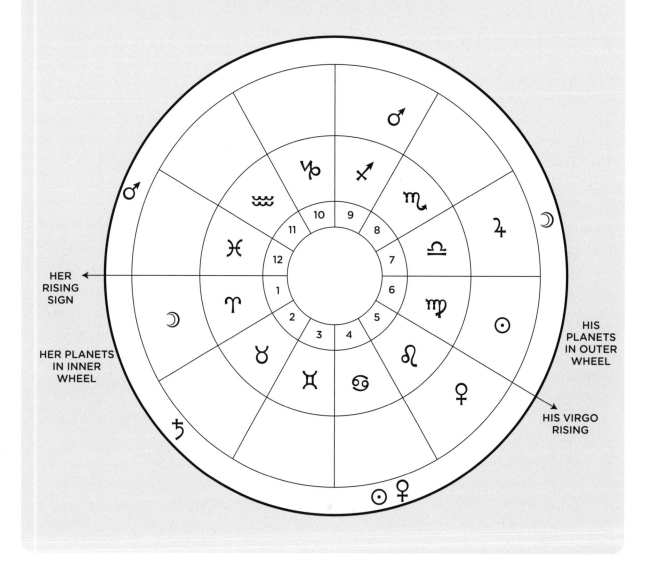

HER RISING SIGN

HER PLANETS IN INNER WHEEL

HIS PLANETS IN OUTER WHEEL

HIS VIRGO RISING

in Pisces, which is searching for something quite profound without being at all sure of what that is. He, too, will never "see" that light of himself reflected in her eyes; he will only experience the winds of Mars swirling around him, not within him.

We have to remember that there are two first house/seventh house polarities in our affinity charts, not just one (unless your partner's seventh house is your first house or vice versa). This means that there is no longer one mirror, but two; the reflections change or are altered, and sometimes the reflection of one becomes so distorted that the reflection we receive of ourselves can turn relationships into messy chaos.

WHEN MS. X MEETS MR. Y

Let's look at another basic example. When Ms. X sees Mr. Y, she instantly "feels" his Scorpio power, which resonates with her own Pluto/moon.

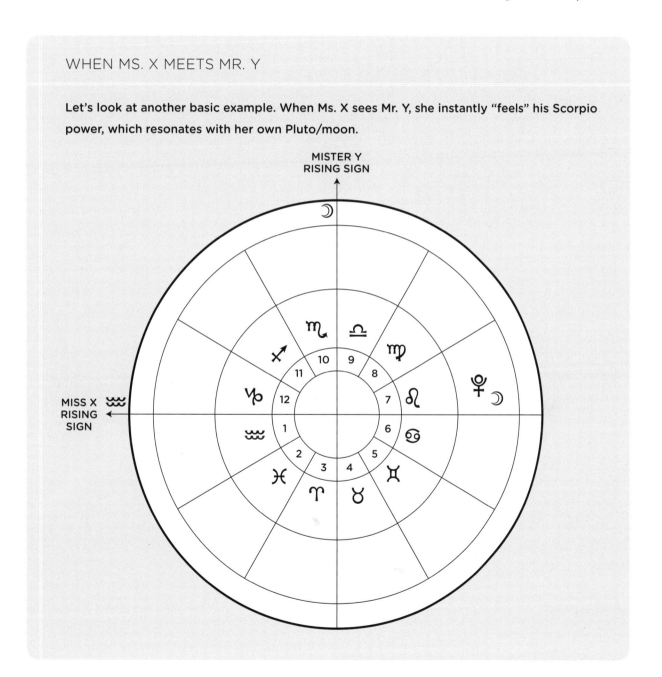

This chart shows Ms. X with Aquarius rising and Pluto and the moon conjunct in Leo in her seventh house. Mr. Y has Scorpio rising conjunct the moon and nothing in his seventh-house Taurus. So how do we interpret this?

We can say that Ms. X gives the impression she's cool, quirky, unconventional, and is everyone's friend. She appears independent, bright, and carefree. Yet although she sees the world as in need of reform—and that includes most of the men in it—out there in her seventh house, her relationships are fraught with power struggles, jealousy, and possession. She is actually far more wary of commitment than just the normal Aquarian-rising person's hunt for unconditional love. In fact, the people who come into her life are usually control freaks themselves, and she seems to repeatedly attract those "wrong" types.

Until she "owns" her moon/Pluto controlling nature, this will probably keep happening to her. Then along comes Mr. Y with Scorpio rising conjunct the moon and a deeply mysterious presence. (When there is a planet also in the rising sign—and usually, say, within 15 degrees of orb either side of the actual Ascendant axis degree—then it will add a powerful backdrop to the rising-sign person's apparent character. Often, the rising-sign impression will mask the true intention and power of the planet in question. So Mr. Y, for all his cool, enigmatic appearance, is probably also twitchy in new situations; he finds himself feeling too much and seeing everyone's dark sides. Alternatively, he may project his lunar moods and instincts onto others, seeing women as overly emotional and not worthy of his powerful Scorpio-rising status. "Out there," his Taurus seventh house fills with possessive sensualists or earth mothers who want to control him.)

When Ms. X sees Mr. Y, she instantly "feels" his Scorpio power, which resonates with her own Pluto/moon. There's an instant affinity, but this is not a romantic idealization or a projection of an ideal onto someone else; it's a deeper sort of knowledge, a sense that behind her Aquarian façade (from Mr. Y's point of view) lies a darker delight, one that he understands all too well. Similarly, Ms. X feels the raw, sexual connection disturbing her Aquarian calm and is utterly amazed by his stunning prince-of-darkness presence. He is fascinated by her intellectual sparkle and lured on by this "mask," so different from his own; he senses they share something so dark that they will become lovers—whatever the cost.

In these two mirrors, then, they have found a part of themselves, even though the mirrors aren't reflecting one another. Instead, they are square to one another, forming a configuration called a grand cross. The tension here is powerful—but within these kinds of reflections can be seen the sparkling jewels of the planets that chain them together, signatures that reveal and underline their affinity to one another, for good or for bad.

Ms. X and Mr. Y are just one example. How do you figure this out for yourself? In chapter 6, we'll start by learning how to interpret rising-sign contacts, which tell us about the initial attraction that's kick-started when two people first meet and about the way both partners perceive the world.

6 The Rising Sign:
The Attraction Factor

When we first meet someone, the first thing we notice about each other is our rising signs. This chapter looks at how your rising sign interacts with other rising-sign contacts in the affinity chart. (Rising-sign contacts to the planets will be listed at the end of each planet's chapter.) Your rising sign is about the way you perceive the world, what you are attracted to, and who or what is attracted to you. It's like looking through a lens that colors your view of the world and all the people in it. For example, if your sun is in Leo, deep down you may have an urge to be the center of attention and shine in the spotlight; but if you are Scorpio rising, you see the world as a suspicious place, an untrustworthy stage on which to show off your talents.

Remember that in love relationships, the rising sign is the first thing that attracts others to you. It reveals the kind of magnetic sway you have on certain people and which types you fall for. If we are lacking in the elemental quality of a person's rising sign, we are usually attracted to that person because they are more of who we would like to be. We want to experience this quality; and what's more, we want to own it. It's like spotting a fabulous outfit in an expensive store while you're window-shopping and thinking, "I must have it; I'll look so good in that!" But most of us can't buy love (although some people do). Most of us attract it to us in order to fill in the missing pieces within us.

SEEING WHAT WE WANT TO SEE

The other person's rising sign is what we "see" before our own eyes, just as much as our own rising sign is how we see the world.

Remember that there are two axes to take into consideration when looking at the affinity chart. You will have to look not only at your rising sign and what contacts it makes to his planets, but also at his rising sign and what contacts it makes to your planets. This is why you may find that his rising sign does nothing in relation to your planets, or that his rising sign is far more important in the affinity chart (making contacts to your planets) than yours is, and so on. And that's perfectly okay. Try to stay open and objective as you discover more and more contacts between charts, whether you discover harmonies, clashes, or challenges.

All rising signs have an "ideal" attached to their way of seeing the world, as well as a darker view of life. With every sign's positive qualities come its negative ones, and so when we look across to our seventh house to that which is "other," we either dress the other with a shining vision of our ideal lover or else we don them with the armor of the enemy. The seventh house is the house where we give away or lose touch with parts of ourselves and look for those apparently missing parts through others.

But what if there are no contacts between either rising sign and the other's planets? Well, all I can say is that this is the mystery of love at work. The initial attraction may be something very deep-seated: It may manifest as a fated sense of having known this person before in another life or a feeling that you've just met your soul mate. And this is where other factors in the chart can create instant attraction, just as the rising sign can. So if you have no rising-sign contacts, don't worry that there's something missing. There isn't; it's just that this is a very different, out-of-the-ordinary sort of attraction.

THE ATTRACTION FACTOR: MISSING ELEMENTS

A person with a rising sign in an element we lack in our own natal chart can be instantly and intensely attractive to us. He or she reacts to life's events exactly how we wish we could—if we only had more of that element. For example, Air rising takes an intellectual approach to life; she wants to know why things are, rather than how things are made. If you have little Air in your own chart, an Air-rising person will fill this gap because he is more of who you would like to be; he appears to be more intellectual, philosophical, and rational than you are. If you lack Fire, then she will seem more extroverted, passionate, and instinctive than you. If you lack Earth, he will appear more practical, creative, or materially minded than you. If you lack Water, she'll appear more sensitive, gentle, and compassionate than you are.

THE RISING-SIGN MASK

Once you get to know the other person better and you begin to see through his rising-sign mask, the initial attraction may wear off—or it may evolve into something more intense because of other stabilizing or harmonious contacts between you. Let's take, for example, a Scorpio-rising person, who, on first meeting, will be seen as secretive, mysterious, and intense. She is likely to attract those who may have Scorpio planets themselves, who can identify with and recognize those qualities. On the other hand, a rising sign can attract people of the very opposite rising sign, the same Scorpio-rising woman falling for a Taurus rising sign, so different in the way he behaves and therefore desirable according to the law of opposites attracting. (For more on the influences of the first and seventh houses, see chapter 5.)

Planets Conjunct the Rising Sign in the Natal Chart

Note that when someone has in their natal chart the rising sign conjunct a planet, within usually a 12-degree orb maximum (the closer the more intense the influence), it will color the viewpoint of the rising sign. For example, if a man had the moon conjunct his Capricorn-rising Ascendant, although he would see the world from a cautious, structured, and containable viewpoint (Capricorn), it would be occluded by the sensitive, changeable flow of the lunar outlook on life. He may seem like a strong, ambitious type on the surface, but he may be moody and unsure of what he really feels behind the mask. Or he might come across as very needy (the lunar influence being more powerful than the Capricorn one) but is in fact strong and ambitious when he can shake off the lunar moodiness. Always take into account any planet on the Ascendant, as it will be a powerful influence on the way the person reacts and behaves in the world.

RISING SIGN/RISING SIGN CONTACTS

The first thing to look at when you've created your affinity chart is whether your rising signs complement one another or create a challenge. When your rising signs are the same, an immediate rapport is often revealed because you both view the world the same way. Other complementary rising signs are those that fall in the same element. Challenges or clashes come from signs that are three signs away or from oppositions. Look at both your rising signs and see if there are any contacts between them. Don't worry if there aren't; it doesn't mean you can't see eye to eye!

Next, from your list of contacts, start with your rising sign and note what contacts it makes to your partner's planets (if any). I have interpreted rising-sign-to-rising-sign contacts in this chapter to help you understand the different energies at work. All remaining rising-sign contacts to other planets are interpreted at the end of each planet's chapter. After you've looked up your rising-sign contacts to his planets, move on and see what contacts his rising sign makes to your planets.

Rising-sign contacts to the other person's rising sign tell us about the moment when you look in the other's eyes and see something that you instantly hook on to or are instantly repelled by.

Rising Signs in the Same Sign

When you have the same rising sign as another person, you immediately get a sense that the other person has the same viewpoint on life, and there's a genuine "twinning" attraction, as you both make the same impression on one another. This feels comfortable and natural. But, like any same-sign contact between planets, if there's too much of a good thing in the affinity chart and few challenges, you may remain stuck in the same mind-set, unable to see life from a more objective perspective. However, chances are you'll have plenty of other contacts in your chart that bring balance to the general impression you have of the world.

HARMONIOUS CONTACTS

When they're the same sign or the same element, these are mainly harmonious contacts:

Two Fire rising signs (Leo, Sagittarius, and Aries) will share a need to be active, to do something, to have a vision, and to dream and project into the future.

Two Earth rising signs (Taurus, Virgo, and Capricorn) will see their world as tangible, materialistic, and filled with problems to be ironed out. They will see life in terms of what needs to be done now, rather than what needs to be done in the long term.

Two Air rising signs (Gemini, Libra, and Aquarius) see life through a lens of logic, rationalizations, and questions. There is always a pro and a con or a detached analysis to be made.

Two Water rising signs (Cancer, Scorpio, and Pisces) go with the flow, and they both see the world through their feelings. In other words, they take very seriously what their intuition says about something or someone.

CHALLENGING CONTACTS

Challenging rising-sign contacts are either three signs away or in opposition. Rising signs that are three signs away are said to be in "hard or difficult aspect" to one another, which translates as a tense or dynamic exchange of energy. This is where elements truly clash since each person will see life from a totally different perspective. That said, this tension can also generate a highly creative, exciting, challenging relationship if other factors in the chart confirm positive energy. Signs that are three signs away often feel drawn to each other as if they have found something they believe is missing in themselves. Let's take a brief look at each of these.

Fire/Water

Fire wants to see action and looks at life as one big opportunity, while Water follows a dream but can't quite believe it could ever be realized. Fire knows how to sweep people off their feet; Water sees where this will lead, hopefully to eternal bliss. Water is easily led astray by Fire's brandishing swords of idealism, and each can reinforce the other's lifestyle dreams.

FIRE/WATER

For example, Aries sees only endless possibilities in life for himself, but Cancer sees only endless possibilities for others. That means Aries will feel like the bee's knees around the Cancer-rising person because Cancer rising will "look after" Aries (and will enjoy it, too). Yet Cancer rising may realize one day that she needs to look after herself as well.

Leo sees herself as the lead player on stage. Scorpio sees the problems backstage, the envious audience, and the menacing taxman and can advise accordingly. Scorpio puts Leo on the throne and becomes the power behind the throne, especially as Leo is happy to be backed all the way. But unless they have other positive affinities in their chart, Leo's self-love may make Scorpio jealous.

Sagittarius sees life as one big adventure, while Pisces sees himself as a mirror of the person he is with. So, obviously, when infatuated with a Sagittarius, Pisces sees life as an adventure, too. It can all go wrong, though, when Sagittarius decides to run a political race: Pisces was convinced that they were going to run away from the rat race, not toward it.

Air/Earth

This is the traditional clash of elements! Air and Earth have great lessons to learn from one another, but only if other factors in the chart can support and lend balance to these very different elemental qualities. Earth is resolute, pragmatic, and ready to get on with the job, while Air thinks long and hard about action and is known to prevaricate and to be indecisive. Put these together, and you might think the result is a fusion of mind and matter—but in fact, it's whether mind can override matter (or vice versa), which becomes the problem.

AIR/EARTH

For example, Gemini and Virgo both see what can be done (Virgo) or said (Gemini) to change a situation to their liking. Off to a good start with a common ground of mercurial curiosity and fascination with knowledge, this could seem an ideal attraction at first. Yet Gemini often tires of Virgo's obsessive self-interest, and Virgo can be infuriated by Gemini's trick of avoiding the truth and being contrary just for fun.

For Libra and Capricorn, their tremendous differences make a formidable business team. But as for romance? That's trickier. Capricorn sees how seductive, charming, fair, and balanced Libra is, and as Capricorn likes life to be neat and tidy, Libra appears to be the perfect match. But depending on other contacts in the chart, it can all go wrong when Libra sees that Capricorn has a ruthless side or when Capricorn sees that Libra's seductive charm is directed toward everyone else, too.

Aquarius and Taurus rising face a difficult challenge because both are stubborn, or resistant to change, and so have a static view of the world. Taurus is possessive and sees a lot of things "out there" that he wants to own—including people. Aquarius sees a lot "out there" that she can reform, particularly outdated conventions. The problem here is that Taurus sees reform as a threat to his stability.

Fire/Earth

The Fire-rising person sees the world as filled with opportunity and has an enduring desire to discover that there is another realm of existence beyond so-called reality. Earth will see the world as finite—what you see is what you get—and will wonder how there can be anything other than what is right in front of one's eyes. If Earth were able to look beyond the tangible, together, they could be highly creative in any joint enterprise. In love relationships, they may never truly agree on their long-term future, as Fire will keep pushing the boundaries, while Earth would rather remain with the ones they know.

FIRE/EARTH

For example, while Aries sees only what she can achieve for herself, Capricorn has plans of greatness—or, at the very least, the power to delegate. Both of these signs have high principles: They are initiators or leaders, and they want to show others the way. Seeing that life and people need controlling, Capricorn will stop at nothing in his quest to do so, while too-hot-to-handle Aries will fear the chains of drudgery and run for the hills.

Leo and Taurus rising resist change and are renowned for the sustained pursuit of their goals, whether in love, work, or battle. Together, they can create a superb relationship in which Leo takes the spotlight and Taurus perseveres to ensure Leo's success. It's a good initial affinity, but Leo may eventually see Taurus bound by his own pragmatism, while Taurus may see Leo as bound by too much self-love.

Sagittarius and Virgo adapt, thrive on change, and can identify easily with one another's worldviews. If their quest for truth is mutual, they have very different viewpoints about what the truth itself is. Sagittarius's truth is about looking to experience the divine in nature, while Virgo is about seeing how to heal others in order to understand human nature.

Air/Water

These combinations have very different perspectives on the world: Air thinks while Water feels. However, these rising signs are often instantly drawn to one another. Air is curious as to how Water sees with almost a sixth sense, and Water wonders how Air can be so detached and analytical about life.

AIR/WATER

For instance, Gemini easily communicates his future desires, while Pisces, identifying with whomever she is with, believes she has the same desires, too. Both see life from a romantic viewpoint, and often this relationship develops into a light, frivolous love affair—the wedding bells will only chime if they can see the same future up at the altar.

Libra and Cancer are attracted by each other's ability to initiate romance, projects, or ideas, even if neither of them can finish what they start! Here, Cancer sees the charming allure of Libra, while Libra sees Cancer's gentle, compassionate outlook on life. Together, they can go far, but Libra's ideals about the perfect partner could be disturbed when Cancer cares more about the lame pigeon in the street than Libra's glamorous new jacket.

Aquarius and Scorpio are notoriously at odds, not just because of the Air/Water challenge, but also because neither is ready to adapt, forgive, compromise, or start again (unless they have stronger planetary aspects by sign in their charts). In fact, since both see life as a need to gain control over others (Aquarius with the power of words, Scorpio through sexual power), they may initially hate each other or fall madly in love simply because they glimpse a strong streak of their own character "out there"—which lures them right in.

RISING-SIGN OPPOSITIONS

Now we're going to look at rising signs that are opposite to one another. These are often the most magnetic, challenging, and life-changing attractions of them all. Let's dive straight in and see how these mirrors work between all the six oppositions of the zodiac.

When we gaze across the zodiac to our seventh house, we are projecting this part of our personality onto the people "out there." So, for example, if you were Sagittarius rising, then Gemini rising would be your opposite sign, and you'd probably find yourself importing Gemini people, behavior, and themes into your world throughout your life.

From a psychological perspective, it seems that we are unconsciously (or sometimes consciously) aiming to become whole to carve out the best versions of ourselves and to try to create balance in our lives. And what you see right across the street from your rising-sign view of the world is the seventh house. It's highly alluring yet strangely foreboding. When you meet someone who has a rising sign that corresponds to your seventh-house sign, you see a new and exciting vista on the horizon, and you crave it desperately. What also happens is that since it's a part of yourself that you sense is missing, you unconsciously want to acquire or import it in one form or another in order to rectify that deep sense of imbalance.

Although this is also true for opposite sun signs and other planets in opposition, it is more so for the rising sign since it is the window from which we view the other. It is also the window from which the other views us. It is our attraction factor.

How can we not be drawn to another's (apparently) different way of reacting to the world if we unconsciously sense that it's what's missing in our own lives? We could name it desire, envy, a craving, or a longing—but whatever you call it, it sure as heck gets under our skins.

Here are the rising-sign oppositions.

Aries/Libra: "Me" or "We"?

If Aries sees the world as one big challenge to be confronted, then Libra sees the world as a place to find compromise and balance. Aries rising looks through a window colored by competition, where rivals outstrip each other for love's best catches, but Aries will win the hand of the one she loves at any cost. Aries sees what's best for herself first and foremost and how to be number one in the relationship. In the early stages of romance, Aries is usually the initiator and is renowned for having little patience, wanting it all *right now*, and romantic love provides the greatest challenge of all. Then along comes the beautiful Libra rising—calm, careful, and unselfish. How strange, how different it is from Aries's own fast-paced, self-centered approach to the world! Then, when Libra starts to let Aries make the romantic decisions, Aries is over the moon to do so—it's in her favor, after all.

The magnetic pull between these two is that Aries rising sees "me in here being adored by you out there"—and Libra rising sees "you out there being at one with me in here." But the tricky thing is that Aries finds it really hard to imagine fusing as a couple because that means she will lose her individuality or her freedom. So when she's faced with her own seventh house—the perfectly unselfish, giving, compromising Libra who seems to be all the things Aries believes she is not—Aries is attracted to someone who appears to understand her fine ego. Libra sees his own seventh-house fiery assertiveness and the lack of compromise that he has missed or denied in himself, too. This can be an exciting, beneficial relationship if there are good contacts elsewhere in the affinity chart. The key challenge worth remembering about this opposite attraction is that Aries looks on life in terms of "me," and Libra looks on life in terms of "we."

Taurus/Scorpio: Tangible or Taboo?

In astrological circles, the Taurus/Scorpio attraction is thought to be steamy, erotic, and emotionally intense. And that's hardly surprising when Taurus rising looks through a window colored by sensual pleasure and Scorpio rising through one of sexual power and intrigue. Together, this is a powerful bond, simply because as fixed signs, neither finds it easy to let go of the other once they've got each other. Taurus wants his senses to be filled with the tangible, earthly delights of love and life, while Scorpio only wants to delve into the taboo and unknown. And if we join the sensual pleasures of Taurus with the sexual demands of Scorpio, we get some pretty steamy stuff. However, outside of the bedroom, Taurus looks for financial and material stability, while Scorpio likes to plunder and undermine that stability by showing that something darker and deeper is at work. This can be one of the most highly volatile—and sexiest—attractions because Scorpio sees life from the dark side of Pluto, while Taurus sees life through the vain pleasures of Venus.

Gemini/Sagittarius: Truth or Fiction?

If Gemini rising sees love from a romantic's viewpoint, then Sagittarius rising takes it one step further and sees herself as the ultimate romantic who journeys through life, taking opportunities—never promising much, but never demanding much, either. The rest of the world is viewed as a place for this larger-than-life romantic to try out her seductive powers. Gemini sees the minute details, while Sagittarius sees the bigger picture, and although philosophically this amounts to the same thing, both will argue to the death if they have to prove a point. Gemini believes he can twist words and reach any logical solution, and Sagittarius is as sure she knows the ultimate truth. This, of course, makes for a lively relationship. Gemini's intellectual expertise is the key attraction to Sagittarius, and Gemini is attracted to Sagittarius's carefree attitude. If Sagittarius looks to discover a meaning in life, Gemini is simply curious about life, and together, they can brainstorm, dispute, explore, and mold their different ways of seeing life if other aspects or affinities are positive. As a couple, they often run before they can walk up to the altar and later realize that Gemini's need to rationalize why sex is better in position A than position B may create tension for Sagittarius, who'd rather just get on with it, enjoying spontaneous sex whenever or wherever she likes.

Cancer/Capricorn: Cool or Calculating?

When the lunar-ruled Cancer rising meets the Saturn-ruled Capricorn rising, there's a deep mutual empathy, although it's rarely voiced between them. Each intuitively senses each other's loneliness and deep-seated vulnerability. Capricorn senses Cancer's need to belong, and Cancer senses Capricorn's need to take control, both generated by their fear of inadequacy. If Cancer is sensitive and takes things personally, then Capricorn protects himself well, his mask as hard and tough as a diamond. Yet when he encounters the gentle, kind, lonely Cancer, he is drawn to her seventh-house serenity like a bee to honey.

Let's look at it through the lens of the office party. The Cancer-rising woman either hides in the kitchen, pours the drinks, or washes up—anything other than expose herself to the noisy masses. How could she compete or be as cool and clever as her Aquarius-rising colleague or as brash and loud-mouthed as her Aries-rising friend? The Capricorn-rising man will hover near the buffet table; he'll say little, but will be ready to eat the finest canapé and drink the best champagne and will have the patience to wait for the right person to pass by who can help him secure his future interests. When Cancer spots this calm, suave approach to life, she's hooked. How she longs to be as cool as a cucumber! (Her seventh house is always full of cool people: Why can't she be like them?) And when the Capricorn-rising man spots the busy Cancer woman looking after everyone else, he is attracted to this caring yet serene angel of goodness; after all, this might be the woman whose presence could help him rule the world.

Leo/Aquarius: Ego or Eccentric?

Leo rising spends a lot of time looking in the mirror, concerned with self-image, being in the spotlight, and looking good in public, while Aquarius rising isn't really concerned about his image too much at all. In fact, Aquarius has no problem with his self-image; rather, he sees himself as just another human being trying to right the world and everyone in it. Whether by saving the world, supporting environmental issues, or planting organic beans, Aquarius is concerned with shaping the world of big egos into compassionate ones. So along comes egocentric Leo, and Aquarius sees how self-absorbed she is, so seemingly unbothered by much around her—and, of course, deep down Aquarius would like to be like that, too. This combination either forms one of the most challenging but rewarding relationships or the most disastrous because both are fixed signs. In other words, neither wants to change their perception of the world: They want others to subscribe to their viewpoints instead. When the proud Leo crosses swords with altruistic Aquarius about egos, self-importance, and how to right the world, it's hardly surprising that both will dig in their heels and insist they are right and the other is wrong. And that's an instant power struggle. This can be a highly exciting and tremendously enriching rapport if other good affinities are in the chart.

Virgo/Pisces: Lost or Found?

Virgo and Pisces are both mutable signs, willing to adapt to each other's apparent differences. Virgo rising is attracted to Pisces rising's dreamy, elusive behavior and Pisces to Virgo's refined and cultivated way of looking at life. Virgo hides her romantic desires well behind a cool approach to everything and everyone. Elegant and usually dressed immaculately, Virgo sees the world with a discriminating eye, and as love can sometimes be a messy—and therefore awkward—game, likes to play it according to the rule book. In fact, sometimes Virgo can be too obsessed with details or manners, or the "right" way to romance someone.

Pisces, whom it's impossible to label or put into a category, proves to be an irresistible attraction, mostly because he easily falls into the role of victim, while Virgo takes on the role of savior. The emotional rescue of others is one of Virgo's best-kept secrets, and Pisces, who swims with the tide and falls comfortably into any role chosen for him when swayed by physical desire and beauty, will be happy to have a new identity bestowed upon him, simply because he doesn't even know what that is. In love, Pisces sees the cool, calm Virgo's romantic longings, and Virgo senses that Pisces needs to be held and healed. This can work, as long as both are aware of their role-playing, with Virgo as the savior of the lost Pisces.

RISING SIGNS AND THE PLANETS

Remember, the most important planet contacts to the rising sign are when the planet is in the same sign as the rising sign or in its opposite sign. The rising-sign person will obviously "get a rising-sign experience," so to speak. For example, King Felipe of Spain has Mercury, the moon, and the sun all in Aquarius, contacting Letizia's Ascendant. Letizia will feel she's making a great impression, and Felipe will find it easy to communicate (Mercury) and align his moods and goals with the impression she makes on the world. He will also get an experience of what his planets represent, perhaps waking up to the presence of that quality in himself for the first time.

Also, the person with the planet in the rising-sign person's seventh house will alert the rising-sign person to a different quality he believes is lacking in his life. This can often be highly desirable to the rising-sign person, but the way in which it's desirable depends entirely on what the planet means in his own chart. The rising sign is an expression of the merry dance we engage in throughout life—but the choreographer is hiding in the wings, personified by all the other planets in the chart. This is why we must now turn to the sun, the core of the natal chart and the symbol of our true identities. This identity is one that often lies dormant beneath layers of "planetary defense mechanisms" and lunar feelings and is brought to life when we meet someone who illuminates that solar center. In chapter 7, we'll see how that happens.

LETIZIA AND FELIPE OF SPAIN'S AFFINITY CHART

Spain's royal couple need to maintain a certain decorum to present to the world, along with a spirit of joint enterprise, which is easily accomplished by their compatible rising signs and suns. Leitizia's airy rising sign communicates easily, and she can be herself while Felipe can negotiate (Mercury) and align his moods (the moon) and his long-term goals (the sun) with her worldview. Similarly, Leitizia's planets in earthy Virgo are in harmony with Felipe's Taurus rising sign, which demands a stable and traditional lifestyle.

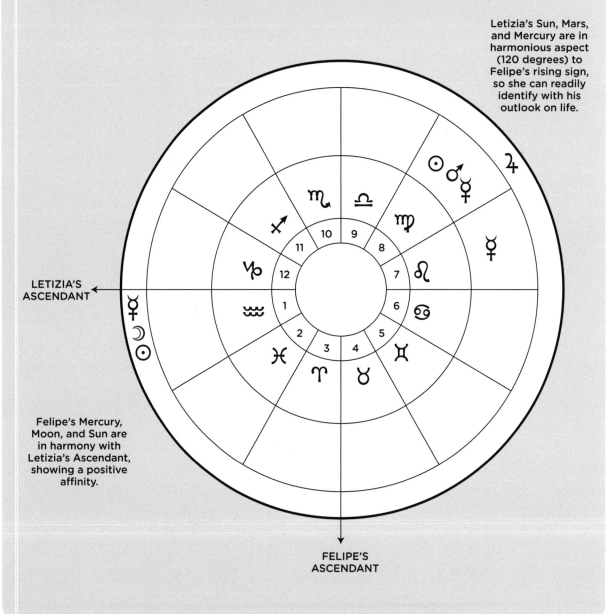

Letizia's Sun, Mars, and Mercury are in harmonious aspect (120 degrees) to Felipe's rising sign, so she can readily identify with his outlook on life.

LETIZIA'S ASCENDANT

Felipe's Mercury, Moon, and Sun are in harmony with Letizia's Ascendant, showing a positive affinity.

FELIPE'S ASCENDANT

7 **The Sun:**
Sacred Light

I n your affinity chart, the sun is a beacon of light that can draw other people to you—but it can create envy and resentment in others as well. This chapter will show you how to interpret sun contacts in the chart— but first, it's essential that you understand the true purpose of the sun and the deeper potentials that are at work behind it.

If you read your horoscope in the newspapers or spend a few minutes clicking around on the casual astrology websites on the Internet, you might think that the sun simply represents our personality traits. You know the kind of lines that are bandied about: "Geminis are fickle; Pisces are dreamy," and so on. But there's so much more to the sun's influence than that. Yes, some of our inner solar light does filter out into these quirks and characteristics we identify with on the surface. What's far more significant, though, is that the sun tells us about what truly matters to us, deep down inside. The sun represents your potential; your will, purpose, and spirit; and your sense of having a calling to a particular vocation, lifestyle, or relationship. The sun is about your sense of you: It says, "I am," and "Here I am." That may sound pretty straightforward, but it's actually a curious, rather difficult quality to grasp because the sun is what we are becoming, and sometimes it takes a whole lifetime to find out what that is.

THE SUN: WHAT I AM BECOMING

Think of the sun, then, as what you are in the process of becoming. It is your future intention, and it could be articulated as "I am," "I want," or "I want to be." For instance, it might say, "I want to shine in this field of work," or, "Here, in this love relationship, is how I want to be individual." And it's the sun that describes our sense of being centered, whether that's self-centered (too much ego) or self-conscious (too little ego). In other words, the solar principle is about our sense of accepting who we are as individuals, and it describes what truly matters to us. That might take a while to figure out: We often think we know when we're younger, but this knowledge is partly shaped by cultural and family attitudes. It's only later, as we start to see ourselves as individuals in our own right—perhaps through meeting an enlightening lover, recovering from a tragic experience, or simply through increased self-awareness over time—that we start to know what matters to us in a profound way.

Recognition

The sun shows us the areas in which we want to be recognized or to reinforce our identities. For example, people with the sun in Gemini may want to be recognized for their ability to adapt to any circumstance and for their lighthearted take on life. But how do we become aware of this need for recognition?

The answer, of course, depends on where the sun is placed by house and also by aspect to other planets in our natal charts. This means that we may find it more or less challenging to seek out that recognition. Here's a quick illustration of what that might look like: If planets could speak, Mars/sun might say, "Look at me, I'm courageous: I will find my potential!" Sun/Neptune would say, "Look at me, I'm a victim. Save me: That seems to be all I am." And sun/Saturn would say, "Look at me. Please? Well, I'm not surprised that you're not looking at me; people usually don't, so why bother?" If we interpret the sun as a symbol of the process of finding our identities, such factors in the chart can either hinder or help that purpose.

The curious thing about the solar "me" is that it's not an easy thing to grasp, which is why our sun isn't something that's visible to another person (let alone ourselves) in an obvious way: Rather, it's picked up in an unconscious way. Plus, it doesn't shine brightly from the moment we were born: It can take most of our lives to be able to step into our own identities, often through a sense of vocation or calling.

THE MYTH: APOLLO

Although the god of the sun in ancient Greek mythology was Helios, Apollo was the true god of light itself, and it is this sacred light that he represents in our birth charts. Apollo was also known as the god of music, truth, healing, plagues, and prophecy, and, with bow and arrow, was the slayer of the great serpent, Python. Apollo was an oracular and omniscient god and was venerated at his temple at Delphi.

I believe Apollo's solar light represents the most sacred part of ourselves and is often the beacon that guides us as we move through life and love. I equate this light to a sacred inner temple, like Apollo's, where the god sent messages to mortals through his oracle. The oracle at Apollo's temple at Delphi was a sibyl known as the Pythia, who acted as a medium for these messages and auguries. Similarly, this inner temple is where we, too, can sometimes get flashes of what we're called to do on life's journey. It can teach us to manifest our true potential—our solar potential. When we listen to this oracle, we discover that this temple is also where our souls reside. And this "soul-centered" place within us shines through when we're listening to our true calling—rather than the expectations of family, culture, or society.

WORKING WITH THE SUN IN THE AFFINITY CHART

So when you meet another person who has the same sun sign as you, things might look great on paper—but there's often a far more challenging energy to the encounter than first meets the eye. There is, of course, a curious deeper sense of an affinity: not just empathy or understanding, but a kind of familiarity or recognition. For example, I notice that the Gemini man I've just fallen for is flirtatious and carefree; as a Gemini woman, I'm flirtatious, too, but I might not like that quality in another person. These solar personality traits are like tiny rays of solar light that radiate from each of us. We may pick up on another person's similar solar energy—but that doesn't necessarily mean we accept it! In fact, we might not identify with it at all; it may feel frustrating or irritating to us.

First of all, look at what contacts your sun makes to his planets and rising sign. But before you begin to interpret or analyze these contacts, think about whether you're sure of your own solar purpose. Is it being brightened and strengthened by your partner's contacts, or is it being tarnished? Think of the sun as the gold within you. In this particular affinity chart, is it being treasured or buried by contacts to your partner's planets?

Next, look at your partner's sun and do the same thing, as objectively as you can. Remember, these are planetary archetypes, so it's not you, specifically, who's responsible for the quality of your partner's solar light—or vice versa. But, for example, if Mars in your chart is at a troublesome angle to his sun, then some angry outbursts may result. But if, say, Venus is in good aspect to his sun, you could temper this with fairness and compromise. Let's look at the ways in which this can manifest.

SUN-TO-SUN CONTACTS IN THE SAME SIGN

There will always be two different kinds of same-sign sun encounters, depending on how conscious the person is of his or her inner hero or heroine (that is, the "I" in the "I am" or "Here I am" statement that's so central to what the sun represents in our lives); on her sense of vocation; or on whether she will import the solar principle from her partner (the woman usually imports it via the man in her life).

The first kind of encounter is one in which the person who is living out his potential to some extent will bring to life the solar light of the other or who might even evoke one of those epiphany or aha moments in which you learn something about yourself for the first time. Alternatively, the person whose solar light is repressed may be so envious of the other that he unleashes all of the dark side of his solar energy in defense or retreats out of fear of being burned alive under the solar furnace of his partner. Let's consider these two examples.

BURNING EFFECT

The man with the sun in Virgo and the woman with the sun in Virgo have just settled down over dinner at a restaurant to discuss their goals and future plans for the very first time. The mood is fairly laid-back: There's wine, good food, and nice white candles. They've been on a few dates before, but they've never really discussed their desires for the future. As with many couples, talking about the future can make them feel like they're getting ahead of themselves. So they start off by discussing the badly-laid-out cutlery and how that wineglass isn't quite as sparkling-clear as it could be. In fact, they seem to have a lot in common, and what matters to them—on the surface, at least—is that life is predictable and things are neat and tidy.

They find out that they both buy free-range eggs, and he says that he likes to boil his for exactly three minutes. She mentions that she likes to put the egg cup on a porcelain plate covered with a linen napkin. They discuss eco-friendly food stores and how important it is to buy good-quality green tea. "By the way," the Virgo man mumbles behind his napkin, "I'm off to the Far East for a few months. My business partner and I just bought a tea plantation, and I need to go out there and check the whole operation. But I hope to see you again when I get back?" Ms. Virgo, who works as secretary in a mediocre law firm, smiles and nods. She responds graciously at first. But soon grace turns to resentment. She starts to criticize everything and everyone, including him, in a defensive attempt to rescue herself from feeling inferior. (The solar principle, even if it's weak and feeble, doesn't like its light to be dimmed by a brighter star in the sky.) He is living out his solar potential (whether he's aware of it or not). She is being burned alive by it. So she makes some attempt to prevent herself from being turned to cinders in his solar furnace and says with cynical but well-armored humor, "Hey, look at that stain on your shirt cuff. Maybe you should buy some stain remover instead of a tea plantation." That's the Virgoan dark side spinning into view.

Same Sun Sign: Enlightening Effect

But what if both people are beginning to live out their sun-sign potential? What if each can see that the other person has begun to identify with what truly matters to her and that their future will bring them together, even if they're living apart? Let's take two Aquarians who are beginning to live out their vocational goals. What matters to them is freedom, an unconventional lifestyle, and humanitarian ideals. The Aquarian man has been out with her on a few dates here and there, as he's very erratic. He's a screenwriter, and he's currently working on an important film script and spends a lot of time working late at night. Then one evening he rings her doorbell, invites himself in for a glass of beer, and they brainstorm about his idea all evening. And it makes Ms. Aquarius think. Well, hasn't she always wanted to be a novelist? And isn't this guy, who seems to know what he's aiming for in life, a professional who's as wise and independent as she is? For the next few dates, Mr. Aquarius enlightens her to her own solar potential. She starts to write her novel, and she also begins to realize that this man will honor her own need for space and independence.

Let's look at some examples of same-element suns. In these cases, if both parties are at least slightly aware of their sun-sign potentials, successful and harmonious relating can result.

HARMONIOUS SUN-SIGN CONTACTS

Same-element sun signs usually get along well. There is an intrinsic understanding and sensibility between persons who share elements in their respective charts. Here's a breakdown of the four different elements and how they may manifest in relationships.

Fire

What matters to the Fire sun signs, if they are living out just a little of their potential, is to look forward to the future, to live and let live, and to be free-spirited, animated by every experience they have. Their optimism is innate, so when two Fire signs meet, they instantly know that they're not going to be pulled down into a mire of pessimistic caution or fear. They boost one another's desire to express themselves, whether it's Leo's connoisseurship of love and romance, Sagittarius's free-ranging, adventurous lovemaking, or Aries's drive to be the top dog in any relationship. Two Fire signs shine together when they are active, dynamic, and firing on all cylinders. But although they can merge successfully, they must also be careful that one doesn't burn the other out. Most importantly, if they can both look deep down toward that sacred inner temple and listen to the messages of the oracle, they will see how vivid their imaginations truly are and how this is so important to both of them for their future happiness. The key word here is *imagination*.

Earth

The Earth signs are fulfilled by crafting and shaping something out of the tangible world. What matters to them, if aware of their solar individuality, is to create, shape, and develop something solid that lets them put their stamp on the world. Whether it's the Taurean artist who creates a sculpture, the Virgo editor who works on a book, or the Capricorn business tycoon who develops a manufacturing company, all of them produce something elegant or useful out of nature's gifts. When two Earth signs meet, they instinctively know that they don't have to do much other than admire the other's life portfolio. Whether they work together in a partnership to create their own business or simply accept each other's talents, this is often a powerful combination in which determination and creativity walk hand in hand. The key word here is *creativity*.

Air

The Air signs have a special gift—although it can double as a curse, too. It's a flickering, niggling reminder that they *must know* who they are, and it lingers at the front of their minds—possibly because people with sun in Air tend to reflect more on who they are than the other elements do. Of course, that doesn't mean all Air signs are diligently attending to their calling from the day they were born—or even when they're all grown up. But air signs like to learn and discover, so when two Air sun signs meet, they play with ideas, and they inspire each other. The Gemini knows that she feels special in a relationship in which she has space to express her ideas; Libra's at his best where there's peace, beauty, and minimal emotional tension; and Aquarius is happiest when she has the freedom to change what she wants to change. Together, they can bring inspirational ideas to light—although, at times, they may be so busy theorizing about life that they forget to attend to its practicalities. The key word here is *inspired*.

Water

The flowing, changeable energy of Water is a constant battle for those with the sun in these signs. The solar principle finds it hard to break through the murky depths of the lunar light (Cancer), the underworld light (Scorpio), and the veil of illusion (Pisces). It often emerges in the individual as a calling for art, theater, music, drama, passionate love affairs, or escapist addictions. The little traits that seep through from the sacred temple come in dreams, fantasies, and often in illusions about love. But when two Water sun signs meet, there is a deep sensitivity, longing, and unconscious understanding that the soul's journey can be fulfilled at last. The solar light may truly shine through these two people since they reinforce each other's sensitivity and spiritual awareness. These signs often embark on a deeply romanticized merger of body, spirit, and soul. The key phrase for the Water signs is *soulful empathy*.

CHALLENGING SUN-SIGN CONTACTS

If it's hard enough for the same sun signs, and sometimes same-element suns, to get along together, then when two suns are in opposition or three signs away, the challenge can really become intense. Why? Well, two solar forces striving to outshine each other is inevitable. So when we meet someone with the sun in the opposite sign, we're both excited, or compelled, to shine brighter than the other person. But we're also fascinated, driven to take some of their shining light for ourselves—not knowing, of course, that this polarity is within us, too. We find their bright light both threatening and desirable, so if we're unable to burn it out, then we import it into our lives by forming a relationship with the person who possesses it.

Fire Sun/Water Sun

When the fiery-sun person encounters the solar-Water person, Water may dampen Fire's enthusiasm (unless there are other positive affinities in the chart), simply because Water tends to identify with her feeling world and doesn't take easily to showy displays of "Look what I can do!" On the surface, Aries doesn't much care what other people think of him, while Cancer, deep down, does care what others think about her; Leo wants to dazzle and impress, while solar Scorpio intends to plunder all egos and all spotlights. Sagittarius puts on a great show of crusading for the underdog, especially those who strive to become top dog, while sun-sign Pisces easily takes on the role of the patsy but never accepts the challenge to make something of himself.

Water Sun/Air Sun

Water is sensitive to every nuance and is aware of every change in energy around her. This deeper sensitivity often manifests on the surface as acutely moody, touchy, or overemotional behavior. Unless the Air sun has Water energy in his own chart, he will grow tired of the Water person's changing moods and feelings. The elusive behavior of Pisces will certainly rouse Gemini's curiosity—but Gemini will get frustrated if she's not getting straight answers. What matters to a Libra sun deep down is to find the perfect relationship or to dwell in a perfectly harmonious world. This will eventually infuriate Cancer, who lives for the ebb and flow of changing love rather than the ideals of it. What truly matters to Scorpio is to discover and experience the dark side of life, while Aquarius seeks to turn every black cloud into an illuminated halo of goodness and purity. This won't gel easily with Scorpio's solar hunt for the taboo and all things "bad."

Air Sun/Earth Sun

In love, the Gemini sun is a romantic lightning conductor, behaving erratically and expecting life to move at a crazy pace. "Let's get there before we decide where to go next," says Gemini, while the Virgo sun says, "Let's plan the whole trip carefully before we even start." It's important for the solar Virgo to take things one step at a time. Even if it takes longer than planned to get things done, discrimination is all. Libra talks of ideals and how love is a wonderful thing, free of conditions or responsibility, while what matters to the Capricorn sun person is that material security, caution, and rules are laid down before love can even get a look in. Finally, Aquarius loves the whole world, not just one person, while what matters to Taurus is that love is defined exclusively as "me and you."

Earth Sun/Fire Sun

What matters deep down to the Taurus sun is comfort, togetherness, roaring log fires, and being head chef, while the Leo sun longs to be on the world's stage, adored by millions and eating in the best restaurants. "Who needs a kitchen unless I'm the star of it?" asks Leo. As for Virgo, he gets obsessed if dates don't go according to plan and sees either a problem or a solution in every detail of life, while Sagittarius doesn't give a hoot about being late for a date: The important thing is that she managed to turn up at all. Capricorn has serious ambitions about love and marriage and the responsibility to take care of one other, while the sun in Aries is, on a profound level, fiercely independent and doesn't want to be responsible for anything other than himself.

OPPOSITIONS

As with all opposing planets, friction, challenge, tension, and rivalry can exist. But often, with two suns, the result can be something fruitful: insight, or a sudden understanding of one's own solar purpose. There's a powerful magnetic attraction here, as the opposite sign represents a part of us that lives in the shadows. When it comes hurtling out of that darkness in the form of another person across the room at a party, we are drawn to it, dazzled by it; our own solar light is diminished for a moment and the unknown side of ourselves is laid out before us like a golden robe. Then we either attempt to squish it all back down into the darkness again or we see that it sheds an intriguing light on our own solar purpose. In fact, it can allow the oracle within us to speak of Apollo's truth; it can encourage us to know ourselves.

So becoming enlightened to your vocation or to what really matters to you in life is a gift that falling for your opposite sun sign can bestow, especially if you discover that there are other harmonious contacts between the two of you.

Aries/Libra

The sun-in-Aries man's solar urge for competition and rivalry is threatened by the way sun in Libra identifies herself with peace at any cost and by her seductive ways and her apparent frivolity around other men. He talks about how he plans to take the world by storm when he wins the next bodybuilding championship, how he trains every day, and how he's so dedicated that he rarely has time for a relationship. She remembers that they had been attracted by each other's perfect bodies at the party—but now the question is, are their outlooks and priorities alike or totally contrary? Her solar self has a glimmer of a vocation—something having to do with beauty or aesthetics, perhaps the desire to become an art historian—and this man's high-octane lifestyle seems to be reminding her of something she knows deep inside: that his kind of life is not for her. So when the Aries man starts talking about freedom, travel, and competitions, she wonders what the hell she's doing there. Surely her commitment to individual purpose centers on a sense of "we" and how important relationships are—right? Whether they can get around the Aries identification with the-self-and-nothing-but-the-self and the Libra identification with us-and-nothing-but-us may depend on other, more harmonious contacts in the chart. Nonetheless, Libra will still have gotten a surprising dose of self-realization.

Taurus/Scorpio

The sun-in-Scorpio woman may not have found her true vocation yet. She only knows that her relationships have been perpetually tainted by unavailable men, dangerous liaisons, or passions that have led her into the darkest of sexual waters. But she's survived. She doesn't quite know what's calling her on, so to speak, but she knows there is something deep within her that's attempting to rise to the surface, like a mythical phoenix rising from the ashes.

When she gets closer to the Taurus man, she finds that he's possessive but seems to be sensible. He is a talented craftsman and has a good business. In fact, he seems to touch a chord deep within her about what matters to her most. Yet she still can't quite grasp what that is. So when he starts to talk about sensual pleasure, nature's treasure, and love's most magical ways, she realizes that all that she truly longs to express (right now) is her most erotic, sexually empowered self. Instead of importing fatally attractive, unavailable men into her life, she can now play out that solar side of herself safely in his arms. This opposition is known for the incredible hypnotic influence between the two people involved. When the solar light of the Earth sun confronts Scorpio's underworld-solar light, they might carry a flambeau of passion as they walk hand in hand to the lower depths of the underworld—or upward toward the light of day.

Gemini/Sagittarius

This is often one of those manic, highly inspirational, and exciting relationships in which both solar lights are flicked on simultaneously by some mysterious force. We can chalk this up to the fact that both are mutable signs, so they're driven to think and act out of the proverbial box. They adapt, merge, part, return, and never take anything for granted. The Sagittarius man's solar light usually shines through his hilarious antics, madcap lifestyle, and his inability to stick to any promise, let alone any form of commitment. So when the sun-in-Gemini woman gets to know him better, she also knows that this relationship's candle could blow out as quickly as it was lit. What matters to her is to have fun, to play, and to show how good she is at transmitting information. She may already be a journalist—or she might be a checkout girl at the cash register—but whatever her vocation, her solar light of carefree, lighthearted living seeps onto the surface, and it's something the Sagittarian man can also identify with. So, if they both identify with space, what's the catch? This is often a highly entertaining, exotic relationship if both have other harmonious contacts. Problems only arise when he'd rather be exploring the world and everyone in it or when her seductive enchantments lead her astray with someone else.

Cancer/Capricorn

A powerful allure exists between these two solar principles, as Cancer usually pushes so many of Capricorn's psychological buttons that she's suddenly turned on to where she's going in life. Let's take a Capricorn man and a Cancer woman. They fell for each other a few weeks ago at a work event. She looks after the HR department (a suitably nurturing vocation), and he is the company's CEO. She has always admired his role and his classy manner. He hasn't really noticed her until now since he's been so consumed with his career. But they each sense something unique about each other that runs deeper than sex or attraction. As they discuss their future, he discovers that what matters to her is to run her own matchmaking company someday. She believes her greatest skill is matchmaking and intuitively understanding how others feel. He's impressed. He's never thought about feelings much before and doesn't identify with his own. So as her solar light shines ever brighter, he's taken aback by her dedication to what matters to her. He has a moment of epiphany and realizes what matters to him: success by the bucketload. Perhaps they'd be a fantastic duo, with business and pleasure walking hand in hand.

Leo/Aquarius

Things aren't so easy for Leo and Aquarius. Here's why. If a Leo man is besotted with an Aquarian woman, it's either because of other contacts between their charts or because she's truly letting his solar light shine brighter than anyone else's—to begin with, anyway. What matters at heart to sun in Aquarius is that the world and everyone in it is happy and that there are no conditions in love relationships. Her solar light might shine through into the real world via her work with a humanitarian cause, and she may have a string of datable but nonexclusive boyfriends. She is innately very good at making the person she's with feel good about himself. This goes to the sun-in-Leo man's head. Yet when they get closer, and he begins to get a nagging sense that she really isn't going to give up her other dates for him, it niggles his solar center. It worries him enough to make him realize that he identifies solely with being in the spotlight—without sharing it with anyone else. How can he ever do that if she has other men in her life? This presents a difficult challenge unless there are more supportive contacts in their charts.

Virgo/Pisces

Finally, we come to a couple who can find much in each other's solar identity that will help them come to terms with their own. In fact, the sun in Pisces is notorious for taking on the identity of the person he's with because he is the master of Neptunian disguise. This is an innate quality, and it is usually totally unconscious. The only thing that sun in Pisces is aware of is it that the person he's with seems right at the time. So when a Pisces man is faced with a Virgo woman, can she shine a light deep into the crevices of his soul to help him know what he's truly becoming? The answer is yes and no.

The Pisces man may well have some kind of suitable vocation, which gets them both off to a good start. He's a musician, nurse, artist, or maybe even a mixologist at a cocktail bar. He's kind and gentle, and other people's energy tends to rub off on him. He's the sponge of the zodiac in that he soaks up everything around him: He's sensitive and often gullible, too. So in the pleasing company of the Virgo woman, he appreciates her ability to tell black from white and her amazing knowledge about—well, everything. At first this useful, observational woman is a delight to the Pisces man. In fact, everything she says or does seems polished, and he finds himself imitating her wise, skillful voice. But the more he takes on the Virgo mask, the more he begins to resist it. There's something deep down inside him that tells him, "Hey, this isn't really me at all!" And this is when the Pisces man can discover that his deep well of illusions is exactly that—an illusion. At the other end of the equation, the Virgo woman may learn that the boundlessness of this man's solar light can bring her to terms with some inner knowledge that she may have always been afraid to truly accept.

THE SUN AND THE REST OF THE CHART

Sun-to-sun contacts are critical in a synastic chart. However, the sun also plays a key role in relation to other personal planets in the natal chart and the way in which it can boost or diminish the qualities of each planet. We'll talk about sun/moon contacts in detail in chapter 9, but for now, let's look at other key planets. When, for example, your sun is contacting the other fiery planets (i.e., planets that rule Fire signs), such as Jupiter and Mars, then sparks will fly and will help to boost your solar light. This also goes for Venus and Mercury, as both are "active" planets. However, when the sun contacts Saturn, as we shall see, your solar light may feel as if it's been turned off or is unable to shine at all.

SUN/VENUS CONTACTS

When the sun and Venus are in contact in the affinity chart, there is an immediate rapport based on the fact that these are both dynamic energies. If the sun shines, then Venus likes to follow suit or take the sun person by the hand and show them how glorious it is to bask in the light of each other's admiration, self-indulgent pleasures, and the joy of mutual happiness.

Maria Callas and Ari Onassis are known for their lifelong passion, and particularly for Maria, a tortured love affair. With their positive sun/Venus, moon/Venus and Venus/Venus cross-contacts, it's hardly surprising they loved each other and sought the same pleasures in life. Although Ari Onassis abandoned Maria to marry "America," or rather, Jackie Kennedy, he often found himself compelled to return to Maria's side (his Sun drawn to Maria's Moon). Maria remained loyal in her love for him until the end of his life (her Moon attached to his Sun). Some say it was a broken heart she died of two years after his death.

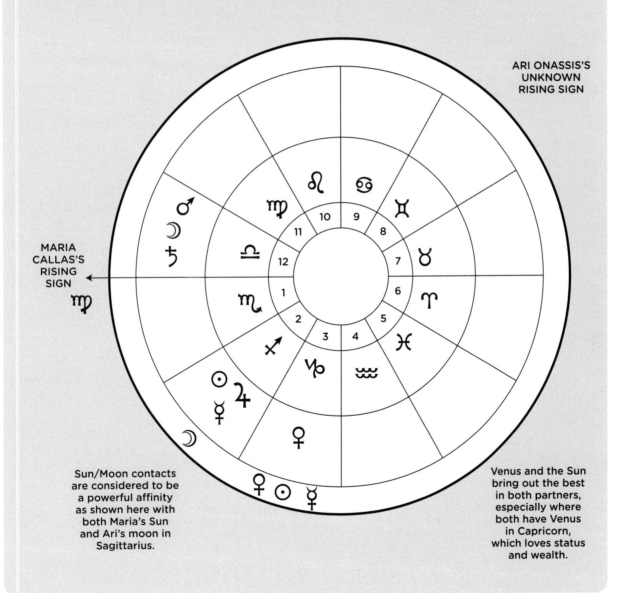

ARI ONASSIS'S UNKNOWN RISING SIGN

MARIA CALLAS'S RISING SIGN

Sun/Moon contacts are considered to be a powerful affinity as shown here with both Maria's Sun and Ari's moon in Sagittarius.

Venus and the Sun bring out the best in both partners, especially where both have Venus in Capricorn, which loves status and wealth.

Harmonious Contacts: Same Sign and Element

This is a classic romantic contact since the Venus person usually has an empowering, seductive influence over the sun person, who hooks into Venus's pleasure-loving ways. This is because the sun is an active agent that embarks on a quest to discover its true sense of meaning or its calling. And so the beautiful, enchanting Venus of another (particularly same sign or same element) invites the solar person's light to illuminate the Venus partner for a while (remember the vanity of the goddess Venus). Even though Venus is a feminine principle, it is also active: It oozes desire and intention and isn't a receptive container like the moon. So most sun and Venus contacts work well together when they're in the same sign and same element. If one partner's pleasure principle and desire for happiness are in accord with the sun person's vocation, identity, and self-development, then these two can work together actively to make the relationship a success. Take, for example, the chart of Ari Onassis and Maria Callas, in which Ari's sun in Capricorn contacts Maria's Venus, and Maria's sun conjuncts Ari's moon. Although they had plenty of ups and downs throughout their relationship, they were always illuminating each other's lives.

Challenging Contacts: Three Signs Away and Oppositions

When Venus is in opposition to the sun, there will naturally be differences between what the Venus person, for example, values and enjoys, and what really matters to the sun person. The problem arises when the Venus person's desire for the finest, most expensive things of life (let's say we're talking about a woman in Taurus) clashes with the Aquarian man's identification with helping the poor and homeless. Unless he's happy to chat about it between the sheets (and has a host of planets in earthier signs), he'll feel like he's being bitten by a mosquito without being able to scratch the itch.

To begin with, oppositions and squares are sexy attractions because of their very differences. But the Venus person usually begins to feel she's not as beautiful (or, rather, that she doesn't shape up to the solar image her partner identifies with) or attractive as she "should" be. This is because the solar person gets on his high horse, desperate to restore his true solar purpose rather than be outdazzled by Venusian vanity. This is often a short-term attraction since the Venus person weaves a spell around the sun person, making him feel as if he is being seduced because his own solar light is shining so perfectly. Later on down the line, the sun person's light begins to dim as Venus tries to steal the limelight and prove that her pleasure-loving ways are more important than his shining light. Unless there are other, more harmonious contacts between them, this is not a particularly good contact for long-term love.

SUN/MARS CONTACTS

Whatever happens in the rest of your relationship, when Mars and the sun are together, an active, dynamic energy is at work.

Harmonious Contacts: Same Sign and Element

Like the sun, Mars is a Fire planet, and this powerful combination can stir the solar person to understand his long-term objectives, while the Mars person gets in touch with her willpower, courage, physical libido, and lust for life. This can be a very sexy liaison—but it can be very challenging and competitive. And chances are that any testing, spirited rivalry behind the scenes will also be played out between the sheets.

Challenging Contacts: Three Signs Away and Oppositions

As with all challenging contacts, this one can pose significant problems for both partners.

First of all, there's a very strong sexual attraction at work here. There's also tremendous vigor, passion, and desire, but unless other contacts suggest strong bonds, this is usually a relationship fraught with points-scoring, through sex, behavior, or attitudes. Competitive yet often compelling, this love affair can be highly impulsive and daring. But there'll also be power struggles and battles, and hot-and-steamy romance could soon turn into a war of nerves. Take care unless other contacts suggest long-term commitment.

SUN/SATURN CONTACTS

This is often one of those "fated" attractions, and apart from Saturn/moon contacts, is one of the most binding Saturn contacts in love relationships. However, this partnership seems to work best when the woman's Saturn and the man's sun are involved, simply because it's usually the man who develops a "vocation" or is more able to act out his solar principle. But don't get me wrong: This match can be just as powerful the other way around, too, since it can mean that the woman's sun slowly "sees the light."

Harmonious Contacts: Same Sign and Element

Again, when the sun person meets the Saturn person, the sun person shines, radiates, and glows with the very qualities that the Saturn person has repressed because they seemed to be difficult or awkward to express. (For detailed information about Saturn, see chapter 13.) But suddenly the Saturn person is faced with the sun person who's (consciously or unconsciously) radiating his or her solar self.

Let's take an example of a man with the sun in Capricorn and a woman with Saturn in Capricorn. He's glowing with pride: He has built a mini-empire for himself in business and is self-confident and driven to succeed. She immediately feels vulnerable in his presence, yet secretly craves what he has. She may be compensating by playing the role of the shrewd businesswoman (even if she's not actually making any money), but if they form a long-term relationship—and this is often the case—she will depend on him to live out her success, and he will be happy to let her do so because it strengthens his solar purpose. This is often one of the most long-term, binding ties in the affinity chart because it leads the Saturn person to understand and admire what she truly can master; and, with admiration, the sun person pushes himself harder to develop his potential.

Sun/Saturn connections in the same element are powerful connections, and to outsiders, it can seem as if both partners are seriously ambitious about their future together. Here, both people have the ability to build a future based on trust and respect. They help each other out in all kinds of practical ways, and even in elements that are more cerebral, like Air or Fire, both people remain grounded and down-to-earth when they're together. If it's her Saturn and his sun, she may need to be prepared to join him in acquiring the skills he's trying to develop. If it's his Saturn, then he's going to have to work hard to draw out the qualities he finds so admirable in her. This is a powerful link, and it can bring success and security to both parties.

Challenging Contacts: Three Signs Away or Oppositions

When the sun and Saturn are three signs apart or in opposition, powerful unconscious defense mechanisms can rise to the surface. It's a bit like a pressure cooker that needs release: Both partners will feel as if they're locked up in a prison, both building walls of defense around themselves to protect their very different quests for achievement. If it's her sun, she may feel cheated out of being who she's really trying to become, as his Saturn takes over a solar role for her. But if it's her Saturn, there may be a more enduring energy as he begins to accept their differences. With maturity and reflection, this can be a powerful connection—especially if other contacts provide balance and harmony.

SUN/MERCURY CONTACTS

These contacts are beneficial when it comes to good communication between you and your partner. It's easy to overlook these contacts to some extent in favor of the more exciting ones that tell us about our sexual chemistry, the way in which we fall in love, or our long-term compatibility potential. But Mercury is all about the way we talk, discuss, and, most importantly, listen to one other—that is, it's about how well we can truly understand and accept our partner's feelings. After all, some of us might sit in a daze staring longingly at our lovers, but without really listening to what they have to say. These are the couples who find, a few years down the line, that what they *thought* they heard and what they *actually* heard were two very different things. That's why Mercury can clue you in on how the two of you will communicate later on.

Harmonious Contacts: Same Sign and Element

When we have same-sign and same-element contacts from the sun to Mercury, we can be assured of a pretty good dialogue between the two people involved. For example, Mercury in Fire is usually quick to jump to conclusions, doesn't think things through, and is often impetuous with words—only to realize later that he may have said something outrageous or indiscreet. Yet this can be delightfully provocative for a Fire-sign person and often gives her a sense of her own inner energy and how combustive and spontaneous it can be when it's triggered by the Mercury person's carefree communicative style. So, for example, when a woman with Mercury in Aries chats with a sun-in-Sagittarius man, her assertive,

If a woman with Mercury in Taurus, for instance, takes time to get her message across (she deliberates, thinks things through, and likes to get the words exactly right), then the man with the sun in Virgo will admire her determined, well-paced self-expression. This may not be the key to the "lust factor," but it's certainly one of the doors to the "wit factor." And whatever Mercury in Earth knows, he knows it well, and so his questions will always get the right answers, and her answers will stimulate his solar desire for ultimate knowledge.

impatient attitude is actually very welcome to the Archer, who likes to get on to the next subject, preferring quick thinking to inertia. The Mercury-in-Aries woman is also much more intuitive than she thinks. However, she will want to rile him into action, which means they can both get into hotheaded disputes.

Challenging Contacts: Three Signs Away and Oppositions

All these contacts are thought-provoking, but they're not easy to negotiate and often aren't a big help in long-term relationships. After all, if we can't communicate with one another or if we seem to be on different wavelengths, then (unless our Mercuries have some affinity between them) we're unlikely to be able to express ourselves authentically. According to the sun person, whatever the Mercury person says seems to be riddled with hidden agendas. For example, let's assume that her Mercury is in Scorpio and his sun is in Leo. He will, initially, be fascinated by the mysterious way she expresses herself, but it won't really fit with his life purpose and his open attitude toward life and love. Sun in Leo identifies with the drama of it all; he loves to be center stage and wants everyone to know his business. Mercury in Scorpio, on the other hand, seeks privacy and won't be at all happy about the secrets of her love life being advertised around town—and this creates an underlying pressure within the relationship.

SUN/JUPITER CONTACTS

The sun and Jupiter are both Fire signs, and, as with the sun and Mars, this provides a powerful creative energy. If both partners can harness it to their advantage, this energy can bring them long-term luck and success in all they do.

Because Jupiter exaggerates all it touches, the sun person becomes more aware of her solar self as a result, and it often provides her with the push or leap forward she needs in order to discover her true potential. The Jupiter person, meanwhile, gets a Jupiter experience, often believing that this is the

Relationship To End All Relationships and may believe he has found his life partner. He just wants to keep feeling divine in the presence of the sun person, but this, unsurprisingly, can lead to excessive pride and self-belief.

Harmonious Contacts: Same Sign and Element

The Jupiter person is just a larger-than-life version of the sun person, and so it's easy to see why they get along so well. There's a sense of optimism between these two and a tremendously exciting energy and magnetic allure. There's also a healthy competition based on beliefs (Jupiter) and purpose. This can be one of those relationships that last for their adventurous spirit and enterprising interest in one another.

Challenging Contacts: Three Signs Away and Oppositions

As with all oppositions and incompatible elements, there is a powerful tension here, and it can be very sexually exciting for the two people involved. But the battle between the two heavenly gods, Jupiter and Apollo, gets played out through silly disputes, sexual power games, or manipulative tactics. They might even blame each other for their luck, whether it's good or bad.

For example, the no-nonsense Jupiter-in-Aries woman, who is direct and to the point, can dominate most men (in the nicest possible way!) with her fiery drive to win yet another challenge and to demonstrate her power. So once he gets up close and personal with her, the highly defensive Venus-in-Cancer man (who has somehow fallen for her charm) not only reacts to her Jupiter "inflationary" influence by feeling even more insecure than usual about what really turns him on, but also wishes he could retreat into his shell and avoid discussing the whole thing. As they flounder in the bedroom, the Jupiter woman's greed for scoring points reaches its climax—but unless either has supporting contacts, it's likely this will be her one and only game, set, and match.

In challenging alignments, the Jupiter person may become highly principled and judgmental, accusing the sun person of being on the wrong track. The danger here is that the sun person will feel that her own goals and self-worth are being bullied or belittled at the expense of the other's beliefs. The Jupiter person may be amused by the game, but it usually ends up with self-righteous, banner-waving wrangles when both partners attempt to outwit or outphilosophize the other.

SUN/URANUS CONTACTS

If the sun is about our solar purpose and Uranus is the planet of awakening, shock, and change, then sparks are sure to fly when these contacts appear in the affinity chart. The Uranus person will want to reform or change the sun person in some way, and the sun person will find the Uranian person a challenge, even in harmonious contacts. But this challenge is one in which both partners are inspired or excited by their encounter. Uranian energy creates a spirited, lively, unusual, and sometimes frustrating atmosphere between two people, but it is never passive, and it is always dynamic. (For more information about Uranus, see chapter 16.)

Harmonious Contacts: Same Sign and Element

When a man's Uranus makes a harmonious contact to his partner's sun, then they'll both feel sparkling and alive, and together, they can create an unconventional twosome. She may want to shine even more brightly on her own but will be ready to try out new ideas and to see herself in a new light. This will be an electrifying rapport with plenty of surprises and inspirational ideas that'll keep both of them on their toes. The Uranian man may even feel ready to give up his whole philosophy of life and follow the sun person around the world. Whichever way the contact, it makes for an unconventional and unusual love affair based on the way in which it can inspire the solar identity of one and the Uranian light of the other.

Challenging Contacts: Three Signs Away and Oppositions

If it's his Uranus and her sun, she could find that he wants to control her or change her solar identity to something progressive or idealistic. She'll be fascinated by him, of course, but will soon discover her own personal goals are being squished out of existence. They both will be compelled to contradict one another, and the more this happens the sooner one will retaliate while the other runs and hides. (Which person does which? That depends on other contacts in their charts.)

For example, when his Uranus in Sagittarius opposes her sun in Gemini, the universe is trying to wake her up to something other than who she really is. On one level, does she dare to change? On another level, it seems as if something magical, radical, and impossible is happening to her. She may ask questions like, What does love really mean? Can there be such a thing as unconditional love? This challenge will provoke the sun-in-Gemini woman to either defend her sun's natural calling by promoting her own ideals above his Uranian vision or to change her perceptions to fall in line with his. But whether this is a change for the better depends on her own Uranian vision, too.

SUN/NEPTUNE CONTACTS

Neptune's paradox is that it longs for something, but it makes it nearly impossible to reach the object of its desire. And that means that contacts between Neptune and the sun can cause us to live in a misty haze of not-quite-attained romance. If your Neptunes are in different signs, and if your Neptune contacts your partner's sun, you may quickly hook into him, seeing him as the living embodiment of all your dreams. But with difficult contacts, the Neptune partner confuses the sun partner by acting seductive and wily; she may never really show her true self to the sun person. (See chapter 16 for more information on Neptune.)

Harmonious Contacts: Same Sign and Element

This couple will bring out each other's sensitivity, and they'll be highly intuitive about each other's desires. If they both have similar goals (i.e., similar sun-sign elements), they'll help each other attain them as long as both partners are caring and understanding. But, as with any Neptune contact, the Neptune person will need to make sure she isn't imagining qualities in the sun person that he doesn't really have. The relationship will be light, sparkling, and romantic, as long as both people don't deceive themselves about what's really going on. (This means you need to look at other contacts to the sun, Saturn, and moon to determine long-term compatibility.) If your Neptunes are in different signs, then the person whose sun contacts the other person's Neptune will feel as if the sun person represents everything she longs for.

Challenging Contacts: Three Signs Away and Oppositions

Let's take an example opposition of a sun-in-Taurus woman and a Neptune-in-Scorpio man. Our sun-in-Taurus woman will find it hard to trust this man. He promises a lot, but can he ever fulfill those commitments? Neptune in Scorpio is filled with yearning: He longs to reach down into the depths of a relationship, to discover a beautiful treasure within, and to steal it for himself. However, Neptune in Scorpio fools himself with impossible expectations. Would a Taurus woman give up what really matters to her—keeping her feet on the ground, maintaining financial security, and having long-term material goals? So, drawn to each other yet misunderstanding one other, he will cast his romantic illusions upon her (for Neptune wants to dissolve all boundaries) and the two will indulge in physical attraction. She senses—quite rightly—that there's something emanating from him that's too seductive, too good to be true. But that doesn't stop her from being led astray—for a while, at least.

SUN/PLUTO CONTACTS

Pluto is both empowering and transformative when it's in contact with the sun or any other of the personal planets. (For more detailed information about Pluto, see chapter 16.) In these contacts, both partners feel as if they can't survive without each other—but not in a good way. A mutual power struggle of emotions, passion, pain, and destruction is at work here, and it's often very difficult for either person to become untangled from the relationship's obsessive quality.

Harmonious Contacts

After decades of looking at synastic charts, I don't think Pluto can ever really be harmonious in the affinity chart. "Easy" contacts, such as trines and conjunctions, are never truly easy, and the force of a dark power always lurks unseen between the two partners. It often manifests as sexual lures, power struggles, codependence, or a sense of restricted freedom. So we'll consider all Pluto-to-sun contacts to be challenging.

Challenging Contacts

Although Pluto is destructive, obsessive, and passionate, when he's faced with another person's (conscious or unconscious) solar light, Pluto is initially blinded by that light. But Pluto is crafty and wears an invisible helmet when he ascends to the earth's surface and faces the light of day. This prince of darkness grins widely at the sun person and beckons, knowing that he can survive—and win—at any game his partner plays. (Of course, neither person is aware that they're part of such a game, but it manifests as the dark power of the unconscious versus the solar energy of the ego.)

So, for example, when the sun-in-Virgo woman meets the Pluto-in-Virgo man, she is instantly attracted to his deep understanding of what makes her tick. He obsesses (more than other signs because this is Virgo, after all) about how hideous the real world is, but how dangerously beautiful and powerful some things in it can be if you "know your stuff." Then, if Pluto were to speak, he might say, "So, you think you're a clever Virgo and you have all knowledge at your fingertips, do you? Well, *I'll* show you what knowledge is." Pluto secretly wants to harness the power of knowledge for himself and abduct it, taking it down to the subterranean depths of his underworld realm. To do this, Pluto intends to overpower Virgo both sexually and emotionally; that way, he'll get to reap all her knowledge himself. Then he'll leave her poisoned and tainted by the darkness she has experienced. This is when her own solar light becomes blinded by a painful, obsessive love for the Plutonian man—and she finds that her ego has been buried under the weight of Pluto's power.

Sure, this description may sound overly dramatic, but if you've experienced it, you'll know that nothing about it is exaggerated. There's no doubt about it: When your sun is in the throes of a Plutonian relationship, it feels as if you're being buried alive. (For more on Pluto, see chapter 16.)

SUN/RISING SIGN CONTACTS

Because your rising sign is all about the first impression you present to the world (as well as the first impression you get of the world when you're born), it plays a significant part in attracting another person via his or her sun. With rising sign/sun attractions, the rising-sign person either feels a strong affinity with the sun person (if in the same sign or element); feels compelled to do battle with him or her (three signs away or opposition); or feels challenged in some way.

Harmonious Contacts: Same Sun and Rising Sign

If your rising sign is the first impression you give of yourself and is the way you show yourself off, so to speak, then the other person's sun unconsciously recognizes this part of itself and lights up in the presence of the other. Without being aware of why, the sun person instantly identifies with this "replica" of itself as the rising sign walks into the room or is spotted across a crowded bar. This is an unconscious but deeply illuminating sense of recognition. Meanwhile, the rising-sign person may not immediately take to the sun person but still knows that something about that person resonates with her own behavior. This is what makes same sun sign/rising sign contacts so mysteriously fated; it's as if both parties know something about the other but aren't really sure what that something is.

As for the sun-sign person, along comes a rising-sign person who represents all that he is trying to be. So the solar "hero" would say of the rising-sign person, "How can she give such a good impression of what I'm spending my life striving to become? And boy, what an impression she's making on me. Behind my own rising-sign mask, I've got illusions, fears, and doubts, and I'm finding it hard to really know who I am. Lo and behold, though, in her presence, I'm beginning to realize that I *do* know who I am! But do I like it?"

In fact, something utterly magical happens to both people here. The rising-sign person encounters the core identity she is acting out on the surface. She is a dead ringer for the sun-sign person's true self, and on the whole, both feel amazing in each other's presence.

Harmonious Contact: Same Element

When the rising sign is the same element as the other person's sun, an easy empathy exists, as well as a magnetic pull from the sun-sign person toward the rising sign of the other. This gentle desire to know more of the rising-sign person is also a hugely attractive one because although these are different signs, they share the same qualities of the element they're in, whether that's passion (Fire), feeling (Water), substance (Earth), or imagination (Air).

Often the sun-sign person will be highly attracted to the rising-sign person, sensing a fellow element regardless of whether the rising-sign person has a totally different sun sign. Then it's a question of whether the sun-sign person's true identity creates tension with the rising-sign element in question. However, the rising-sign person will key in to the elemental quality of the sun-sign person as happily as if she's been given a pot of gold. This immediately makes the rising-sign person confident and content to carry on projecting this impression, no matter what truly lies behind that painted veil. If the sun-sign person feels a sense of recognition and purpose, the rising-sign person will feel that keeping up appearances is worthwhile.

Remember, sun-to-rising-sign attractions offer the sun person a chance to really know themselves, and they can offer the rising-sign person affirmation, too. This is why this kind of attraction is likely to last a lifetime—as long as there are strong affinities between other planets. However—and isn't there always a catch?—incompatibilities can arise, particularly from the rising-sign person's point of view. If her own sun isn't being expressed or if it gets swallowed up by her overpowering identification with the other person's bright solar light, resentment can begin to undermine the relationship. The way in which this operates depends, to a great extent, on the rest of the affinity chart, so you'll need to look at each partner's sun in relation to other planets in the chart to see whether it's being supported or eclipsed by larger-than-life planets like Pluto (who wants to bury the solar light) or Neptune (who idealizes the solar principle).

Challenging Contacts: Oppositions

In challenging rising sign/sun contacts, particularly oppositions, the rising-sign person's seventh house "out there" is embodied in the solar identity of the sun person, who becomes a vehicle for the missing energy of the seventh house.

And we get into tricky territory here. Once you get the sense that the rising sign can be defined as "what you see and how you see life" and the sun is "what matters to you and how you shape your life," you'll understand how this can create either amazingly challenging relationships, with electricity and sparks flying left and right—or, alternatively, a tense, confusing mix of incompatible energies.

Opposites attract, and none more so than the rising sign of one person opposing the sun of the other, who immediately gives the rising-sign person a dose of his own estranged seventh house.

As with all sun contacts, we can assume that usually we aren't consciously aware of, but have a vague sense of or niggling feeling about, what matters to us if we're the sun. So when we're faced with the opposite rising sign, the thing that matters to us may start to work its way out of the darkness, provoked by the startling realization that the rising-sign person presents a challenge to what matters most to us. For example, let's take a Libra sun and an Aries rising. If the Aries looks at life from a purely subjective viewpoint, so that the world is all about "me," then the Libra sun is all about sharing and caring—the absolute opposite of a self-centered ego. This stand-alone, egotistical Aries rising is a big threat to what matters to the Libra sun—pleasing others rather than just the self—but Aries is curiously attractive to Libra, too. The question is, does the sun in Libra know that this is what matters to her? Perhaps not.

Challenging Contact: Three Signs Away

In this case, the sun person will be more likely to feel the tension, being faced with a rising sign who acts, behaves, and gads around the place in a way that has nothing to do with what matters to him deep down. And this usually means that he'll simply retreat, but not always. Remember that there's something magnetic about people who are very different from ourselves—and this is even more true when the sun is in opposition to the rising sign.

SUN/MOON CONTACTS

We'll talk about sun/moon contacts in detail in chapter 9. Let's move now from the goal-oriented brilliance of solar light to that of the moon, which represents the most precious, softest parts of ourselves. Incompatible moons can cause us to experience feelings such as resentment, self-pity, or anger that can lead us into tense, tricky relating, while compatible moons signal that we understand each other's feelings and can support, nurture, and accept each other. How well does your moon work with your partner's? Chapter 8 will show you how to find out.

8 The Moon:
Attachment and Need

The truth is that our needs and desires may not always be in tandem, both in our own natal charts and in the affinity chart. This chapter focuses on the moon, and it'll show you how to work with the moon's subtle energies to create successful relating.

We may be lured to one another by our rising signs; we may fall under the spell of another person's Venus, or we may be physically tempted by his Mars or her Eros. But the moon can either provide an anchoring bond that's vital to a successful relationship—or, if your needs, comfort zones, behaviors, and reactions don't connect with the desires or needs of the other person, it can cause real havoc.

THE LUNAR SELF

The moon represents the most fragile, vulnerable parts of ourselves. Think of it as your inner infant, hungry for comfort and nurturing. In a sense, it still wishes that its mother were there to care for it, as she was when it was living in ignorant bliss inside the womb. And once we are out of the womb and away from the breast, we attach ourselves to consistent habits, those things that will sustain us whether we were nurtured by a fearsome mother or a weak one. For bad or good, then, the moon signifies that which is instinctively reliable. It also describes how we sustain or nurture others. Problems arise when one person's comfort zone doesn't gel with her partner's, and this is often when the moon's neediness takes over from the Venusian ideals of romance.

THE MYTH: SELENE

Let's take a moment to consider the myth of Selene, the goddess of the moon in Greek mythology. Selene fell in love with a shepherd, Endymion, and because she wanted him all to herself, she cast a spell over him that lulled him into an eternal sleep. The only time he awoke was when she came down from the sky to wake him with a kiss and make love to him.

This tells us something about the moon that we may not want to hear. The moon's needs can also be possessive; like any planet, it too has a dark side that can manifest as greediness—or it can react in a subversive, underhanded, and even threatening way when its sensitive boundaries are pushed. So we need to carefully consider our moons and their contacts in our affinity charts.

WORKING WITH THE MOON IN THE AFFINITY CHART

It's important to remember that if the moon is in contact with an outer planet in one of the partners' natal charts, it will have a powerful effect on the relationship. Look at your own moon placement in your chart and any aspects or configurations that touch the moon to help you understand where your moon is coming from. Then do the same with your partner's before you analyze the contacts in the affinity chart. If we can be open about our own lunar needs or issues, then we can learn to accept our differences, too.

We really have to look at the whole affinity chart to understand the effects of the two moons, rather than just looking at your moon in its relationship to your partner's planets. This all makes for serious thinking about interpreting the chart as a whole, and of course, making adjustments and balances to see where you can successfully work or play with someone and where difficulties can arise between you. For example, your moon may be conjunct his sun, which is a sign of mutual understanding and empathy: Your needs will be met, and his solar identity will be reinforced. But if his moon is square your Pluto, his feelings will be plundered—according to him—and he'll never feel at home in your company. He'll prefer to keep his distance instead.

Same-Sign Moon Contacts: A Mixed Blessing

On paper, same-sign moon contacts look like good things, and in certain ways they are. Surely they indicate that you and your partner must have similar feelings and an ability to react intuitively and to understand one another—right? Yes, that's a good start. But equally, if we resonate with the lovely, nurturing side of the moon, we may also be horror-stricken at its darker, more suffocating side. When we begin to suspect that our own habitual reactions and negative sensitivities are coming to life in our partners, we are also forced to come to terms with these qualities in ourselves. But compassion, tolerance, understanding, and true empathy can help us to accept the dark side of the moon—within both ourselves and our partners.

This usually takes time, and it can take hard work, too. But the good news is that this most private, fragile part of yourself is more likely to be accepted and encouraged by your partner when it's in positive aspect to another planet, particularly Venus, sun, Mars, or Jupiter, or when your partner's moon is in a different sign but is within the same element.

TOUCHY-FEELY

Let's take two people with the moon in Cancer, its natural home. The man with the moon in Cancer may resist or fight his feeling world, to some extent, simply because men are generally taught to be unemotional, strong, and stoic in the face of adversity and to react to life in an intellectual, analytical, or rational way. So the moon's touchy-feely side (especially in Cancer) is something he may have suppressed or blotted out with his analytical mind. When he meets a woman with the moon in Cancer, all of this changes. He senses her vulnerable side; he understands her feelings; and he responds to her reactions and behaviors and realizes that maybe he, too, has feelings. And this can be both a blessing and a curse. It's a blessing if he can work with this deeper, less rational side of himself and can see that he and his partner can be both comfortable and comforting together; it's a curse if he ends up rejecting his feeling world and plays the crabby game of blaming his black moods on her or casts her as the moody one in the relationship.

Harmonious Contact: Same Element

When both moons are in the same element, both partners will intuitively understand each other, and this will add an immediate sense of familiarity, security, and emotional harmony. However, if one person is feeling down or depressed, those feelings can easily rub off on the other person, which can lead to a situation in which one partner blames the other for how he or she feels.

But generally speaking, when both moons are in the Fire signs, a high degree of intuitive understanding exists. In the Air signs, there are great opportunities for the couple to explore and discuss their feelings rationally. In Earth, they are both capable of keeping their feet on the ground and staying in the "real world," instinctively knowing when is the right time to make plans or act on ideas. In Water, they'll be so tuned in to each other that they can get overly emotional; you might even find them crying over a weepy film together.

Challenging Contact: Three Signs Away

When your moons are in clashing elements (or in opposition), two very different sets of needs and behavior are at play. These relationships may be difficult to sustain unless there are important positive contacts that can bind the partners together. But do keep an eye out for any positive contacts between the moon and Venus, which can help to bring pleasure into the equation and true value surrounding lunar feelings. The Venus person enables the moon person to understand that her feelings are as valuable as the things the Venus person loves.

It's a very sexy relationship on the surface, but the undercurrents of different emotional needs will make things feel tense and inhibited for one person or the other. The result is that the couple will unconsciously try to resolve the imbalance through their sexual relationship. When it comes to sex, excitement is one thing—but this kind of energy can become frantic and can create a tension that's volatile and dangerous, all the more so because it's hidden underneath a calm exterior. Often one partner will start playing underhanded games because he feels isolated or because her needs aren't being met. Look to see whether the moon makes other, more harmonious contacts that might reflect more mutual understanding.

Challenging Contact: Oppositions

Here, again, we're talking about very different emotional needs, behaviors, and comfort zones, which may test the relationship sooner rather than later.

For example, let's take a woman with the moon in Leo and a man with the moon in Aquarius. The moon in Leo, as we've noticed before, needs to shine by being on a stage of some kind. If she's not in the spotlight or on center stage, either she'll react by robbing someone else's spotlight or she'll want to possess that stage for herself in the same way that Selene possessed Endymion's beauty.

So along comes the Aquarian moon man, who isn't at all interested in the fiery passions of the Leo woman and her precious spotlight. They may have fallen in love in the first place through some great Venus dynamics in their charts, but now, a few months or so down the line, they begin to think about moving in together. The moon-in-Leo woman suggests that they sleep at *his* apartment for a change (they've been at hers on and off for the past few weeks since she just loves to show off her fancy lingerie, sparkling wardrobe, lines of designer shoes, and her pristine kitchen) and says that she'd love to see his tank of piranhas. Instantly, instead of feeling excited, the moon-in-Aquarius man feels uncomfortable. His moon is under threat, and he feels defensive. A swarm of butterflies surges through his belly. He agrees, of course, but he's dreading the event. To be honest, he pays little attention to domesticity, and his home is more like an alien spaceship than a human dwelling. He never did get that leaky faucet mended, and he's sure there's something growing in the fridge. "Maybe come over tomorrow night?" he says. "I need a night in alone; you know me." Our nondomestic god smiles, but inwardly he's panicking about how much cleaning he has to do. And yes, she does understand his need for a night alone. She knows enough about his needs to anticipate that. So the following evening she shows up at his place, dressed in her most seductive outfit. He's on edge. He's run an old vacuum across the ragged carpet, sprayed some deodorant around the bedroom, and wiped the dust off the coffee machine. In this newly uncomfortable habitat, he feels totally unable to be himself. She picks up on this, sensing his change of tempo. Maybe her need for glamorous surroundings and luxury won't be met with a mucky pig like this guy? He, too, is nervous, cagey, not himself, and for that reason, he finds himself unable to even have sex with her that night. No one's happy. See how edgy moon oppositions in the affinity chart can be?

MOON/VENUS CONTACTS

When the moon contacts Venus in the affinity chart, the scene is set for a sensitive undertone to mutual pleasure, especially when in harmonious aspect. The Venus person will be able to enjoy himself around the moon person, whose habits and behaviors are compatible with his. However, the moon partner often gets the niggling sense that she's responsible for her Venus partner's happiness. If the moon partner's own Venus isn't being rewarded, resentment can build up. When the moon and Venus are in challenging aspect to one another, the result can be a competitive or rivalrous energy between the lunar, caretaking, mothering quality inherent in one partner and the sexual Venus quality within the other.

Harmonious Contacts: Same Sign or Element

If other contacts between the two people are harmonious, the relationship can really feel indulgent and mutually beneficial. In the same sign, this indicates sensual understanding and gentle, harmonious compatibility. Both partners will be able to express themselves without feeling vulnerable and can enjoy the same pleasures in life. If it's his moon, he'll see the Venus woman as the one who wields the seductive power in the relationship; if it's her moon, she'll find herself playing a role that's a cross between a mother figure and a femme fatale.

In the same element—for example, with her moon in Sagittarius and his Venus in Leo—he'll find his greatest pleasure in passionate lovemaking. This makes him feel special, and she'll feel comfortable around his fiery, motivated flow of sexual energy. This can make for a luxurious, opulent kind of love and can help stabilize already-compatible relationships.

Challenging Contacts: Three Signs Away and Oppositions

Again, the partners' very different values and needs will have to be taken into account here, but with acceptance and realization, there is always room for compromise and progress.

For example, when the Venus-in-Cancer man gets to know the moon-in-Aries woman better, a clash of values erupts. She needs emotional independence and has to be the boss in the relationship. He values a woman who is tender and caring, someone whom he can be close to and who understands his feelings. But the moon-in-Aries woman objects because she needs to be free-spirited, not held in a tight grasp: The Cancerian values of homey domesticity are light-years away from the moon's refusal to be tied down. The result may be mutual retreat or coldness, or even manipulation, as both partners engage in a hurtful game of trying to blame the other person for their lack of fulfillment.

MOON/MARS CONTACTS

Although it's not thought to be a trigger for long-term love, moon/Mars does make for a lively, vibrant kind of relationship, and it can temper more difficult aspects with an electrifying physical buzz that vibrates between the partners. The moon reacts to the action of the Mars person, so if they're in compatible elements, they naturally get moving in the same direction and with a similar purpose—although it's usually the moon person who tags along since the Mars person likes to take the lead.

Harmonious Contacts: Same Sign or Element

When the moon-in-Pisces man, for instance, meets a Mars-in-Cancer woman, the moon man instinctively feels at home in her company. And although she's not usually the most dynamic Mars sign around, she soon leads the way in the bedroom, keeping the Pisces moon amused, enlivened, and feeling good about himself in her presence. They are stimulated by each other's company and want to get out and about, be a little more daring, and take risks together—whether that means playing the lotto or revealing their feelings to one another.

Challenging Contacts: Three Signs Away and Oppositions

Although this can be a sexy kind of attraction, there's also an underlying sense of tension because the moon's needs are very different from the Mars person's drives and passions. This is not an easy contact since the moon's needs are often repressed or even rejected at the expense of the Mars person's will and ego. For example, if his moon is in Pisces and her Mars is in Sagittarius, he'll certainly feel that he's been rescued by a damsel in shining armor! But the last thing the Mars-in-Sagittarius woman wants is to be someone else's savior. That's when she'll start making all kinds of promises she can't keep, and he'll play the "poor me" game to try and win her back.

MOON/SATURN CONTACTS

Like Saturn and the sun, this is another long-term relationship indicator and often denotes that "fated" feeling that can arise when two people first meet. (See chapter 13 for more information about Saturn.) Problems crop up later down the line, when the moon person, who is very much at home with her own acutely personal behavior, habits, and needs, continues to act without consideration for all the Saturn person's "effort," according to the Saturn person, who feels criticized and discouraged. If the moon partner behaves in the way she does because it's natural to her, the Saturn person will have a hard job coming to terms with it. He might be able to pretend for a while—until his own moon knocks on the door and demands attention, that is. That's when the Saturn partner will turn to emotional castration in order to control the moon partner. Both may turn cold or blame one another for their lack of intimacy and so on: Much depends on how both sets of Saturns balance one another out in the affinity chart.

Harmonious Contacts: Same Sign or Element

Take a Libra-moon man and a Saturn-in-Libra woman. Here, the moon-in-Libra man is naturally peace-loving and feels he belongs in a cozy sort of coupledom. The Saturn-in-Libra woman may have had many relationships throughout her constant quest to get Libra right: The ideal of the perfect couple constantly eludes her. But the very fact that she feels so inadequate about this makes her crave it all the more. Then along comes this man who lives and breathes harmony, peace, and equality. And she falls in line with it: She assumes the correct loved-up, happy-in-coupledom guise and convinces him that she's as perfect as his moon needs her to be. But even when she's made all the right moves—even when she's walked up the aisle with him—she may feel she's conquered her Libra-moon man, but she hasn't filled the gaps that remain within her.

Even though this is a powerful hook for both of them, his never-ending references to coupledom and his constant complaints that the place isn't as clean as it should be (for the moon, if the kitchen's clean, so is the relationship) will drive the Saturn lady to drop the perfect-woman disguise and to resort to her independent attitude or to "frigid" Saturnian behavior in an attempt to control him. But if she can accept that her greatest fear stands before her and that she now has a chance to overcome that fear, then they could become the perfect couple—her own long-standing dream.

Challenging Contacts: Three Signs Away and Oppositions

Whether three signs away or in opposition, this is a very compelling contact and a powerful attraction of different energies. The stern Saturn person can't resist trying to control that which is not in his nature (unless both partners have the same moon signs). The relationship can mature slowly, but the main problem is that the moon's needs are completely alien to the Saturn partner's struggle to make the best of himself. The moon partner will feel dominated and forced to act against her own instinct. If it's his moon, he may see his partner as a mother figure or assume that she behaves "like a mother" and might begin to resent the authoritative, parental role she has come to represent. The result, of course, is that she'll begin to act out this role—precisely because he has projected it onto her. They've got a tough road ahead unless both parties are aware of their differences.

MOON/MERCURY CONTACTS

When one partner's moon aligns with the other's Mercury, habits, behaviors, feelings, and communication meld together, either to create an easygoing platform upon which the relationship can evolve, or, in the case of challenging contacts, to create edgy, nervous, or restless energy between them.

Harmonious Contacts: Same Sign or Element

This is the home of good communication. The moon person will respond naturally to the Mercury person's views and will feel comfortable with her ideas, mind-set, and problem-solving ability (depending on the sign or element involved). The moon person will also be comfortable expressing his own needs and feelings, and they'll both have the honesty and openness to enjoy a few mind games, too. There's often a childlike, sweet-but-smart quality to the relationship. In fact, they often act like a couple of kids, laughing and joking about life. All of this isn't necessarily an indicator of long-lasting commitment, but it's a brilliant match when it comes to enjoying each other's company and generally getting on with life together.

Challenging Contacts: Three Signs Away and Oppositions

When the moon and Mercury are three signs away or in opposition, partners' feelings and thoughts are contrary, and they'll both have trouble communicating and understanding one another. Resentment can build up around the moon's need for emotional expression and around the Mercury person's rationalizing response when provoked by these edgy lunar feelings (unless the Mercury person has a same-element moon). This contact can cause both people to have inner doubts and insecurities and can prevent them from communicating with total honesty.

MOON/JUPITER CONTACTS

Jupiter inflates and exaggerates whatever it touches, so when it's in the same sign or element, it makes the moon person's feelings swell up like a balloon. Both partners experience love (or, rather, the emotional nature of love) as limitless, and their rapport is dynamic and carefree. But the excessive nature of this energy might need something more solid to back it up: A nice heavy bonding contact, such as Saturn to the sun, would do the trick. Yet there's so much *joie de vivre* between the two people that it'll take a lot to keep them apart.

Harmonious Contacts: Same Sign or Element

This placement is liberating, stimulating, and mind-expanding. Let's take two Fire signs as an example. Both feel warmth and passion, but they also get excited about progressive plans for the future and have a liberated sense of who they both are. A woman with the moon in Aries will be able to tune in to exactly what the Jupiter-in-Sagittarius man adores about life, what he believes in, and what he's best at. Equally, he'll become "more" of his Jupiter, and, like Zeus, will want to ravish, enjoy, and indulge in the party she creates around him. Both will feel romantic and boundless; they'll be wooing, cooing, and rushing around making travel plans. A good example of this is Brad Pitt's Jupiter, which is conjunct Angelina's moon in Aries. Essentially, exciting sparks may fly and will offset the difficult "three signs away" challenge from Brad's Capricorn moon, as shown in the following chart.

Brad Pitt's Jupiter is conjunct not only Angelina's moon, but also her own Jupiter and Mars in Aries. With so much fiery energy, exciting sparks fly around reinforcing the powerful opposition between their two suns. In this chart we can see challenge and adventure (two opposing suns), impulse and daring (Jupiter contacts to Mars and the moon). This also offsets the difficult "square" tension from Brad's Capricorn moon, which is far more cautious and defensive. Angelina's Saturn and Venus in Cancer crave love, affection, and a sense of belonging. Although Brad's Capricorn moon reacts by being cool and defensive about his feelings, his Venus wants to be desired, it wants to show off the best of itself, and sensing this deep desire, encourages Angelina's Saturn to "crave" what he has. This is a provocative relationship, where we can see how so many contacts create a cauldron of swirling reactions.

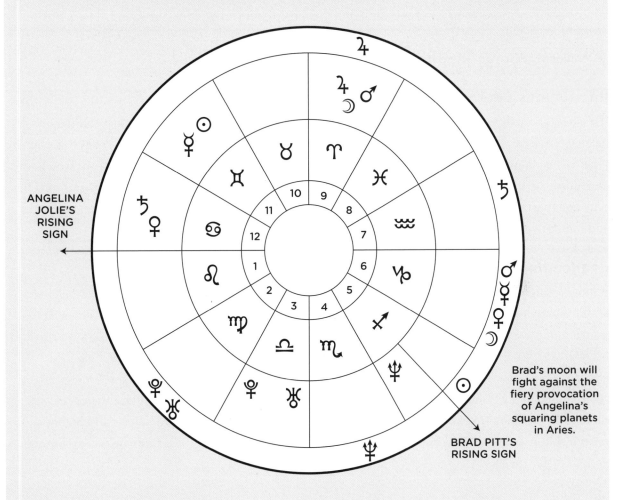

ANGELINA JOLIE'S RISING SIGN

Brad's moon will fight against the fiery provocation of Angelina's squaring planets in Aries.

BRAD PITT'S RISING SIGN

Challenging Contacts: Three Signs Away and Oppositions

When Jupiter and the moon clash, the moon partner overreacts and may feel inferior or picked-on in the Jupiter person's presence. Then she becomes edgy and senses that she's in danger of being overwhelmed by someone who's both pushy and too good to be true. Let's take a man with Jupiter in Gemini and a woman with the moon in Virgo. He just wants to gush on about the state of world politics, while she'd rather be sorting out the internal affairs of her workplace. The Jupiter man will also niggle her sensitive spot, reinforcing her insecurities. (For example, his Jupiter-in-Gemini way of exaggerating every fault into a major disaster will make her even more obsessive about order and perfection.) This, in turn, will cause him to think that she's too reactionary and oversensitive, and he'll eventually seek more time and space alone.

MOON/URANUS CONTACTS

This is often a very sudden, very sexy attraction that begins with an exciting encounter. There's usually an inspirational, electric, dynamic energy between the partners at the outset, especially if there's a generational difference between them.

Harmonious Contacts: Same Sign or Element

If it's her moon, then he'll respond to her instinctual nature by idealizing her femininity—although he may not be at all interested in her needs unless there are other important contacts at play. If it's her Uranus, his moon will feel comfortable around her laid-back, nonpossessive Uranian energy, which—depending on other factors in the affinity chart—gives him a chance to rationalize his feelings, too. This puts both partners at ease, and the unpredictable mind games they both play will keep them inspired and innovative in their sex life.

Challenging Contacts: Three Signs Away and Oppositions

A long-lasting rapport isn't easy to achieve here since Uranus and the moon create an unpredictable erratic energy together. The moon needs a sense of belonging—but Uranus doesn't! This contact often signals a purely physical relationship and allows the moon partner (particularly if it's the man) to avoid his own emotional vulnerability. If, for example, she has the moon in Cancer and he has Uranus in Capricorn, she may find him overbearing, pushy, and self-important, and her needs and feelings might get trampled on by his ideals and expectations. But if both partners are aware of their differences, this can be a hugely mind-expanding (and sexy!) contact. It might manifest as a stimulating and highly quirky relationship based on a freedom/intimacy dilemma: The more she chases, the more he'll run—but the more he runs, the more he wants to come back for another go.

MOON/NEPTUNE CONTACTS

The moon, like Neptune, reflects the deeper undercurrents of our dream, fantasy, and soul worlds, and so harmonious contacts between the two can create a romance that's deeply bonded and almost surreal. (For more information on Neptune, see chapter 16.)

Harmonious Contacts: Same Sign or Element

This is a deeply sensuous, often mystical attraction. Both people may feel as if they've known each other in another life, world, or place, and an uncanny psychic link exists between them. They share an acute sensitivity, and if other contacts indicate harmony, this can add a powerful spiritual and mystical energy to a long-term relationship. Both partners feel comfortable in each other's presence, and, although they can spend a lot of time idealizing one other, the moon person usually adds a grounding energy that creates a mellow, peaceful balance between them. This contact usually invokes a beautifully compelling, compassionate, warm, romantic relationship.

Challenging Contacts: Three Signs Away and Oppositions

What's not so warm and fuzzy is the challenge Neptune's deeper realms present to the moon's natural sensitivity. Here's an example of her Neptune in Sagittarius square his moon in Virgo. Now this is a man who needs to know exactly where he is at all times. Chaos will not do. His drawers are full of socks that are paired by color, and he feels comfortable with a woman who looks perfect and preens herself regularly. When he meets the Neptune-in-Sagittarius woman, she is far from perfect, but there's something so boundless about her that he wants to contain her, to hold her, to show her how you always know where you are when you have a map in front of you. She needs to know all this, doesn't she? But our Neptune-in-Sagittarius lady longs to be free of all commitments and boundaries. She wants to run with the wolves; she romances the explorers and magicians of the world, and when she meets this precise, discriminating Virgo-moon man, she'll either turn around and run or attempt to seduce him into believing she's exactly what he needs. Because Neptune can drown out the moon's needs, the result might be a dangerous game, depending on other contacts in the chart.

MOON/PLUTO CONTACTS

Pluto transforms whatever it touches, but it wants to bury or annihilate whatever it touches, too. So, for example, when Pluto comes across the moon—the gentlest, most tender part of ourselves—it not only causes emotional pain but also transforms the moon person in the most dramatic, obsessive way. Plundering Pluto rapes ferociously, cuts deep, rips out your entrails, and then asks, "Okay, how do you feel now?"

Yikes. For example, let's take a woman with Pluto in Sagittarius and a man with the moon in Gemini—a nicely juicy opposition. So when the rapacious Pluto woman comes screaming out of the underworld to snatch the lighthearted, laid-back moon-in-Gemini man from his home, the moon is terrified at first—and rightly so. Still, he can't resist her and becomes compulsively and sexually drawn to the very thing that threatens to destroy his dancing moonbeams. Why? Well, we often meet people who give us this kind of Plutonian experience, perhaps to show us what we need to transform in our inner worlds and to reveal the dark side of whatever planet Pluto touches. In this way, then, even though we may have been psychologically or emotionally violated by the invisible god who persecutes all, his dark possession paradoxically liberates us from our own darkness, too.

So the Pluto-in-Sagittarius woman's invisible god steamrolls over the moon-in-Gemini man's chattering moonbeams, and he might head for the hills fast. But it's more likely that he'll trip over her sexual enticements and fall into his own lunar burial pit. On the other hand, it could wake him up to the fact the even a moon in Gemini has feelings that can be ripped apart by the power of the underworld god.

MOON/RISING SIGN CONTACTS

Like all moon-to-other-planet contacts, even if there's a positive moon-to-rising-sign contact, the rising-sign person may have a totally contrary moon placement, and this can create additional tensions when the rising-sign person's own needs aren't being met. That's when appearances are truly deceptive. So it's always important to look not only at the moon placements and contacts for both people involved, but also, in the natal chart, the relationship of each person's moon to her own planets.

For example, your partner's moon may well encourage your rising-sign impression to feel comfortable in his presence, but it doesn't necessarily make you fall in love with him. The moon is more about parental love—empathy, nurturing, emotional reactions—not the passionate throes of sex and desire. That said, the moon does seem to play a huge part in long-term relationships, although, curiously, moon/rising sign contacts are often more tense and challenging than you'd expect. Let's find out why.

Harmonious Contacts: Same Moon and Rising Sign

The rising-sign person shines like a beacon of light; she expresses qualities inherent in the moon-sign person, and so the moon-sign person feels comforted and is reassured that the two of them belong to the same clan. An easy attraction is sparked at once since the moon person feels he can nurture her and be nurtured by her.

So far, so good. The problem is, though, that the rising-sign person will often get her rising-sign experience, so to speak: An initial attraction is quickly established, and she'll understand her partner's needs, but she may not be able to actually meet those needs. (However, this is less likely to happen if the rising-sign person's own moon is compatible with her partner's.)

Take, for example, a woman with Leo rising and a man with the moon in Leo. To feel secure, he needs to be the center of attention; he reacts passionately to what others think and say about him. He thrives on exclusive love, on a woman who feeds his ego and delights in building a nest around him so that he can rest assured she'll be loyal and true forever. But the Leo-rising woman likes to impress the social throng with her glamorous outfit and her new hairdo. She gives the impression that she's center stage, loyal, and true—as long as her partner is there to support her, too. Doesn't this sound like they're heading for a mighty clash of egos? Won't they exhaust themselves by feeding each other's egos? And isn't it likely that Leo rising will eventually find that demanding moon-in-Leo man a little too tiring—unless she happens to have a giving, nurturing, moon in Cancer and is willing to let her leonine lover roar to his heart's content? It's very possible.

Harmonious Contact: Same Element

When his moon is in the same element as her rising sign, the result is an easy exchange of energy—although, as with the same-sign moon and rising-sign example previously, the moon sign might feel resentful later on in the relationship. For example, let's take the moon in Water and Water rising. There's an easy identification from the moon-in-Water person, usually with a deeper, unspoken acknowledgment hovering between the two. Water rising sees life "through a glass darkly," and so, when the vulnerable moon-in-Water guy appears in her space, she intuitively knows how to behave around him. He, too, picks up on the sensitive image the Water rising sign exudes. If she has Cancer rising and he has the moon in Pisces, for instance, he'll feel comforted by her caring presence and the way she helps others, especially a lost soul like himself. As for her, she can't resist saving him from—well, whatever he thinks he needs saving from!

Challenging Contacts: Moon/Rising Sign Oppositions and Three Signs Away

As with all oppositions to the rising sign, the moon can create powerful or reactive feelings for the moon person: For the rising-sign person, this can be either a wake-up call to what she unconsciously believes is lacking in her life or a curiously compelling—or repelling—attraction. (If both partners had their own moons in the same element, they'd probably feel at ease with such a challenging stranger.) For example, Earth-rising people give an impression of—you guessed it—earthy sexiness, and exude that comfortable, safe quality that's highly attractive to Water-sign moons: The moon person, who usually feels anything but safe, can finally relax in the presence of someone so solid, reliable, and consistent. The Earth-rising person is hunting for quality in a relationship, but will the watery moon person's hypersensitivity to every act, gesture, or comment begin to unnerve Earth's pragmatic take on life?

Remember, these are attractions based on the way the moon person reacts to the rising-sign person's presence and whether, depending on other factors, that's enough to create and sustain a deeper, longer-lasting relationship. And as with other planetary inter-aspects, things get tense when your rising sign is three signs away from his moon and vice versa. For instance, when a Taurus moon meets Aquarius rising, they often react defensively to one another. The Aquarian wants to shock, to bend the rules, and to play an awkward game of romance, but that means the Taurus moon doesn't know where he stands—and Taurus moons like to stand on firm ground.

Now we need to look at the moon and the sun in relation to one another in the affinity chart: Chapter 9 will be your guide.

9 Sun/Moon:
Reflecting Each Other's Light

Now that you've established any contacts between your sun and your partner's sun and your moon and his planets and vice versa, you're ready to look more closely at the sun and moon together and discover how they operate in tandem in the affinity chart.

Sun/moon contacts are vitally important in relationship astrology. A powerful (harmonious or challenging) sun/moon contact can be a powerful catalyst within the affinity chart because the sun, as you've already seen in chapter 7, is about your soul and your true identity, while the moon represents your deeply personal feelings, habits, instincts, and reactions. So when they are in a positive cross-aspect to one another in the affinity chart, the moon person usually augments the qualities of the sun person by making the sun person feel at home, so to speak, while the sun validates the moon's feelings and habits.

That said, not all great relationships have sun/moon contacts, so if you don't have any sun/moon contacts in your affinity chart, don't worry: It doesn't necessarily mean that you and your partner aren't compatible.

WORKING WITH THE SUN AND MOON IN THE AFFINITY CHART

Many synastry books have a lot to say about how glorious same-sign sun and moon contacts are. They claim that it's a key to enduring love and commitment; and that it causes two people to become profoundly fused—that is, united or merged and basking in a glow of alchemical love. And it's true that there is something alchemical at work because when we deal with the sun and moon together, we're aligning the masculine and feminine principles together as One. I do think that sun/moon contacts are essentially beneficial when in harmony—but I also think there's something odd going on among these same-sign sun/moon contacts: Unless your sun and his moon are in similar elements as your moon and his sun, one partner is going to lose out on having his or her lunar needs met. Keep this in mind when you're interpreting your own (or anyone else's) cross-aspects between sun and moon.

An example of a double whammy of powerful sun/moon contacts in the affinity chart is that of Elizabeth Taylor and Richard Burton. Here, Burton's Scorpio sun is conjunct Taylor's moon, and her Pisces sun is opposite his Virgo moon. There's a powerful interplay of light and dark, validation, hidden truths, and power struggles.

Sun and Moon in the Same Sign: A Double-Edged Sword

You already know that when two planets are in the same sign, the result is a potent, highly concentrated mash of similar energy, creating an instant bond between the partners. And the moon is about nurture, support, belonging, comfort, and emotions. So the moon feels safe around the same-sign solar person; it's happy, very much in its comfort zone, and is willing to nurture the solar person to help her achieve her true vocation or solar purpose. But at what price the moon person's own needs—and, more importantly, at what price the moon person's own sun? Unless there are mutually receptive suns and moons both ways—that is, he has the moon in the same sign as your sun, and you have the moon in the same sign as his sun—things might get a little tricky, particularly for the moon person.

We've already talked about the "same-sign claustrophobia" that exists between the sun/sun and moon/moon. For example, if we both have the sun in the same sign, there'll be rivalry over who can express or manifest the best of that sign; if we both have the moon in the same sign, we'll feel niggled when we see our own emotional needs laid out before our very eyes. But we're also talking about power dynamics. One partner may hold the balance of power in the relationship, while the other might begin to feel resentful, less compassionate, and less nurtured. Here's how that happens: The moon person's habits, behaviors, and reactions in daily life unconsciously signal to the sun person that his solar potential is worth living out. (Not that there's anything wrong with that; the moon person just does it naturally!) So without realizing it, the moon person confirms the messages her partner is receiving from the depths of his "solar oracle." And as her partner's solar light shines through, the moon person will, at first, feel splendid in her role as nurturer. But questions might creep in: What is the moon person getting out of

ELIZABETH TAYLOR AND RICHARD BURTON'S AFFINITY CHART

This affinity chart is strangely harmonious and powerfully challenging. It is made up of both superb compatibility and mutual empathy, but also has envious imaginings and dark, undermining power struggles. Their sun/moon contact in Scorpio suggests that the dark delights of this sign brought out their best and their worst sides. Equally, Liz was able to empathize with Richard's Saturn (his vulnerability) in Scorpio. Married to each other twice and divorced both times, their turbulent affair was addictive and insatiable (moon opposing sun attracts and detracts). Richard's apparently 'oh so noble' moon in Virgo was bedazzled by Liz's Pisces planets, and she found him powerfully attractive yet melancholic (Scorpio sun/Saturn), astute (moon in Virgo) but jealous (Saturn in Scorpio). Together, however, they created one of the most tumultuous and passionate love affairs of the twentieth century.

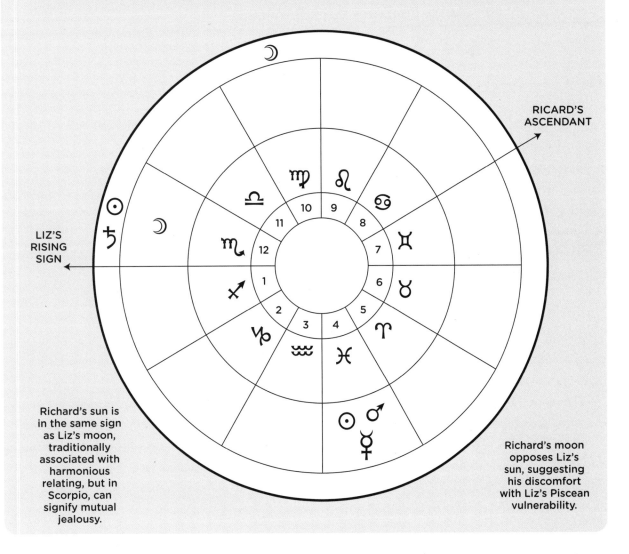

RICARD'S ASCENDANT

LIZ'S RISING SIGN

Richard's sun is in the same sign as Liz's moon, traditionally associated with harmonious relating, but in Scorpio, can signify mutual jealousy.

Richard's moon opposes Liz's sun, suggesting his discomfort with Liz's Piscean vulnerability.

OVER THE MOON OR IN IT?

Here's an example of a man with the moon in Sagittarius and a woman with the sun in Sagittarius. Our moon man will be over the moon—no pun intended!—to encounter such an outgoing, fun-loving, spirited woman who, if she's living out her solar potential, will view life as one big adventure. He, of course, will nourish and encourage this because he has the same instinct for exploration and excitement. Together, they connect to the Sagittarian love of freedom, and this mutual inspiration can help them achieve a long-lasting rapport. Wait a minute, though. Are the moon-in-Sagittarius man's solar goals being encouraged? If he is living entirely "in his moon," he will eventually resent the fact that he can't live "in his sun" in this relationship because his solar identity is being ignored. And what about the sun-in-Sagittarius woman's lunar needs? Is she being nurtured in the way she needs to be? At some point, these questions will need to be addressed.

this relationship? If she is supporting the sun person, giving him the backup that allows him to shine, what—if anything—is he giving her in return?

Of course, that's not the only possible outcome. If the sun partner is already living out his solar potential, then the moon person may continue to feel contentment around this shining light, as long as she can identify with her own solar purpose, too. As always, it depends upon the signs involved as well as the other contacts in the affinity chart.

So when you're interpreting contacts like these, look at both sets of moons and suns and how they can blend together.

Harmonious Contact: Same Element

A different sign within the same element allows the moon person to thrive without worrying about whether his solar partner's identity will overpower him. He'll ride on her sunbeams, sure; but his lunar light will still be able to shine brightly. Here are a couple examples.

The moon-in-Aries man, for instance, quickens the pace of a Sagittarius woman's desire to get out of the rut she's found herself in. (Perhaps she's not being true to her solar identity because of transiting Saturn in her chart.) He supports her quest to move on and out—either with or without him—but this doesn't compromise his lunar energy at all. His moon, fast-paced and restless, feels at home with her desire to take a trip around the world and back. As long as he can continue to honor his own solar principle, both partners will benefit from each other's qualities.

Similarly, when the sun-in-Virgo woman meets a moon-in-Taurus man, she knows that help is at hand. Ms. Virgo's aim is to become a top editor at a publishing house, and this man isn't just supportive of her career; his behavior around her is also both practical and constructive. He's content when he's doing the cooking, fiddling with his car, or nurturing her ambitions, and he's pretty reliable when it comes to looking after their finances, too. As for Mr. Taurus, he feels good around her because he knows he can trust her judgment: She's not going to upset his sense of security. As long as he also has a mutually harmonious sun (and as long as she has a harmonious moon), this could be the kind of firm, stable relationship that'll sustain them both in the long term.

If the airy sun requires space, knowledge, and ideals in order to breathe, then the airy moon will provide a safe place in which the sun can explore her solar light. The moon-in-Gemini man is quick-witted and mischievous and thrives in a lighthearted, carefree environment. He isn't acquisitive and prefers space to clutter, but he feels most at home when he has his own library—or, at the very least, when all his books line the walls of his living room. He feels comfortable among airy people: They make light of life, too. So the woman with the sun in Libra is to be treasured. Her solar destiny is to beautify the world or the people in it: The moon-in-Gemini man feels comfortable with this, and she finds that his fun-loving behavior boosts her own airy identity. With other mutually supporting contacts, this one could keep the two of them amused for a very long time.

The moon feels more comfortable in Water than the sun does. So it's inevitable that the sun-in-Cancer man will get a massive burst of support from the moon-in-Pisces woman, who understands exactly why he finds it hard to express his feeling world. Like all men, men in Cancer face the problem of living in a world that frowns upon male displays of emotion. And this is particularly tough for Cancer men, who truly "feel" their way through life and, unconsciously or not, attempt to cover up their deepest reactions and emotions because it draws them down into a side of themselves they'd rather ignore. But as the moon-in-Pisces woman empathizes easily with his solar impetus, she can bring him to realize that his destiny is essentially about his power to show gentleness in the world. He may be evasive, crabby, and might have mother issues (he either hates or loves her)—but the moon-in-Pisces woman will go with his flow. She won't be put off by his moods, and she'll always be sensitive to his neediness. And they'll both feel free enough to let each other wander a little. Cancer needs to go away and come back again in order to feel that he belongs, while Pisces needs to get close so that it's okay for her to back away again when she needs solitude.

Challenging Contacts: Oppositions and Three Signs Away

When the sun and moon are three signs away or in opposition, it's fairly obvious that the sun person's identity and potential will conflict with the behaviors and habits of the moon person. The opposition may present the sun person with the possibility for really getting in touch with her solar destiny, simply because being faced with her opposite forces her to reach deep within herself. But misunderstandings are inevitable, too, as both partners will be plagued with self-doubt and mistrust of one another. Of course, if there are good contacts between sun and Venus and rising sign and Jupiter, the sun person's sense of solar power or the moon person's attitudes and habits may be modified or reinforced.

One simple example of an opposition is a man with the sun in Aries and a woman with the moon in Libra. The man with the sun in Aries is fairly confident on the surface. He is independent, has never married, and has become highly successful in his career. He lives a fairly strict lifestyle: He works out every day and jogs every weekend. He certainly finds the moon-in-Libra lady attractive as she walks into the room, smiling at everyone she meets. He's taken with her civilized behavior and her lack of arrogance: It's oh-so-different from his own egocentric identity. He's never really gotten on well with intellectual types, but now he is charmed by the delightful way she chats freely with others—and never a hair out of place, either. As for her, she finds him macho and unbearably arrogant. As she watches him mingle with a group of adoring women, her moon (the most sensitive and fragile part of the self) almost feels bruised by his brash approach to others. She can't bear the sense of conflict he's brought to her peaceful world. He niggles her at her sensitive core, and she can neither forgive him for that nor tolerate his presence, so she turns on her heel and walks out of the party. But there's another possible ending to the story: If he were to follow her, and if he had, say, the moon in Air or another planet in Libra, then she might turn to him and use her lunar power to lure him to her.

Now it's time to turn our attention from the empowering light of the sun and the moon to the planet most closely associated with sexual pleasure and desire: Venus.

10 Venus:
The Heart's Desire

S ome say that the key to successful loving is whether or not both partners have the same personal and sexual values, and, as you'll see in this chapter, Venus describes our ability to give and receive pleasure. It's about how we go about making ourselves and other people happy—but it's also a symbol of how we *take* pleasure. In this way, then, it represents the kind of beauty or aesthetic that animates our senses and brings us to life. In our charts, Venus is a mirror for how vain or self-conscious we are (our sense of self-value), and it shows us how (and why) we attract lovers. Ultimately, along with Mars and Eros in the affinity chart, Venus reveals our patterns of seduction as well as how sexually compatible we are with others.

So when it comes to intimate relationships, Venus is the planet that tells us whether we'll be able to find happiness in the arms of another person. Venus is about sensual and sexual fulfillment rather than emotional happiness (the moon) or the joy of idealized romance (Neptune).

THE MYTH: VENUS

The Greek goddess Aphrodite (known as Venus in Roman mythology) was carelessly vain and jealous and embodied both sexual power and female wisdom. And the manner of her birth is inextricably linked to her creative sensuality: She rose from the foam created when the severed genitals of her father, Ouranos, fell into the sea. (Isn't this sea foam a great metaphor for the waves of pleasure we experience in physical relationships?) Self-centered Aphrodite was married off to ugly, lame Hephaestus, the god of blacksmiths, but she rarely shared his bed: She much preferred Ares (or Mars, in Roman mythology), the virile, potent god of war. In a way, Venus has the job of "civilizing" other planets it contacts, such as taming Mars or seducing Jupiter, so that she can get her way. However, she can also do this by wily, sensual, and underhanded means, just to prove that no one is fairer or more refined in the art of seduction than she is.

VENUS IN RELATIONSHIP

Venus represents an attraction factor that's different from that of the rising sign. It's specifically about pleasure and how we draw others to us, rather than a presence or an impression. What's more, it's a dynamic, bright, extroverted energy, and so most contacts between the rising sign and Venus are bound to create a physical and sensual affinity in either the long or short term. With Venus contacts to other planets and the rising sign, we feel good about ourselves—ebullient and abundant. But when two Venuses clash, it's either because two egos are striving for dominance or because one feels inferior in the presence of the other. Venus is skilled in the art of seduction and self-love, so when they're out and about, each half of the clashing Venus couple might flirt with strangers at the bar in order to attract each other's attention—or they might try to score points off each other by seeing who gets more attention from the opposite sex.

Let's start with how Venus acts as a significator of your pleasure principle and sexual values. When your Venus and his Venus interact by aspect, the result can either be a great sense of mutual pleasure or an imbalance or challenge in your sex life.

Harmonious Contact: Same Sign

This is an excellent contact that can help boost a loving and sexually stimulating relationship since the two of you will form a creative, mutually beneficial physical rapport (as long as your Mars contacts aren't too challenging!). Whether both your Venuses lie in Taurus, Aquarius, or Pisces, you'll both have the same pleasure principle, so you'll be able to indulge together without having to make compromises. Each of you understands what the other wants, which fosters compassion, sexual satisfaction, and pleasurable companionship.

But is there a downside to all this mutual understanding? Yes: Too much of a good thing can spoil that good thing. So when you encounter a great contact like Venus/Venus in the same sign, check out your other contacts to see what might modify, subdue, or add a smattering of erotic challenge to the highly subjective signature of same-sign planets.

Harmonious Contact: Same Element

When the two of you have Venus in the same element, the result is a more balanced feel to the relationship. The claustrophobic tightness of the same-sign Venus contact changes to a mutual understanding of the qualities you both value, but with a little breathing space.

In Fire: *Lively and Sexy*

Venus in the Fire signs have a lively, sexy approach to love. They both value passion, adventurous sex, and a provocative or flirtatious style of romance.

In Earth: *Sexual Sensuality*

When both partners have Venus in the Earth signs, they value the sensuality of sex; they love one another's touch and enjoy indulging in luxurious living and becoming experts in sexual techniques.

In Air: *Power of the Mind*

Venus in the Air signs chatter like birds and have imaginative sex, but they're also happy to spend hours in deep conversation or exploring new ideas or social haunts. They value erotic mental stimulation and are happiest when indulging in lighthearted romance, erotic thoughts, and the power of the mind.

In Water: *The Dreamers*

They both know the depths of their feelings and the value they place on the sexual act itself. Both partners want to experience an emotional, all-embracing kind of love, in which they merge as one and dream the same dreams.

Challenging Contact: Three Signs Away

When Venus is in different elements, a very different set of values comes into play. But that's not necessarily a bad thing: When your partner's pleasure principle is unlike your own, it can create a highly potent, magnetic type of attraction. We all know that opposites attract, and Venus values are equally desirable when they're unfamiliar. They present endless possibilities: Could alternative values or forms of pleasure make us happier than we ever imagined? To test these tantalizing waters, then, we attract a lover who possesses these very values. This is when clashes can become challenges—but sometimes it's the most vividly clashing affinity charts that prove to be the longest-lasting ones.

Sexually, however, it's possible that both partners will never be truly satisfied, and this is where the most conflict or tension can arise. For example, she may adore slow, sensual massages and lengthy foreplay (Venus in Taurus), while he may prefer a sexy romp in the countryside or spontaneous sex in the boardroom (Venus in Aquarius). Although short-term fun is guaranteed, unless they have some strong, supportive contacts between their sun, moon, or Saturn, the relationship could fizzle out as quickly as it began.

When Venus is three signs away, you can expect a clash of values and sexual-pleasure principles. Although Venus is more willing to embrace such differences than, say, Mars, who wants to fight them, Venus is still vain and possessive and can be acutely defensive.

Aries/Cancer

Pleasure for Venus in Aries is fast and furious, challenging, and prioritizes self-pleasure. Cancer likes to tenderly care for her partner and is a willing accomplice in the art of giving Aries pleasure. But eventually, Venus in Cancer feels left out of the equation and can resort to manipulative tactics because she's not being satisfied herself and because what first seemed a better way to love isn't so great after all.

Taurus/Leo

The Venus in Leo lover likes to take control, dominate, and be center stage. Demanding and stylish, some element of glamour and sophistication in the bedroom is a must for her. Venus in Taurus is happy to oblige with all the accoutrements and quite likes the idea of sharing champagne in bed, too. But Taurus values pleasure for the sake of pleasure itself, while Leo values sexual happiness because it's a way to show off. Once the initial fascination has worn off, these two will test each other with their very different sexual needs.

Gemini/Virgo

Both like mental stimulation, but these two Venus placements are worlds apart when it comes to what gives them pleasure. For Gemini, love and sex is an entertainment, a world of text messages and "now you see me, now you don't" games. Love is fun and frolicsome: Even sex is to be taken lightly. The romance of it all comes first. But for Venus in Virgo, there's no wild sense of "being in love with love;" it's all carefully planned, and pleasurable dates are arranged as if they were business lunches. Sex is not as unpredictable and spontaneous as Gemini would like it to be.

Cancer/Libra

If Venus in Cancer values emotional intimacy in the bedroom, a warm embrace, and a sense of belonging, then Libra prefers lighthearted romance and the ideals of love, not the clinginess of Cancer's possessive desire. Venus in Libra will initially think that the close bonding of the Cancerian bedroom is an ideal he can aspire to, but it might get too hot and steamy for Libra's light touch.

Leo/Scorpio

Venus in Leo wants the world to know about her sexual relationship and how madly in love she is with her partner. Meanwhile, Venus in Scorpio values privacy, discretion, and keeping the door firmly closed on the sex act. What's more, the bright, glittering passion of Venus in Leo doesn't gel with Scorpio's darker interest in power and taboo sex. They can, however, truly give each other a sexual run for their money.

Virgo/Sagittarius

Taking a traditional approach to courtship and sex, Venus in Virgo wants to throw a net around his lover, simply so he "knows where he stands." But Venus in Sagittarius really doesn't want to stand still for long, nor does she like being a caged bird. This is a Venus who wants space, adventure, and, most of all, a no-strings spontaneity in love: She doesn't want to be sieved for information every time she walks through the door.

Libra/Capricorn

Venus in Libra's ideals and seductive charm can cast a spell over Venus in Capricorn. However, Capricorn takes a long time to trust anyone before he'll let them near his bed. Libra's romantic notions will begin to dry up in the cool earthiness of Capricorn's need to experience and organize love rather than just imagine or idealize it.

Scorpio/Aquarius

Airy, unpredictable, and quirky Venus in Aquarius may well be curious to discover why Venus in Scorpio is obsessed with sex, power, and money. Sexually, Venus in Aquarius takes pleasure from mental stimulation over and above emotional closeness (unless she has a load of Scorpio planets herself). Likewise, Scorpio may be intrigued to discover whether Aquarius really is as unconditional about love and sex as she makes out: When he finds out the truth, he might retreat as quickly as the famous sting in his tail.

Sagittarius/Pisces

This one often works—to begin with, anyway. Being mutable signs, they go with the flow and adapt to one another's needs; that is, they keep changing. Venus in Sagittarius is capricious, makes promises, and doesn't fulfill them; Venus in Pisces is elusive and gets led astray by people and ideas. Pisces dreams, while Sagittarius has great visions. Venus in Pisces values the enigma love presents and how it's a merger of spiritual and physical selves. Venus in Sagittarius longs to gaze at the stars from a sleeping bag with her lover beside her—but will Pisces be able to keep up on the journey? Much depends on the other contacts in the affinity chart: Other reliable, consistent contacts may help keep them on the same path.

Capricorn/Aries

If Venus in Capricorn takes pleasure from extensive foreplay, a lengthier romance, and a lifelong commitment, then Venus in Aries will tire quickly of the slow romantic game and the time it takes to get from the dinner table to the bedroom. Between the sheets, Aries wants it fast and furious; Capricorn prefers slow and serene. Perhaps they can find a balance together?

Aquarius/Taurus

There's a challenging difference of pleasure principles here as Taurus wants complete sensual indulgence, warmth, and human contact, plus slow arousal and the joy of sexual marathons. Of course, the only kind of marathon Aquarius takes pleasure in is a conversational one. However, Venus in Aquarius has an unpredictable sex drive and can shock even a Taurus with bizarre ideas of where to have sex (ever tried swinging from the chandeliers?).

Pisces/Gemini

Although Venus in Gemini gets bored quickly with Venus in Pisces's dreamy, laid-back lovemaking, both are adaptable and creative enough to take pleasure in sex in different places. Pisces prefers to be the submissive partner, and although Gemini enjoys the chase and the sparkling romance of it all, taking a dominant role can seem a bit too much like growing up. (Remember, Gemini is a child for life.) However, both are romantics, and the light side of love can be a huge mutual attraction—however irresponsible the relationship may become.

Challenging Contact: Venus/Venus Opposition

Like all oppositions, the attraction is based on what the other person seems to have that you lack. If you had Venus rising in Virgo and he had Venus in Pisces (which means his Venus is in your seventh house), then this would be a double attraction—from both the rising sign/"what you see" viewpoint and your values when it comes to sex and pleasure. His Venus would not only be magnetically attracted to your rising sign, but would also have a powerful attraction to your Venus. Always bear in mind that these double-whammy contacts and attractions can add weight and substance to both the initial romance and the long-term commitment.

Aries/Libra Opposition

If Venus in Aries is all about her own pleasure, then Venus in Libra is all about her pleasure, too—but only if pleasing her pleases him! The paradox of this opposition is that both are genuinely out to satisfy themselves, but the Libran Venus has refined the art of compromise to such an extent that the pleasure he gives must be comparable to the pleasure he gets. What an attraction this is, though! Aries is all out for sexual power, and Libra is willing to submit to it. Cue sparks flying. This can be a hugely rewarding relationship if other inter-aspects are complementary or supportive of long-term commitment.

Taurus/Scorpio Opposition

Venus in Taurus is renowned for sensual empowerment, Venus in Scorpio for sexual power; together, they merge, devour, gratify, indulge, experiment, and turn away from the social scene, preferring the privacy of the boudoir. Theirs is an intensely sexual affair, but it's also one in which possessiveness and jealousy can turn the whole thing into a dark, codependent, greedy mash-up. If, however, there are strengthening or highly positive inter-aspects between sun, moon, and Saturn, then these two power-mongering Venuses could enjoy a mutually empowering pleasure principle.

Gemini/Sagittarius Opposition

Flirtatious by nature, both these Venus signs are led astray by a beautiful face. They hate to feel trapped and are more fascinated by the thought of sex and the games it involves than the act itself. Venus in Sagittarius is turned on by seducing strangers, spontaneous sex, and the adventure of it all; Gemini is turned on by sexy phone calls, messages, and other erotic entertainment. Together, they enliven one another and give each other plenty of space, too. Their major challenge is that if they give each other too much rope (unless they have more stabilizing planetary aspects between them), they might get hung up on someone else en route to that dirty weekend away they've been planning.

Cancer/Capricorn Opposition

Venus in Cancer is careful, sensitive, acutely emotional, and has a pleasure principle that ebbs and flows with the cycles of the moon. Venus in Capricorn takes the whole idea of pleasure and its value extremely seriously. They're both defensive about their sexual desires, but when these Venuses meet, they (unconsciously) recognize something very special in each other. Cancer values emotional closeness, while Capricorn is anything but emotionally close for fear of losing control. Instead, Capricorn gets pleasure from sensual luxury, serious lovemaking, and being the boss. This can allow Venus in Cancer to feel wanted, who, in turn, may be able to open her arms without fear.

Leo/Aquarius Opposition

Venus in Aquarius has an unpredictable sexual appetite and can't be quite sure what turns him on until he's tried everything in the sex manual and beyond. Venus in Leo is only concerned with self-pleasure and knows exactly what turns her on. Although they are fascinated by each other's opposite values—Leo's vain self-interest, Aquarius's love of all—they may still fight in the bedroom. Aquarius likes to surprise and be surprised in bed, while Leo would rather get right down to the nitty-gritty. It's a competitive relationship, in which Leo thrives on the glamour of it all, while Aquarius would prefer to analyze their sex life over the breakfast table. But it's quite workable if other planetary activity suggests a stable affinity elsewhere.

Virgo/Pisces Opposition

While Venus in Virgo likes an orderly route to the bedroom, Pisces takes an elusive and sometimes wiggly one. Venus in Virgo secretly yearns to be wilder and more sexually carefree—all things that Pisces appears to value and enjoy. The problem with Venus in Pisces is that sometimes he just doesn't know what *does* give him pleasure or why it's so easy to feel so happy with just about *anyone*. Being led astray is Pisces's *bête noire*, and Venus in Virgo will find it hard to value his disappearing tricks and the seductive airs he puts on with strangers; after all, she values privacy and refined sexual techniques. She may be able to persuade Pisces that this is the best way to make love since Adam met Eve, but ultimately, Virgo yearns for a perfect union of mind and body—an ideal Pisces might not be able to live up to. It's a challenging opposition indeed.

VENUS/MARS CONTACTS

See chapter 12 on Venus and Mars.

VENUS/SATURN CONTACTS

This is one of the most difficult contacts to deal with in the affinity chart. When affectionate, pleasure-loving Venus confronts vulnerable Saturn, strange things happen. If Venus expresses himself in a loving, all-embracing way—the very qualities Saturn struggles with the most—then this contact produces envy, suspicion, or inhibited behavior from Saturn. (See chapter 13 for more detailed information on Saturn.) Venus, after all, is about how we relate and give and take pleasure in the "real" world. It's also about why we feel happy, loved, and good about ourselves around our partners. Saturn, on the other hand, is where we feel most uneasy with ourselves and others. When confronted with Venus's delightful antics, Saturn is usually shocked into overcompensating; that is, Saturn will begin to act like Venus in order to appear better qualified in all of her innate sexual or sensual arts—and, therefore, to be one up on her.

While certain aspects discussed below are a bit more favorable, I qualify that no Saturn contact is ever truly harmonious with Venus because it requires so much work and effort, challenge, and acceptance to work through the defensive games (unconscious or otherwise) that the Saturn person presents. So let's first look at Saturn to Venus in the same sign.

CONFRONTING THE SHADOW

Let's consider a man with Saturn in Gemini and a woman with Venus in Gemini. Of course, she's delightful; she seduces, flirts, dances, laughs, and enjoys a good social lifestyle. When she meets the Saturn-in-Gemini man, he immediately feels socially clumsy: He's wary of her lighthearted, carefree attitude, and something inside him wants to either fill himself with this energy or restrict it. He may already have begun to master the art of the buffoon, but now he'll adopt the guise of a Venus in Gemini and will play the lighthearted game. But as the game progresses, he may, deep down, turn Gemini's lightness into a much darker version of itself, in which flirtation is disloyal, charm is shallow, and loveliness mere vanity. He'll secretly envy her as time goes on (if other contacts suggest long-term bonds), and this in itself can make him feel he is bound to her, dependent on all the qualities that he lacks in himself.

Harmonious Contact: Same Element

This is slightly easier, as the Saturn person senses a like-minded attitude: Even though it brings up her vulnerability, it's not quite as intense. In the Fire signs, for example, the couple could draw on their visions of an ideal world and their progressive ideas for their future together. In Earth, material aims and joint career moves will be the focus of their attention, and the Venus person will love hearing about Saturn's plans. In Air, ideals, ideas, transmission of information, and harmony will be valued by both. In Water, feelings and emotional stability will be vital to both partners.

Challenging Contacts: Oppositions and Three Signs Away

Venus/Saturn contacts can also play out in Saturn controlling Venus through financial obligation, particularly when three signs away and when different energies are involved. For many Saturn affinity contacts, what arises—and, often, what ties the two partners together—is an inner sense of guilt. But with openness and honesty, there's always room for negotiation in any Saturn contact: It just takes willingness, self-knowledge, and acceptance.

With the opposition, the Saturn partner exudes coolness and distance. For Venus, love isn't easy here because the Saturn person represents (or is attempting to represent) something contrary to Venus's values. This means that both may feel frustrated or blocked out but are somehow bound to each other in an uncomfortable way. It's as if both partners have their wrists chained together, but they're not facing one another in their bondage; they're back-to-back. And that means they're no longer mirroring one another. The result is a compelling but emotionally exhausting relationship. But if there are better contacts in the chart, both partners may be willing to negotiate their needs within this relationship.

VENUS/MERCURY CONTACTS

On the whole, Venus gets along with Mercury. In our natal charts, because the planets are never more than 78 degrees apart, they usually add a lighthearted, sweet-talking feel when they're in conjunction or sextile. But what if your Mercury opposes or squares his Venus or vice versa? In that case, the way you communicate doesn't gel with his values, or the things he takes pleasure in don't sit well with your values. On the whole, whether they're harmonious or challenging, these contacts tell us about our ability to share our partners' interests.

Harmonious Contacts: Same Sign or Element

This is characterized by mutual acceptance and an ability to share common interests. Both people can freely talk about their values and ideas with warmth and honesty. There are no power trips or mind games, just good conversation, plus a common bond of understanding. Venus may fall in love with Mercury's mind, while Mercury will be infatuated with Venus's seductive aura. This is a gentle contact and a useful one if you are looking for a lighthearted, no-strings kind of relationship. It's hardly bonding, but it does give both people the chance to communicate and listen with fairness, truth, and honesty.

Challenging Contacts: Three Signs Away or Oppositions

Here's where the intellect tries to overcome the natural urges of Venusian love. While the Venus partner may be discovering romance through Mercury's mind, she'll have a tough time finding love through Mercury's heart unless there are other good supporting contacts to Venus. The problem arises when the lack of "heart" from the Mercury partner remains a dark shadow in the relationship and when the Venus partner ends up resenting Mercury's rational mind-set. The Mercury partner may not even notice that Venus needs more personal indulgence and romantic seduction, and, unless they have strong bonding or sexually exciting contacts in the chart, the pair will soon find that Venus is drawn to someone who allows her to talk about what really pleases her, rather than what Mercury *thinks* pleases her.

VENUS/JUPITER CONTACTS

If Venus is about sexual pleasure and Jupiter about exaggeration and the desire for more, then when these contact one another in the affinity chart, the result can be some pretty mind-blowing sex. Both Mars and Jupiter are Fire planets in that they rule two of the Fire signs and, as such, are active, dynamic agents. Mars gratifies the Venus principle and is concerned with libido, ego, and lust, while Jupiter has grandiose ideals of how perfect and beautiful sex should be and wants more than the mere desires of the ego. So when coupled with Venus, pleasure isn't just about physical arousal or orgasm; it's about beautiful, bountiful experience that unites mind, body, and soul.

Venus and Jupiter in the Same Sign: Hitting the Jackpot

There's nothing sexier than when Venus and Jupiter are in the same sign. The Venus partner feels as if he's having an out-of-body experience in the presence of the Jupiter person: Suddenly, his own way of giving and receiving pleasure seems to be augmented, inspired, and given grace—as if he's found himself on stage getting applause and acclaim for his beauty. Jupiter, too, gets a divine experience in the company of the Venus person: The ideals and fantasies in which she's always believed can finally come true. Venus blows Jupiter's mind, just as the Jupiter person exhilarates and animates Venus.

Harmonious Contact: Same Element

When Jupiter and Venus are in the same element, there's a grand and spectacular sense of carefree love, romance, and sex—and maybe even long-term commitment, depending on the rest of the chart.

In Fire: Powerful Love

With Venus and Jupiter both in Fire, passionate dreams are the key to the success of the relationship, and a competitive but exciting aura often surrounds the two when they're out and about. This fiery

For example, let's take a look at same-sign Jupiter/Venus in Capricorn. Venus in Capricorn is serious about sophisticated pleasure, sensual indulgence, and lingerie to die for (both Capricorn men and women love the feel of silky fabrics in the bedroom). She's hunting for a successful lover who can make her feel glamorous or rich, and when she meets the Jupiter Capricorn man, her senses are enriched and all her seductive wiles are on red alert. Sexually skilled, stylish, and suave, the Jupiter man works hard to be the best lover around, and when he meets this divinely discrete, graceful, tasteful woman, he knows instantly that they're going to make the right kind of love. He imagines them soaking in a gold-tapped bath in some fantasy penthouse suite, and as she dances closer to him in her cool, informed, calculated way, he knows this is going to be the beautiful experience he's dreamed of. She, too, will take all the pleasure she can in the hope that this experience is even bigger than his expense account. It can be an enriching relationship if other beneficial contacts support it.

energy also filters into the bedroom, and the Venus person may want to show Jupiter that he can be the dominant partner in bed. They both feel free in each other's company, and it's this kind of powerful love that keeps the relationship vivid and alive.

In Earth: *Hardworking*

When Venus and Jupiter are in Earth, sexual pleasure is bliss, but establishing joint objectives and goals is highly valued, too. Sharing their wealth or generosity (the money-minded, security-conscious side of Earth Venus and Jupiter) or setting up a business can all be offshoots of the impulse toward bounty, both in lovemaking and the material world. They can create a well-organized lifestyle in which they'll never have to worry about money as they achieve their mutual goals.

In Air: *Delightful and Fun-Loving*

Venus in Air takes both intellectual and erotic pleasure from the mind. And Jupiter in Air has plenty to say on that front. In fact, Jupiter in Air is playful, lighthearted, hugely romantic and idealistic, and wants peace at any cost. Together they'll enjoy pillow talk all night, make love all day, and will swap roles, indulging in whatever wicked thoughts cross their minds. Their ideals of the perfect lifestyle can be grounded if they have enough backup from other contacts.

In Water: *Magical and Emotional*

In Water, Venus indulges in the pleasures of merging body and soul. Jupiter in Water, similarly, has grand designs for transformative, out-of-this world oblivion. Together they'll understand each other's moods; they'll sob on each other's shoulders over a dead bird or sit side by side on a beach under a full moon and imagine themselves among the stars. Both are generous and sensitive, and, if other planetary contacts are good, can form a magical and often mutually healing relationship.

Harmonious Contact: Opposites Attract

Although oppositions generally create challenging and provocative energy in the affinity chart, when such planets as Venus (love) and Jupiter (abundance) are in opposition, passionate flames are more likely than damp squibs.

When Venus is opposed by Jupiter, there's a powerful attraction of opposites, in which personal values are challenged by a profound belief system. This is a subtle difference, but when it comes to love, it's a very important one. Here's why: Hopefully, our interaction with our romantic partners validates our personal values (Venus), but our larger spiritual belief systems (Jupiter) have little to do with other people and are sustained by an unconscious connection with our own souls. So when other people's very different personal values cross swords with our individual senses of purpose and meaning, we feel provoked to defend our territory. And Jupiter takes issue not only with the value Venus places on pleasure, but also with her sense of vanity. (Don't forget that, in addition to sexual and sensual pleasure, Venus also represents how vain or self-conscious we are about our bodies.)

Jupiter, known as Zeus in Greek mythology, was more interested in proving he was the ultimate divine sex bomb among goddesses, nymphs, and mortals alike than actually caring about the females he ravished. So when Jupiter is challenged by the preening self-love of Venus, he wants to show off his divine omnipotence (that is, his ideals about life and love) or wants to compete with Venus to find out who wins the prize for Most Seductive Deity. This can lead to some of the most potent and dazzling love affairs—but whether a long-term commitment will flourish depends, as always, on other contacts in the affinity chart.

Fire Venus/Air Jupiter

Venus in Fire glamorizes life and love. She takes pleasure from dramatic sex (Leo), potent lovers, and beating rivals (Sagittarius). She's dominant in the bedroom, which is strewn with torn sheets and empty bottles of wine (Aries). For Jupiter in Air, sex isn't about writhing bodies; it's about erotic thoughts (Gemini), pure spirits connecting in a romantic embrace (Libra), or enough space to breathe between tender kisses (Aquarius). Both find amusement in the other person, and Venus in Fire is often the one who becomes so fascinated by Jupiter's antics that she finds herself addicted to his exuberant spirit. Meanwhile, Jupiter begins to see that spontaneity in love is as inspiring as idealistic thoughts.

Air Venus/Fire Jupiter

True, the Fire Jupiter man is unreliable—but he's unstoppable when he's on a mission (Sagittarius) or when he's possessed by the drive to seize whatever's there for the taking (Aries). In fact, this Jupiter guy (Leo) is most like the god himself, who ravished the mortal Semele via a lightning bolt, causing her both instant sexual gratification and instant death. (Gulp.) So the Venus-in-Air woman must take care when playing with Jupiter in Fire. Not that this guy is about to burn her up: He'll just burn her out with his superabundant desires. Venus in Air takes pleasure from lightness of the mind (Gemini)—think sexy messages and thoughts—romantic fantasies (Libra), and challenging sexual techniques (Aquarius), so this relationship can be fun, lighthearted, and often a quick starter. If other beneficial contacts are present, it can make for a hugely exciting relationship that's based on romance as an escape route.

Water Venus/Earth Jupiter

The Venus-in-Water man is private (Scorpio), cautious about revealing his feelings (Cancer), and considers pleasure to be a deeply personal way of revealing himself to another person (Pisces), so he rarely takes sex lightly. (That said, he can also be hugely promiscuous as compensation for his vulnerability!) For the Jupiter-in-Earth woman, love and sex are a means to an end (Taurus); they are big physical events that move her toward finding true meaning in life (Virgo). She's extremely indulgent and can become the dominant partner in a love affair (Capricorn), drawing the Water man into the delights of sensuality and out of himself. This can be an eye-opening experience for the Water man and a pleasurable challenge for the earthy Jupiter woman.

Earth Venus/Water Jupiter

If Earth in Venus is about total physical, sensual indulgence, Jupiter in Water believes that life and love are part of a greater scheme and that sex isn't just the merger of bodies but a total merger of souls (Cancer), divine power (Scorpio), or an escape to other realms (Pisces). So when the Jupiter-in-Water woman is invited to take pleasure in Earth's worldly sexuality, she'll find this sensual, gutsy lover quite a challenge to her otherworldly love style—unless she has a good dose of Earth planets herself. Both partners can benefit from each other's different values and beliefs, and this can be a highly indulgent, possessive-but-delightful blend of the sacred and the profane.

Challenging Contact: Three Signs Away

Venus and Jupiter clashes are unlikely to promote a stable physical relationship and can even hinder it because the Venus pleasure principle is not at all helped by Jupiter's drive toward omnipotence when it's triggered by Venusian rivalry. Don't forget, if Jupiter "inflates and exaggerates" whatever it contacts, then Venus is going to become ultradefensive about what she values or what kind of sexual pleasure she needs and will become even more "in Venus," so to speak, in her attempt to free herself from dominating Jupiter. In fact, Venus will always want to do things her way while greedy Jupiter wants to do things his way. But if there are other positive contacts in the chart, this tension may be subdued or diminished.

Now that we've looked at Venus to Mars and Jupiter, let's take a look at what happens when Venus makes contacts to the outer planets. Brace yourself: You're about to come face-to-face with a darker, fated sense of love's mysterious ways in the affinity chart.

VENUS AND THE OUTER PLANETS

Where sexual chemistry is concerned, there seems to be a fated, almost cosmic sexual connection between two people, particularly when Venus is in a powerful contact to Uranus, Neptune, or Pluto.

VENUS AND URANUS

So when it's in contact with the other person's Venus (unless he or she has a Venus contact to the same Uranus sign in his or her own chart), Uranus wakes up Venus's self-image and romantic values. Uranus is also about radical reform, surprise, electrifying energy, and buzzing idealism. If you were each born in a different approximate seven-year generation, then the visions and ideals of your partner's Uranian influence will be very different from your own—in which case, instead of waking you up to your Venus, your Venus principles will either be broken down or, like the famous Bond martini, shaken and never stirred.

Another type of awakening is far more sexual. In the ancient Greek myth of Ouranos, the god of the heavens was castrated by his son, Cronus (or Saturn, in Latin), to stop him from fathering the terrible monsters that he hid inside Mother Earth. As his genitals fell to the sea they created foam, from which arose Aphrodite (Venus), as we've already discussed on page XX. This mythical tale, then, is a metaphor for the great sexual interplay between Venus and Uranus in the affinity chart. The Uranus person awakens the Venus person to a brand-new world of sexual pleasure; Venus is as new to this world as if she's just risen from the sea. In sensory terms, this is an intense, out-of-the-ordinary physical attraction. But what happens to the Uranian person? She, too, is woken up to something profound. Often the Uranian partner will break up an existing relationship, will wake up to this newly found sense of divine sexuality, or will become aware of what rebellion and freedom mean to her. Depending on the individual natal chart, though, this can be experienced as either a gift or a curse. It's a gift if Uranus develops the ability to evolve as a person and accept herself and others; it's a curse if she can't free herself from negative patterns of behavior.

Harmonious Contact: Same Sign

When they're in the same sign, Uranus can't resist Venus's seductive charm, while Venus feels totally enraptured by this exciting, unknown energy that's producing such a powerful sexual spark. In our charts, Saturn doesn't act as a conscious energy; rather, its effect is to pull us into the transpersonal, or unconscious, realms of our existence and to compel us to behave in ways we might find contrary to our Venusian principles. It can also bring about breakthroughs in our love lives via unexpected means.

So, in general, same-sign Uranus and Venus contacts lead to adventurous, unpredictable sexual relationships. If it's your Venus, you'll compare him to an electrifying sex god; if it's your Uranus and his Venus, the spark between you will depend on your own sexual inventiveness and how you're able to adapt it to his style of loving.

Harmonious Contact: Venus and Uranus in the Same Element

In the same element, Venus and Uranus create a dynamic and exciting frisson of sexual electricity. There's an unconscious bond between the two, even though the sensual or romanticized qualities of Venus may not always gel with Uranus's universal energy. But both partners do empower one another to expand—or, at least, to tweak—their sexual perspectives.

In Fire: *Dramatic and Demanding*

In Fire, Venus is dramatic, self-absorbed, and highly demanding, and when she meets the Uranian Fire person, there's mutual excitement and a frenzy of sexual activity, coupled with the Uranian Fire partner's need for freedom and space. This can make for a seductive, arousing sex life, in which both Venus and Uranus will be utterly insatiable.

In Air: *Adventurous and Unpredictable*

The winds of change blow erratically through Uranus in Air's love life, with her desire for experimental sex, for trying out the new and different, or for remaining in a permanent state of arousal via erotic imagery or literature. The Venus-in-Air person immediately relates to this, and together, they will discover all the delights of the mind first and the body second.

In Earth: *Chains of Love*

Uranus is not comfortable when bound and chained in Earth energy; after all, Uranus was the god of the heavens and feels more at ease in Fire and Air. So when Uranus meets the sensual Venus/Earth person, both partners feel as if they're plummeting headlong into the ground, but they're powerless to resist: Venus in Earth willingly opens her sensual arms, while the Uranus person erupts into sexual life like a volcano. However, the Uranian person might want to escape back to his lofty heights when he feels chained to the rocks of Venus's possessive love.

In Water: *Emotional and Claustrophobic*

Venus in Water is changeable, emotional, secretive, and dreamy. When Uranus in Water hooks into her mysterious charm, an easy flow of sexual energy results, even though the Uranian partner may not like drowning in the claustrophobic waters of emotions. Venus will be fascinated by Uranus's attitude to sexual freedom but may not be able to sustain a relationship with his eccentric behavior for long unless the two of them have other supporting contacts.

Let's take, for example, a Uranus-in-Scorpio man and a Venus-in-Scorpio woman. Her Uranus is in Libra; she's a couple of years older than he is and doesn't have the collective Scorpio energy in her own chart. So the Uranus-in-Scorpio man unconsciously attempts to shake up the depths of his lover's feelings to wake her up to her own hidden power. The Venus-in-Scorpio woman, who values personal power, sexual depth, and the most orgasmic part of herself, is electrified by a part of this man that seems like a sort of divine accomplice. It's part of who he is yet seems to be separate from him, too—and the feeling it provokes in her is definitely out of the ordinary. When she's in his presence, she's always sexually aroused. Likewise, although he's not aware that he's brandishing his Uranian sword, he realizes through this woman's sexual darkness that all the gifts he carries can be transformed into something life-changing—something verging on the supernatural. Both partners will sense this nearly supernatural energy and call it sex. And it is—but it's also a schism that divides them from what they've known before and a catalyst for sudden sexual awakening.

Challenging Contacts: Oppositions and Three Signs Away

When we come to oppositions and three signs away, that sense of awakening disappears (unless the Venus person has Uranus in the same sign as the Uranus partner). Instead, there's more of a shock or a shake-up of all the Venus partner's romantic values. This often leads to the stormiest—but often the sexiest—relationships: Think short-term, madcap flings and one-night stands. But once that initial spark has been sated, the Uranian person is usually the one who cools off. Venus's very different style of loving (unless the pair have other mutually beneficial contacts) may contradict Uranus's sense of awakening to her own magical side, or the "divine rebel" within her. This can be a highly magnetic physical attraction, but unless there are other longer-term contacts in the chart, it can fizzle out as quickly as it began.

VENUS/NEPTUNE CONTACTS

Neptune and Venus contacts are more harmonious than most other cross-aspects to Neptune, simply because Venus is happy to seduce and be seduced. In fact, she wants to out-seduce Neptune with his wily ways and deceptive behavior. Venus sees Neptune not so much as a threat as a wonderful catch, and she longs to prove that her sensual (Taurus-ruled) and pure (Libra-ruled) love will always win out over the chaos hidden in Neptunian waters.

Harmonious Contact: Same Sign

Say we've got a guy with his Neptune in Capricorn conjunct her Venus in Capricorn. If Neptune lures us into believing that something's for real, then the man with Neptune in Capricorn is swayed by class, beauty, money, and glamorous women. He's also skilled in the art of traditional courtship, knowing that it's the "disguise" that'll help him get what he wants. That's what lures his Venus-in-Capricorn date into believing that all this is, indeed, for real. After all, he *wants* it to be real, and Venus in Capricorn does, too. And it just might be. If he has other Earth signs that can pull him away from his Neptune self and if he's truly capable of "making something" of his life, then Venus in Capricorn will warm to his overtures.

Venus in Capricorn is a realist. She wants sensual delights, imagines herself rolling around on a bed of Monopoly money (or, even better, real cash!), and has a very definite image of her ideal capable and successful lover. Venus stirs his longings; in turn, he stirs her desire for the skilled pleasures he's acquired as if by magic. And if, by magic, they should have other supportive contacts, that's a good thing: It may add a safety net to the glamorized ideals inherent in this relationship.

Harmonious Contact: Same Element

These two vibrate to the same romantic tune and have similar loves and longings. It's a romantic, dream-like, and often highly creative combination if other supporting and grounding contacts are present. And even if it all fizzles out as quickly as it began, this will be a memorable and deeply enriching romantic involvement. The only problem with same-element Venus/Neptune contacts is that the couple may swaddle each other in a cocoon-like existence for a while, but that could be deceptive, as Neptune will find it very easy to seduce, beguile, and capture the Venus person's heart. But is it really what Neptune wants? Take both Neptunes and both Venuses into account here, as well as any other contacts involved with these two planets.

Challenging Contacts: Three Signs Away and Oppositions

Let's imagine—and why not, since we're in Neptunian territory here?—that it's your Venus. His ideal image of romantic bliss will be defused by your very different sensual and sexual values. Somehow you don't quite fit the image he has created, and although he may be drawn to you romantically, he'll begin to feel he has to give you up in order to feel comfortable with his own dream. And the more you chase him or long for him, the more quickly you'll lose sight of him: He'll vanish into the night, fearful that you might see through his disguise. This contact is a very difficult one when it comes to long-term loving—but it's often a compelling attraction that leads to some kind of sacrifice on both sides. (And sacrifice isn't necessarily a bad thing: It can yield profound realizations about what's actually important in life.)

VENUS/PLUTO CONTACTS

In the affinity chart, Pluto contacts always create a powerful, unconscious hold over the two partners. Particularly with Venus, it's one of the most potent indications of compulsive desire, obsessive and jealous love, and the most torrid, sexually driven affairs. (See the section on Pluto in chapter 16 for more detailed information on Pluto.)

The tragic love affair between the strong-willed writer George Sand and composer Frédéric Chopin reveals a powerful Venus/Pluto conjunction in Pisces. Sand and Chopin were lovers for many years—Sand was a kind of femme fatale in Chopin's life—but as he became weakened by illness and plagued by family jealousy, Sand became more of a resentful nursemaid and dictator toward Chopin, calling him "a beloved little corpse" in their last years together.

As with all contacts between charts, it's very important to look at what effect his Pluto has in your chart and vice versa in order to determine whether there's any imbalance—or any balance at all—and to get a glimpse of who has the upper hand in the relationship.

Obsession and Clandestine Love

In my experience, it's usually the Venus partner who's obsessed with the Pluto person. Venus will feel as if she's completely consumed by the attraction; ultimately, then, the Pluto partner is in control of whether the relationship will last. Remember that Pluto will "bury" the planet it touches (in this case, Venus) in its dark underworld. It will abduct all of her seductive power; it will "rape" Venus of her qualities. Venus, feeling consumed by her rapacious Pluto partner (who may not even be aware that he possesses these qualities), will be drawn to that darkness in an attempt to reclaim her own power. It's admirable that Venus wants to transform her sense of being devoured into a sense of being loved—but it's also a tall order since Pluto holds the reins here.

If Pluto is about secrets and Venus is about love, then a Pluto contact in your affinity chart might also be a sign that you're having a clandestine relationship—a secret love affair. In fact, it's this secretive aspect of Pluto that often provides the attraction factor, for it seems that anything that is hidden or unknown acts as a powerful lure for humans in general.

Pluto is concerned with compulsion, taboo, and the shadows of love, while Venus is love's looking glass: So when these planets meet, even in the same sign or element, the result is something highly potent, transformative, arousing—and deadly. With complete openness and emotional honesty between the two partners, the Venus person is likely to have a transformative experience, and the Pluto person will be given a sense of his own power. But the question is, will it last? Can it lead to a healthy, successful, long-term relationship?

GEORGE SAND AND FRÉDÉRIC CHOPIN'S AFFINITY CHART

Eccentric nineteenth-century French writer George Sand was thought to be more passionate about seduction itself than the man she was after. However, she was a good companion to many of her lovers, and mothered Chopin through the last years of his life. The affinity chart between Sand and Chopin reveals a powerful Pluto contact between them, with Sand destined to become a femme fatale in the eyes of his family. Note that it is Chopin's Venus and sun which hooks into Sand's Saturn/Pluto opposition, which was already a struggle within her own chart—personal defenses undermined by the underworld's archetypal power. Compelled to both love her and be overpowered by her, Chopin provoked her into resenting him (her Saturn opposite his Venus), yet wanting to conquer his creative talents, soulful imagination (her Pluto conjunct his sun in Pisces), and Piscean vulnerability (Venus in Pisces). So what does she do? Like anyone overwhelmed by Pluto being brought to life in their chart, she rules him, controls him, takes his life-force away from him through love. This is not to say Sand is to blame, rather that the Plutonian archetype is more powerful in us than we can ever imagine.

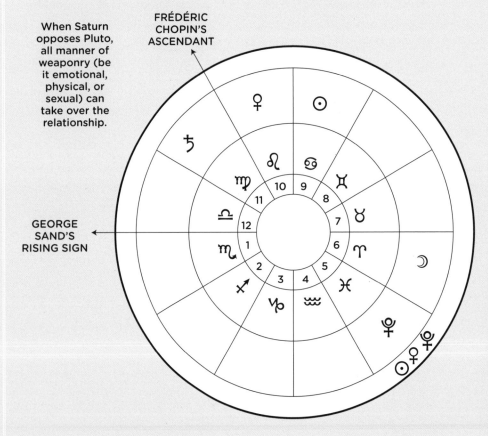

When Saturn opposes Pluto, all manner of weaponry (be it emotional, physical, or sexual) can take over the relationship.

FRÉDÉRIC CHOPIN'S ASCENDANT

GEORGE SAND'S RISING SIGN

A double whammy of Pluto contacts in the affinity chart (When both have Pluto in the same sign as well as Pluto aspecting personal planets) often overwhelm the individuals concerned, and emotional or even physical power struggles result.

A NEAR-DEATH EXPERIENCE

Let's take, for example, a woman with Venus in Libra and a man with Pluto in Libra. For Pluto in Libra, finding harmony, peace, and beauty at any cost is a matter of life and death. And when Pluto meets Venus—a living, breathing example of this pure ideal, a living model of beauty and peace—he's consumed by a desire to seize it and run away with it. The ruthless Plutonian essence of this man is like Hades himself, galloping across the fields of wildflowers on his black horse. He swoops down on his prize; the earth opens before him, and he plummets back into the underworld. When the Pluto archetype is awakened in us, it will go to any length to wield ultimate power. Pluto is compelled to overpower and possess that beauty and to keep it hidden away in the safety of his underworld.

Similarly, the Venus-in-Libra woman is drawn to this man's power and his irresistible darkness. But gradually, her Venusian appreciation of the wide world beyond his embrace begins to eat away at the Pluto man's dark power. He becomes obsessive and wants to possess her at any cost. So Venus begins to feel trapped and powerless, and, like Persephone, she longs to return to the light of day, to the real world of air and light and sun. She's had enough of his deathly existence. And this battle for power might go on for a very long time, depending on other contacts in their chart.

Challenging Contact: Venus/Pluto in the Same Sign

When Venus and Pluto are in the same sign, it indicates that this is one of the most subjective, claustrophobic, nonnegotiable, exclusive relationships imaginable—particularly from the Lord of the Underworld's point of view. For Venus, it's like being throttled and buried alive, while Pluto's never felt so powerful, and he doesn't want to let go of that sense of power. Often both partners are also involved with a third party, which adds a dash of envy and rivalry, a heightened craving for power (for the Pluto partner), and, for the Venus partner, the sense that all of her values in terms of love and pleasure are being ripped apart in the darkness. This can be a transformative relationship for both people, but only if both can accept and understand the depth of the experience.

Challenging Contact: Venus/Pluto Opposition

With Venus/Pluto oppositions, we are in darker territory: We're in Pluto's underworld, and he gets to decide if Venus will remain there with him, leave him to return to the world, or be annihilated forever.

Here's an example from Greek mythology. In the story of Orpheus's visit to the underworld to rescue his lover, Eurydice, Orpheus plays his lyre before Persephone and Hades to put them into a trance. Beguiled by his music, they agree to let Eurydice return to the upper world on one condition: She must follow behind Orpheus, and he must not look back at her even once on their journey. If he does, she will disappear forever. Sadly, Orpheus mistrusts Hades and looks back to make sure Eurydice is following him—and as he turns, he sees her vanish forever. This is because Pluto doesn't warm quickly to intruders, and he's keen to test them to see if they are worthy of his attention. And if they fail that test, they'll lose what's dearest to them, just as Orpheus did.

Similarly, when Pluto is threatened by an outsider—like a goody-two-shoes Venus in opposition—Pluto immediately acts not only to protect himself but also to wield total power over Venus. In fact, Pluto wants to be very sure she follows the path he's set out for her: No deviations allowed.

So in a Venus/Pluto opposition, Pluto is under threat from an outsider. The abduction scenario is no longer a straightforward kidnapping in which Pluto knows exactly what his role is: This time, an uninvited stranger has entered his underworld, and he doesn't take too kindly to the trespass. So what happens when a woman with Pluto in, say, Scorpio is faced with a man with Venus in Taurus?

Immediately, as in any opposition, the attraction is magnetic, but it can be obsessively provocative, frustrating, hypnotic, or devouring. Her Pluto survival mechanism operates (at an unconscious level) by keeping her in control of her emotions at all costs, but when her deepest self feels threatened, she must somehow change the stakes: She must steal, plunder, and do whatever else it takes to ensure she remains in power. Her Pluto is under threat from this intruder who delights in turning on the light—both in the bedroom and outside of it.

Challenging Contact: Three Signs Away

Similarly, when three signs away and in incompatible elements, there's a sense of intensity and lust, of a power struggle that's never resolved—not even in bed—and there's an underlying friction between the couple. If it's her Venus, she feels she'll have to give up all the things she loves most (the upper world) to be with him (in his underworld). Sexual attraction is the main force of this contact until jealousy or possessiveness seeps into the relationship's cracks. Yes, the bed will rock, too, but the upheavals and turmoil involved will be testing and exhausting unless they have other, more supportive contacts.

Do take Pluto/Venus contacts very seriously. They can add drama, intensity, and sexual passion to any relationship, but they can also lead to power struggles, jealousy, and love triangles. Usually, it's Venus's obsessive desire for powerful Pluto that creates the binding, destructive side of the relationship. But once Pluto begins to wield too much power (unconsciously or not), the Venus partner will begin to resent not being able to express her Venus qualities in the ways she'd like to. So just as the goddess Venus herself would, she turns to another lover who may be able to mirror her vanity, beauty, true pleasure, and happiness in a more liberating or compassionate way.

Harmonious Contact: Venus/Pluto in the Same Element

In the same element, a similar energy exists: There's powerful mutual passion and a battle between earthly values and shadowy empowerment, but there's a little more room for Venus to breathe. Don't forget: It's unlikely that you will ever meet anyone with Pluto in Aries, Taurus, or Gemini due to Pluto's slow-moving nature, so here's a brief rundown of what to expect among the elements.

In the Fire signs, Pluto takes control through the power of passion, dragging Venus's love of spontaneity and sexual carelessness into dangerously clandestine waters. Often these two are already involved in a long-term relationship, and it's this that keeps the relationship simultaneously alive and in danger of death: The pair are living on a knife's edge between routine love and irresponsible passion. In Air, the power of ideal love takes over both people, and this constant search keeps the Pluto partner feeling powerful while Venus, too, is tantalized by the pursuit of the perfect relationship. In Earth, Venus is at home, and she's all about sexual sensuality, but Pluto wants to plunder Venus of her riches. Sexually, bittersweet delights abound, but Venus will feel compelled to want more while Pluto will be pushed to *take* more and more control in order to bear the burden of human love. With Pluto in Water, there's only one way to bear this awesome sense of empowerment, and that's to take it on an emotional level. This is where Venus may play a game with Pluto's feelings—but if so, it'll be a game that's characterized by a deeply magnetic, transformative attraction.

Same-sign and same-element Venus/Pluto contacts often occur between people who are already happy in a relationship (or think they are); in these cases, Venus will be compelled to transform or to live out her Pluto power in other ways. If other contacts between the charts are positive or suggest long-term links, then this can be a truly "sacred" or cathartic relationship—although this is entirely dependent on how much power the Pluto partner has and how willing he or she is to understand this struggle.

VENUS AND RISING-SIGN CONTACTS

A powerful Venus contact to the rising sign is often suggestive of a major physical attraction. Of course, this can often happen before we've realized that the rising-sign person might not be all she seems beneath that charming façade. Your Venus sign tells you what kind of beauty you're looking for in the other person—whatever it is, it's the kind of beauty that gives you pleasure. If your rising sign makes a positive contact to his Venus, then sparks fly, the ground moves beneath his feet, and you understand just how to make him feel happy to be alive.

Harmonious Contact: Venus and Rising Sign in the Same Sign

When Venus falls in the same sign or same element as the rising sign, there's an immediate rapport and instant attraction from the Venus person to the rising-sign person. Both are dynamic energies and side with solar energy. Yes, Venus may be a feminine principle, but that doesn't mean it's submissive; it's dangerously sexy when it's in Fire; explosive when it's in Air; torrid when it's in Water; and indulgent when it's in Earth. It's totally unlike the passive energy of the moon, with its lunar reactions and urges and its needy side.

BITTERSWEET DELIGHT

Say you're a woman with Venus in Scorpio, and your partner's rising sign is Scorpio. You'll instantly know how to please the Scorpio rising-sign side of your lover. He'll view the world and present himself to it in exactly the same way that you "please" both the world and yourself. And that means there's a strong and powerful affinity at once. This may not be a lifelong bond, but you'll both appreciate and understand each other's attitudes toward love and sexual pleasure. Here's how that might look.

The Venus-in-Scorpio woman is intensely passionate about sex and longs to feel empowered by that pleasure. But whether she's involved in an obsessive power game or indulging in a delicious, expensive piece of dark chocolate, she is also secretive, probing, intimate, private, and hypnotic. As for the Scorpio-rising man, face him with a wall of graffiti, and he'll notice words like *sex* and *taboo* rather than *romance* or *beauty*. That's because he doesn't look for the beauty in things; he looks for the darkness in them, and he recognizes it quickly in the Venus-in-Scorpio woman. Both are seduced by each other's mystery and dark view of love. The Venus woman is intrigued by his refusal to look her in the eye—surely she has enough seductive power to turn his head?—and he's bewitched by her natural mystique, which aligns so well with his own impressionable one.

Challenging Contacts: Oppositions and Three Signs Away

When Venus is in opposition to the rising sign, there's an extremely powerful attraction from the rising-sign person to the Venus person. This isn't just about lust; it's about a grass-is-always-greener desire to have what your partner has just because it seems more appealing. Also, because Venus falls in the rising-sign person's seventh house, Venus is seen as Something To Be Desired. And unless the rising-sign person has Venus in the seventh house herself (which would be a Venus/Venus contact; see chapter 10), this desirable quality is tossed into the air in front of the rising-sign person like a juggler's ball.

From the Venus person's perspective, the very presence of the rising-sign person is contrary to all that he values, and he intends to win her over by the most seductive means possible. (Remember, Venus wasn't only vain; she was also intent on being the most beautiful of all the goddesses and went to great lengths to prove her point in the famous story of Helen of Troy.) The Venus person, then, will attempt to persuade the rising-sign person to value the same things he values.

When Venus is three signs away from the rising sign, and therefore in incompatible elements, the value of the Venus placement disturbs or provokes the rising-sign person to maintain her perception or outlook on life. This can create an uncomfortable atmosphere in which the rising-sign person will, unless she has supporting contacts between her own Venus and her partner's planets, become resentful or jealous of the "show" of value that the Venus partner puts on. "Look at me, and how I am," Venus seems to command the rising-sign partner: "My way is the right way, and you know you want to agree with me!" And that hardly makes for a harmonious, supportive partnership.

Now that we've explored the highs and lows of Venus in the affinity chart, let's turn our attention to the power of the planet Mars. Sure, you've already seen Mars interact with the sun, rising sign, moon, and Venus—but now it's time to see what else this lusty planet does to two people in love.

11 Mars:
Excitement and Libido

This chapter is all about how Mars, the feisty planet of sexual conquest, operates in the affinity chart. We'll be looking at the interaction of Venus and Mars in chapter 12, but first we'll need to see how Mars provokes, competes, or wrestles with desire when it contacts another person's planets.

If Venus is about how we give and take pleasure, and about how we value pleasure and physicality, then Mars is all about how we go about getting what we want; it's about how we assert ourselves, our drive, and our ambition. Mars is the chase and the conquest, and this Mars energy reveals both what we find sexually exciting and the sexual "scent" we emit to attract partners. (If Venus represents pleasure, then Mars is how we go about "feeding" Venus, or satisfying that pleasure.) And in our affinity charts, it can be the trigger for pure lust and physical desire.

MARS: THE MYTH

Like his father, Zeus, Ares (Mars in Latin) was outrageously promiscuous and fathered many of Aphrodite's children, including Fear (Phobos), Terror (Deimos), and Harmony (Harmonia). Greek writers like Hesiod were ambivalent toward Ares; most of them thought he was a lout and hardly worthy of his lofty status as one of the twelve Olympian gods. It was only when he was assimilated into Roman mythology that he became a warrior with authority and had a new role as a guardian deity. Ares embodied the physical strength needed for military success as a destructive and overwhelming force as well as the libido necessary for fornicating with so many nymphs, goddesses, and half-mortals. However, in Homer's *Iliad*, Zeus reminds Ares—to his face—that he's more hateful to Zeus than any other god. (Ouch.)

So here we have a violent god who's hated by his father, desired by Aphrodite, and who has sired Fear and Terror, his accomplices in battle, as well as the goddess of peace and harmony. Well, it's not hard to see that Ares wants to prove something. He wants to show the world that he isn't going to sit around twiddling his thumbs when he wants something; instead, he'll head straight into battle in a number of different ways, depending on what kind of armor he's wearing (read: your Mars sign).

WORKING WITH MARS IN THE AFFINITY CHART

Venus describes what gives us sensual pleasure, while Mars tells us how we seduce in order to reward our Venus with fuel for that pleasure. In a way, Mars is about how we "penetrate" the love of another person with our own power under the guise of our libidos. Mars can create sexual excitement, lust, and desire—but it can also create fiery disputes, sullen silences, cold hearts, and fear of our own passions. Since this is such a potent contact in the affinity chart, let's see how it plays out in the same sign or same element.

When two Mars are in the same sign in the affinity chart, physical energy is strong and arousing. For both people, the quest for getting what they want becomes a game to see who can arouse, provoke, or challenge the other person to action—in their sex lives, or, perhaps, in their work lives. However, a double dose of the same personal planet can lead to overload or to a highly subjective, suffocating quality, as we've already seen with Venus. Look to other contacts between Venus, sun, and moon to see whether the Mars energy might be a little dissipated or balanced in the affinity chart.

NOW YOU SEE ME, NOW YOU DON'T

Here's an example of a couple with Mars in Gemini. Quick to rise to each other's bait, they act a bit like a jack-in-the-box: "Now you see me, now you don't." In this case, the double trouble of the Twins is amplified, and the energy can be unreliable and unpredictable yet highly arousing. A seductive game of chase is played to keep the energy moving; it's as if neither partner can pause for breath, testing each other to see who can outwit the other. Together, they act like a cheeky, giggling pair of tricksters, and neither knows whether the other is what she really seems to be. Depending on other planet contacts, this can be a sparkling, hilarious courtship. Once they've danced around the social scene and gotten bored with the endless sext messages and dirty phone calls, they'll have to be quick about finding new and exciting ways to stimulate each other—before someone else does.

Harmonious Contact: Same Element

Having both Mars in the same element is often more exciting than having two in the same sign since the couple will have similar physical drives but with different qualities or flavors to them. Still, sometimes too much of a good thing can present problems: Each partner will have to keep up with the other in terms of libido, and if that doesn't happen, the result is likely to be a hefty dose of frustration.

In Fire: *Passionate and Spirited*

Mars in the Fire signs is characterized by challenge, rivalry, action, and, above all, a fast and furious desire for winning the game of seduction. Mars is comfortable in the Fire signs because it is a fiery action planet itself, so it increases sexual desire and the thrill of the chase—and, if in good contact to the other person's Venus, can create the most passionate and sustained sexual relationships. In Aries, Mars acts fast and demands much; in Leo, it wants complete dedication; and in Sagittarius, it insists upon the freedom to come and go.

In Earth: *Limitless Libido*

In Earth, Mars wears the most exquisite armor when he's on the hunt. Mars in Earth is physically strong and has a powerful desire to prove his sexual potency and relentless libido. Mars people are driven to show their physical prowess (in Taurus), their sophisticated sexual finesse (in Virgo), and their consistent desire to give their partners the best of themselves (Capricorn).

In Air: *Mindful Delights*

Mars in Air is concerned with escaping the physical, earthly realms of sex for the high delights of the mind (Gemini). In fact, it's the thoughts, ideas, and longings of desire that motivate and give rise to a lighthearted yet dizzy, and sometimes confused, physical libido (Libra) and the unconventional libido and sexual expression of Aquarius.

In Water: *Seductive and Elusive*

As a Fire planet, Mars rests uneasily in the Water signs. Its fiery flames are easily doused by the churning ocean. It flounders between waves of feeling and the higher realms of passion, and it can build up into a tsunami of both all at once. This tremendous flow of energy is often suppressed or denied, or it can suddenly emerge when triggered by another person's planet, particularly if it's another Mars in Water. These two will instantly sense the churning feelings of libidos that are driven by profound emotions. Both have the desire to seduce, either in an elusive, mysterious way (Mars in Pisces), a calculating, cautious way (Mars in Cancer), or an enigmatic way (Scorpio).

Challenging Contact: Oppositions

Like any opposition, Mars against Mars is where fights break out and challenges become either powerful attractions or complete turnoffs. (Turning off the lights is another option.) I've seen many long-term affinity charts in which oppositions from Mars seem to keep the two people on tenterhooks. They're alive and vibrant, or they're constantly fighting for their physical space as a significant way to hold a relationship together. Our example chart on page 142 shows the fiery interplay of two Mars in opposition in the affinity chart of King Henry VIII and Anne Boleyn. Note that Henry's Mars is also conjunct his Ascendant—a fiery, volatile bait for his seventh-house bedfellow!

ANNE BOLEYN AND KING HENRY VIII'S AFFINITY CHART

The interplay of two Mars in opposition here is not the only challenging aspect between these two volatile people. The usually discriminating Virgo rising, Henry VIII, was probably led astray by his fiery moon in Aries and his volatile Mars. Mars in his own natal chart also squares Jupiter and Neptune, pulling him in all kinds of seductive directions. Anne's sun in Taurus was a powerful lure for Henry's Venus in Taurus (not shown here) but the true sexual challenge came from Anne's Mars which falls in his seventh-house. This not only enticed and fired up Henry's sex drive, but also it provoked angry outbursts (from Henry) and impulsive and dangerous behavior (from Anne). Henry's weakness was his attraction to beautiful women (natal Venus on the Midheaven and Mars square Neptune) and when he met Jane Seymour, Anne became a thorn in his side. Her lack of male offspring and erratic behavior was enough for Henry to get rid of her, and she was accused of being an adulterous witch. Their turbulent relationship was finally over when Henry ordered her execution.

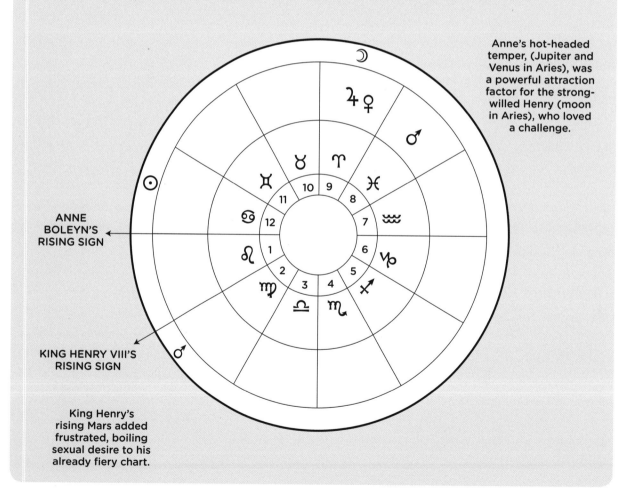

Anne's hot-headed temper, (Jupiter and Venus in Aries), was a powerful attraction factor for the strong-willed Henry (moon in Aries), who loved a challenge.

ANNE BOLEYN'S RISING SIGN

KING HENRY VIII'S RISING SIGN

King Henry's rising Mars added frustrated, boiling sexual desire to his already fiery chart.

Aries/Libra

The Mars-in-Aries person is naturally a leader, potent, fast-paced, and determined to have it all now rather than later. Faced with a placid Mars, he may well become infuriated and frustrated by the Libra Mars's lack of drive and initiative. But on the upside, this gives the Aries Mars person a chance to lead the way, to show off his sexual skills, and to decide when, where, and how to arouse his partner. Mars in Libra will follow this lead at first, excited by the wild, forceful energy and perhaps fearful of it; either way, it's definitely a force that needs to be cultivated and civilized. This is when their Mars will clash, as Aries is all raw potency, while Libra is purified and civilized. But if they have other positive contacts in the affinity chart, this can make for an exciting—if slightly unstable—physical attraction.

Taurus/Scorpio

This is a notorious opposition, mostly because one is deeply sensual while the other is deeply sexual. Together, the grounded Mars in Taurus is overwhelmed by the intense libido of Mars in Scorpio. This can make for a totally compelling attraction and a battle of wills; but once they're in a physical embrace, not much can pull them apart, except when Taurus digs in her heels and won't be controlled by Scorpio's compulsive sexuality. Depending on other planetary contacts, this can be either a complete disaster or a sexual obsession that both partners are unable to relinquish.

Gemini/Sagittarius

The fleeting, scattered, and often unreliable libido and will of Mars in Gemini is challenged by Mars in Sagittarius's rampant and totally exaggerated sex drive—so much so that the Mars-in-Gemini person will either flee before things get too hot or the Mars-in-Sagittarius person will tire of Gemini's unpredictable whims and desires. But it's a laugh a minute if they can keep up with each other. If there are other powerful contacts in the affinity chart, these very restless and constantly inconstant people just might stay together for longer than a one-night stand.

Cancer/Capricorn

Mars in Cancer takes a while to initiate sex, but once her libido is aroused, she has a profound sex drive. However, Mars in Capricorn is more direct, earthy, and demanding, so Mars in Cancer may scuttle away in search of some much-needed peace just when Capricorn least expects it. This can lead to tension, plus a seesaw quality to their sex life that'll probably please Mars in Cancer more.

Leo/Aquarius

If Mars in Leo is uninhibited about his sex drive, Mars in Aquarius isn't quite sure what hers is all about. Sure, Aquarius feels aroused and gets turned on by various sex techniques and positions, but she's more aroused by what goes on in her mind than what's actually happening in bed. However, Mars in Leo will fight for sexual dominance and will lead Aquarius down a very enticing and exciting sexual road.

Let's take, for example, a woman with Mars in Taurus and a man with Mars in Leo. The Mars-in-Taurus woman is strong and earthy, and when she goes after what she wants, it's with an unmatched determination. Her libido is slow, sensual, and silky-smooth, and she doesn't like to be hurried (unless she has Venus in Aries). In fact, her libido is driven by a gradual buildup to good, if simple, sex. The man with Mars in Leo is blatantly fired up with passion most of the time. He's a spectacular showman but can assume that he knows it all—including how to turn a woman on. The key here is that he wants to dominate and to show he means business. Equally stubborn (they are both fixed signs), she wants sex her way, while he wants it his way. He wants to be the boss; she wants to prove she can bring him down to earth and take over the role. He'll retaliate; so will she. So when a belligerent, earthy Mars meets an inflamed, fiery Mars, the carnage can be considerable—unless they have far more harmonious contacts in their chart.

Virgo/Pisces

While Mars in Pisces takes time to get aroused and has a highly changeable sexual energy flow, Mars in Virgo wants clear-cut, defined sexual boundaries. Virgo polishes her performance and likes predictable and earthy lovemaking. Together, they may take turns being the submissive partner and will enjoy their (very!) spontaneous sex. However, Virgo may tire of the Piscean lack of motivation and his many excuses for escaping from Virgo's earthy reality check in the bedroom.

Challenging Contact: Three Signs Away

When Mars are three signs apart, there's sure to be a clash. This can lead to a highly competitive and compulsive desire to win the game of love, and it may result in verbal disputes or mental and physical provocations. If there are beneficial or harmonious contacts in the rest of the chart, then the couple might be able to live with two raging Mars—both out to get what they want in a big way—but only if they're open with one another and understand why these two energies don't get along.

MARS/SATURN CONTACTS

If it's his Mars and her Saturn, then this is where a roving hunk gets stopped in his tracks; he'll be married and tamed before he knows what hit him. Initially, this is a sexy connection, and if both partners work at achieving something other than just good lovemaking, it can bring both of them long-term success.

Apart from the possibility of harmonious contacts between the sun, moon, and Venus to Saturn, Saturn contacts can be considered only as challenging ones. Such is the nature of the planet's influence.

So what's really going on with Mars and Saturn? If Mars is about passion, ego, sexual potency, and libido, then Saturn is about withdrawal, frigidity, and fear. So when the Saturn person meets the Mars person, who uninhibitedly displays all the qualities the Saturn person restricts, Saturn is compelled to control, dominate, or at least join in somehow with this buzzing energy. To that end, the Saturn person immediately cloaks herself with the same qualities that Mars projects, and they get sexy beneath the sheets. They probably fall in physical love with one another and imagine that they'll live happily ever after. And yes, it is a powerful bond. But once Saturn has conquered Mars, she begins to grow tired of playing the role. Suddenly, Saturn doesn't want sex anymore, doesn't get turned on by the same things as Mars, and maybe even sleeps in a different bed. This is, in fact, part of Saturn's master plan since the beginning: Conquer, then retreat.

So once the Saturn-in-Virgo woman, for example, has been able to prove how sensually delightful she can be in the bedroom (and she's probably even more adept than her Mars-in-Virgo partner), she retreats or turns cold. The Mars-in-Virgo man is hurt, frustrated, and begins to generate a little emotional friction to provoke a reaction from the cool, distant woman who used to massage his back with aromatic oils and would always change the sheets on Sundays. Many couples continue in this vein, with small, nit-picky quarrels and displays of irritation—if they have more loving, constant ties in their affinity chart. Yet if they can rise to the challenge and mutually accept this difficult contact, then our chilly Saturn woman might realize that her problem is a fear of fear itself, not envy of the man she married.

MARS/MERCURY CONTACTS

When Mars confronts Mercury when it goes questing, either a strong fascination develops or a conflict of intellect versus sexual power arises. Whatever happens, this is usually a sign of an active, lively, stimulating, and very sexy relationship.

Harmonious Contacts: Same Sign or Element

The Mars person is usually drawn to Mercury's wit, humor, and conversational style. That's because Mercury's means of expression makes Mars feel empowered by his own elemental energy. Similarly, the Mercury person feels confident about what she says and finds it easy to express her sexual desires and to turn her words into actions. Intellect plus lust equals results here; plus, both partners use competition to inspire each other. Although they may disagree on many things, they energize one another, too; Mars enlivens the Mercury person's mind, and Mercury stimulates Mars's famous libido.

Challenging Contacts: Three Signs Away or Oppositions

With such different energies at work, both will unconsciously try to bring down the other by pointing out their faults or weaknesses. This is a conflict of intellectual prowess versus sexual power, and the Mars person often feels that the Mercury person is too clever or too smart for him. Accusations may fly thick and fast: "We're not on the same wavelength," insists the Mercury partner, while Mars condemns Mercury's bright ideas and her lighthearted approach to life. It is a very difficult contact when it comes to long-term commitment.

MARS/JUPITER CONTACTS

If Mars is about lust, desire, and getting some action, then Jupiter inflates these qualities to such an extreme that both people often end up burning the candle at both ends and firing each other up with endless ideas for the future. This can be a brilliant contact if both partners have a reasonable amount of Fire in their own natal charts. Both these planets rule Fire signs, so it will be harder for folks with a heavy weight of, say, Air or Water planets to deal with this volatile combination.

Harmonious Contacts: Same Sign or Element

This is an exciting, intense relationship: Both people may be especially physical or sporty, and if so, they can indulge in the good things in life together. It's often a hot, exciting relationship, too, but both partners can burn each other out if too many sparks fly. The Mars person will give Jupiter the impetus to develop her ideas and plans for the future and will boost her desire for an ideal lifestyle. If realistic goals are in focus, then there's a great opportunity here for both parties to achieve something as a pair. In the end, it's equality of mind, spirit, and lust for life that will hold these two together.

Challenging Contacts: Three Signs Away or Oppositions

Impatience and risk pervade this relationship, and each person can feel frustrated by the other's very different ideals regarding love or their individual pathways in life. This can start as a highly magnetic sexual attraction, as each tries to prove a sexual point—but it can fizzle out quickly if no other supporting contacts exist. Individuality and self-importance run high, which means this match can turn into a battle between Mars's will and Jupiter's adventurous spirit. Expect strong differences of opinion, and know that both partners will be compelled to worry about their own personal identities instead of spending that emotional energy in forging a loving bond. This one isn't easy unless there are more harmonious, gentle contacts elsewhere.

MARS AND THE OUTER PLANETS

As we've noted, Mars is a warmongering brute, and when it contacts the outer planets in your own chart, it becomes the Machiavellian sidekick that activates (and aggravates) the outer planets' collective issues. So what happens when Mars contacts someone's outer planets in the affinity chart? Well, Mars is usually all about lust and sexual chemistry, but in this case, the Mars person is provoked into defensive or aggressive behavior in order to protect itself from the unconscious collective power at work. As for the partner with the outer planet, he or she will be forced to come to terms with the workings of that planet in his or her own life.

MARS/URANUS CONTACTS

There's a magnetic attraction between these two planets. Mars is driven to prove a point while Uranus is ready to change it, reinvent it, and dazzle Mars with its shock tactics.

Harmonious Contacts: Same Sign and Element

This is by and large a favorable contact when Mars and Uranus are matched either in sign or element. Let's take a woman with Mars in Virgo and a man with Uranus in Virgo. Mars in Virgo likes to take control in the bedroom, mostly so that she can maintain her own cool. The Uranian Virgo man will begin to indulge in her classic coolness, but Uranus's nature is to upset the proverbial applecart, so he may want to change the pace (depending on his own Mars) and may even show her a new set of sexual techniques to whisk her out of her comfort zone. Sexually speaking, they're at ease with one another to begin with, but unless their affinity chart reveals more bonding contacts, things will end with a whimper, not a bang.

Challenging Contacts: Oppositions and Three Signs Away

This is an extremely volatile, unstable relationship. Both partners are on edge. There may be instant physical arousal between them, but power games may eventually cause friction in their sexual and intellectual relationship. If it's his Uranus, he may turn away when she least expects it or may disrupt her daily life with his unpredictable plans. Neither person will play fair, and although this can be extremely provocative, it's not usually beneficial for a long-term contact.

When Mars and Uranus are in opposition, this provocative, volatile energy seems to be the glue that holds the two people together. Neither of them feels they can contain their attraction for the other—but can they trust one another? Is there any love at all, or is this all just physical madness, a fated attraction that can only spiral out of control? The good news is that if both partners are prepared to take a risk and trust each other (and if they have other supportive contacts between Venus, moon, and sun), this could be a long-term bond—if a physically quirky one.

MARS/NEPTUNE CONTACTS

If Neptune takes on the guise of the planet that triggers the contact, then when Neptune comes across Mars, she'll immediately set about charming the pants off him before he's had a chance to hunt her down. If they have other grounding or supportive contacts between them, this can lead to a more successful long-term relationship. But like any other Neptune contact, if one or the other begins to sense deception, then disillusionment and betrayal can outweigh compassion. As with other Neptune contacts, there are no real harmonious contacts here: just challenging ones.

Here's an example of a same-sign Neptune and Mars. When the enchanting Neptune-in-Libra woman meets the Mars-in-Libra man, she's fascinated, gullible, and ready to fall into his arms as she gazes into his beautiful eyes. (The Neptune-in-Libra generation is one that idealizes love and romance and attempts to make the dream a reality—only to become disillusioned later on. This is a planetary archetype with high expectations when it comes to love relationships.) So this woman is jolted into her Neptune by a lusting Mars, and she finds herself playing the role of ideal lover quite well. And he, too, has been seduced, lured, and mesmerized. To begin with, this is a gift, a splendidly beautiful thing, but the archetype of Neptune dissolves desire (unconsciously) because its purpose is to dissolve everything into a fluid, numinous state. So eventually, each partner may feel that the other person is never really there, and distance may grow between them.

MARS/PLUTO CONTACTS

Again, as with all Pluto contacts, there is no such thing as a harmonious contact. So let's look at how Mars, the warrior of the zodiac, deals with the subversive power of Pluto.

This is where two different types of "fighters" take each other on. Get ready for a passionate battle of wills that's second only to the Saturn/Pluto contact on page XXX; it can create the most sexually intense, explosive, and obsessive relationship imaginable. Both partners augment each other's desire, and there's always the danger that this physical liftoff can turn from pure sexual obsession toward violence. (Not always, though: This depends very much on other factors in both natal charts and whether one person's natal chart is already angled toward violent behavior.)

Pluto's intense desire to win at all costs, combined with Mars's natural competitive spirit to *strive* to win at all costs, often makes for an immediate sexual attraction. Which means, of course, that this battle will get played out between the sheets. This is another one of those "fated" attractions that can affect the life of a third party, like a wife or husband, an existing lover, or even a close friend: After all, in his fight for survival, Pluto pits himself against everyone.

Again, both people will feel like they can't live without each other and will compete not only in the bedroom, but just about everywhere else—like in their careers or among their friends. There may be blazing rows and crazy emotional scenes, all generated by Pluto's obsessive need for control and Mars's desire to prove he's not scared of the god of the underworld. "I can deal with anything you throw at me," Mars tells Pluto. "So come on, let's fight to the death." And they often do just that. Of course, this doesn't mean death in the literal sense; it signals the transformation and rebirth of one or the other—usually the Mars person, who finds that Pluto's military tactics are far from fair. Mars is open and direct as he goes into battle. He wears magnificent armor, shows his sword, and honors his opponent. Not Pluto: He's secretive, subversive, and often dishonest.

It sounds scary—and it is. But both partners will be changed by this extreme, emotionally torrid relationship. And perhaps, with a lot of honesty and trust (and a few gentler aspects in the affinity chart), the Mars person may be able to live out his physical desires without resorting to Pluto's dark side. As for Pluto, she admires Mars's strength, and if Mars can resist being pulled down into Pluto's murky depths, they can work together to achieve a powerful, energized, sexually exciting relationship.

MARS/RISING SIGN CONTACTS

Here, the rising-sign person signals to Mars that physical attraction is everything, while the rising-sign person either sees a like-minded energy or glimpses something it aspires toward. The Mars person finds the attraction empowering and/or provocative enough to feel threatened and, therefore, to act appropriately.

Harmonious Contact: Same Sign

So when your Mars comes across its doppelgänger in the form of a man with the same rising sign, it's inevitable that you'll be physically attracted to him. You'll be able to relate easily to this physical re-creation of your own desire and libido, but whether his own Mars and Venus are compatible with yours is another matter altogether (see chapter 12).

The rising-sign person will realize that the impression he's making on the world is highly sexual and desirable. At the same time, Mars sends out signals (either unconsciously or not) to show that she feels pretty damn hot and bothered, too. Mars wants to compete with and conquer the rising-sign person and knows how to win him over since these battle tactics come naturally to her. (Things may fall apart in the wash, though, once the physical attraction has worn off—unless there are enough supporting contacts to keep the relationship together.) The bedroom is usually the battlefield since sex is the only way that Mars can win at a physical game without resorting to an actual wrestling match.

Potency and passion (in various degrees, depending on the sign) are like flashing neon signs when the rising sign is the same as his or her Mars sign—and it is these Mars-to-rising-sign contacts that often spark an instant physical infatuation between people who may already be in other relationships. This, in turn, causes love triangles and all other kinds of geometry that they don't teach in college. Here's how that might look.

A DARK PASSION

Let's take, for example, a man with Scorpio rising and a woman with Mars in Scorpio. Mars-in-Scorpio women are passionate and headstrong, but in a secretive, undermining kind of way. Mars in Scorpio seduces subtly and hypnotically. She will gaze into his eyes without revealing much about herself at all, but he'll feel like she knows everything about him, including the color of his underpants. When he goes to the men's room, she'll sneakily browse through his book or newspaper or might even take a quick glance at his cell phone to find out more about him. What's she doing? She's gathering ammunition, ready to enter into battle to seduce him into feeding her Venus (wherever that is in her chart), and this is a form of possession, power, and control. She knows that the force is with her: Nothing will stop Mars in Scorpio from getting what she wants. In fact, his very cool, distant-yet-compelling presence has stunned her; he appears to be potent, sexual, and intense, and that matches her dark passion perfectly. His private parts really are private—as are hers—and she's sure she knows exactly how to turn him on and win the game. At the other end of the Scorpio sting in the tail, the rising-sign Scorpio man immediately feels sexually attractive in her presence. The impression he's making on her makes him feel good; it's erotic and highly desirable. So together—as long as there are other good contacts between them—this can be a very high-proof physical relationship.

Harmonious Contact: Same Element

Similarly, for same-element rising sign and Mars, you can be pretty sure of positive and beneficial contacts—taking the other planets into consideration, as usual—which are particularly important for initial physical attraction. And they can add to longer-term beneficial contacts, too.

For example, Mars in the Earth signs are naturally physical and have powerful sex drives and high libidos. Their sexuality depends on slow, sensual arousal and lengthy foreplay, and visual stimulation is as important to them as tactile arousal. They select partners with discretion and need to know exactly where they stand before making a move. (However, if the Earth rising-sign object of their desire has a more powerful Mars, they may not get a chance to put their own will into action, which will frustrate them!) Now, when an Earth Mars meets an Earth rising sign, a nearly tangible physical force rises up between them. It's easy for the Mars person to seduce the rising-sign person as the two of them slowly and carefully build up a sensual, lustful desire for one another.

Challenging Contact: Three Signs Away

As always with three-signs-away aspects, the rising-sign person feels threatened by the very different energy she senses (unless she has Mars in the same sign or element as the Mars person) and will struggle to maintain her viewpoint or perspective. She may even find that the way she usually behaves suddenly seems ridiculous, weak, or inappropriate. The Mars person, for his part, is determined to "battle" with the rising-sign person, simply because her ways are so contrary to his own desires (unless Mars has the same rising sign, that is). This can cause discomfort and tension, but it can also cause a sexy encounter that can lead to resolving the conflict in the bedroom.

WILDLY CIVILIZED

Let's take an example of a Virgo-rising woman and a Mars-in-Sagittarius man. As the efficient, organized, and highly civilized Virgo woman makes polite conversation with a group of intellectuals about organic farming and South American rain forests, the Mars-in-Sagittarius man is ready to butt in and offer a few home truths (according to him) about what life is really about. Yet amazed by her grace—and conscious of her perfect makeup and smart handbag and shoes—he finds her irresistibly attractive. Still, there's something almost too clean and untainted about her. He needs to change all that; so, like any crusader, he will show her the wilder, sexier side of life and will prove to her that she has fire in her heart just like he has. Whether she runs a mile or is fascinated by his all-or-nothing *Mission Impossible* streak depends on other, more favorable contacts in their chart—but this can be a hugely compelling attraction.

Challenging Contact: Oppositions

When Mars falls in the rising-sign person's seventh house, fireworks go off. This time there is a testier challenge: a huge provocation. Can the Mars person's dynamic aura really attract the rising-sign person's eye, or will it disturb and repel her? When we meet people who live out our seventh house for us—and especially when a planet like Mars is involved—we are provoked, stimulated, or challenged, and we may attempt to stand up to the other person in order to defend ourselves and our viewpoints or opinions. But Mars wants to assert his ego and conquer what he meets, so when Mars is confronted with its opposite rising sign, it makes sense that it wants to overpower that presence. How? Through pure physical lust. Of course, a challenge can easily become a clash when Mars's will is set against the rising-sign person's desire to maintain her self-image—but here, the two partners usually end up making love, not war. That's because one or the other will instigate sex to achieve a physical release from the erotic tension; Mars is driven to play out the challenge in some sense, while the rising-sign partner is driven to impress him in response.

A good example of Mars opposing the rising sign is her Mars in Gemini opposite his Sagittarius rising. How would their first encounter unfold? His Sagittarius rising enjoys a challenge; love and sex are an adventure, an opportunity to play, to take chances, have fun, and make no promises. Mars in Gemini goes about getting what she wants by being a great conversationalist, telling all kinds of tales, and (selfishly) kidding around about all the men she's known before. She's aroused by his knight-in-shining-armor approach and his genuine lust for life, and she's determined to win him over with her witty repartee and physical allure. As for him, he feels good in her presence; his Sagittarian knight is coming alive within him, and he's quite sure that this fling is certain to amuse him for a while.

We've explored the feisty energy of courageous Mars, so let's take a look at Mars and Venus in combination. That's what chapter 12 is all about—plus, it'll introduce you to the asteroid Eros, an indicator of erotic triggers.

12 Venus, Mars, and Eros:
Sexual Attraction

Welcome to one of the most important cross-aspects in the affinity chart when it comes to sexual compatibility— the interaction between Venus and Mars. In the simplest symbolic terms, these planets represent female and male principles, respectively. Venus is about pleasure and love and the things that give us a sense of happiness—including sex. Mars is about feeding that Venusian sense of pleasure and describes the way in which we go and get what we want. And when Venus and Mars get together in the form of contacts in the affinity chart, they reveal the way you and your partner chase and seduce one another and the way you give and take pleasure—both in and out of the bedroom. In this chapter, we'll see these dynamics in action.

VENUS AND MARS IN THE AFFINITY CHART

Be aware, though, that if you have no contacts between Venus and Mars—whether his Venus to your Mars or his Mars to your Venus—it doesn't mean that you're not physically compatible. It may simply signal that you're in this relationship for other reasons (maybe even life-changing ones!) apart from the physical aspects of love alone.

Harmonious Aspect: Venus and Mars in the Same Sign

When your Venus and his Mars (or vice versa) are in the same sign, then it's the Mars partner who'll be doing the seducing. Venus will feel his presence like a hot, passionate, buzzy physical energy. She'll feel good about being herself—and in fact, she might even feel like she's being overwhelmed by desire. It's almost as if the Mars partner has cast a spell of infatuation over her. This classic sign of physical compatibility means that sparks fly, and the heat is so intense that both partners instinctively know how to please and seduce each other.

And a great example is in the affinity chart of David and Victoria Beckham, where David's Mars is conjunct Victoria's Venus (and Jupiter) in Pisces, and Victoria's Mars is conjunct David's Venus in Gemini. This means David's Mars is also three signs away from Victoria's Mars, and her Venus is three signs away from his Venus. So there's sexual tension from the challenging contacts, but there's also sexual understanding, mutual adoration, and seductive passion from the same-sign contacts. It's a powerful combination.

VICTORIA AND DAVID BECKHAM'S AFFINITY CHART

With the delightful energy between both David and Victoria's Venus and Mars, there's a real sense of mutual physical and sensual understanding. The combination in Pisces adds romance, secrecy, and sensuality to their sexual harmony, while the Venus and Mars contact in Gemini adds sparkle, humor, and variety to their sex life. However, David's Mars is also three signs away from Victoria's Mars; while her Venus is three signs away from his Venus, so there's also sexual tension from the challenging contacts. Natally, Victoria and David both have Venus square Mars, so we can see how they mirror each other too, in a way where they may have both had issues about what they really want from sex. Together, they can exchange sexual confusion for sexual understanding, mutual adoration, and seductive passion. It's a powerful combination.

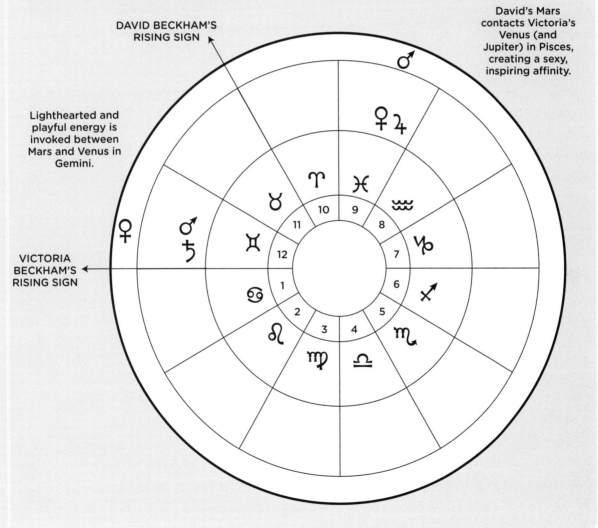

David's Mars contacts Victoria's Venus (and Jupiter) in Pisces, creating a sexy, inspiring affinity.

DAVID BECKHAM'S RISING SIGN

Lighthearted and playful energy is invoked between Mars and Venus in Gemini.

VICTORIA BECKHAM'S RISING SIGN

Harmonious Aspect: Venus and Mars in the Same Element

When they're in the same element, Venus and Mars are sexually dynamic. Mars is usually the more dominant sexual partner unless Venus is in contact with the power planet, Pluto, which puts Venus completely in control (to find out why this is, see chapter 10). Here are some examples of what happens in the early stages of a love affair when Venus and Mars are activated.

In Fire: *Dramatic Adventure*

The Venus-in-Fire person intuitively knows how to please Mars, but a competition may arise over who seduces whom (both Venus and Mars in Sagittarius just want to get on with it; Leo likes to show he can take control; and Aries just wants to be dominant). If they ever do make it to the bedroom—or, more likely, to the nearest empty parking lot—the Mars person will usually assume the dominant role (even Mars Fire women need to show they can lead the way). Both will get a tremendous libido boost from the adventurous techniques, surprising locations for sex, and their mutual love of drama and passion. This is one of those compulsive, crusading, rampant affairs that, if other contacts are beneficial, can lead to a long-term relationship.

In Air: *Game-Playing Seduction*

Mars in Air lures the Venus-in-Air partner with his seductive small talk, direct questions, and ability to stay rational in the face of passion. This is pure fascination for Gemini Venus (a devotee of clever small talk); safely abstract for Aquarius Venus; and a sign of a fun love affair for Libra Venus. Venus in Air is actually sneakily dominant; she plays games with Mars and so is often one step ahead in the game of seduction. So just when Mars in Air thinks Venus isn't interested in sex, she surprises him by being very ready for it. Together, they'll spend the night in lengthy foreplay and sexy pillow talk.

In Earth: *Sophisticated Sex*

In love with the finer things in life and delighting in the purest forms of physical indulgences, Venus in Earth is easily entranced by the classy seduction techniques of the Mars partner. Mars in Capricorn hunts for a sophisticated lover; Mars in Taurus hunts for someone who can pour champagne into the right kind of glass; and Mars in Virgo seeks someone with a straightforward yet refined attitude to love-making. Venus in Earth fits the bill perfectly. She'll usually be the submissive partner, letting Mars take control. Theirs is a sensually empowering sex life that will be hugely satisfying for both of these fans of class and sophistication.

In Water: *Hypnotic and Mystical*

Mars in Water is notoriously manipulative when on the hunt. In Cancer, Mars hovers, circles, retreats, and never dives straight into the sack; Mars in Pisces tempers his moves according to the Venus partner's mood; and Mars in Scorpio seduces by being mysterious. In fact, all Water Venus signs are alluring, hypnotic, and magical. Venus in Cancer is sensually magnetic; Venus in Scorpio is empowering; and

Pisces is enigmatic. So together, Venus and Mars can get misty-eyed, indulge in intense mergers, and whip each other into a passionate frenzy. (As long as they have supporting contacts in the affinity chart, that is.)

Double-Crossed Aspects

Remember that, as with any other contacts between two different planets in the affinity chart, we have to look at two sets of Venus and Mars inter-aspects: The placement of his Venus in relation to your Mars is just as important as the placement of your Mars in relation to his Venus.

Therefore, we need to take a closer look at the way the combination of both dynamics can make or break a sexual relationship when all four positions are taken into account. To make it easy, I'm going to describe these double cross-aspects with key words to help you understand the numerous possibilities that can arise in the affinity chart.

However, if by any chance you *both* have both Venus and Mars in the same element—in other words, if all four planets are in the same element—then this is a powerful reinforcing energy, which makes for a highly magnetic, sexually fulfilling attraction. If you have at least one Venus and Mars contact in the same element between you, the energy will still be highly arousing and exciting, but you'll need to look at what the other Venus/Mars pair are doing in the rest of the chart.

Here are some examples with a brief interpretation. This way, you'll be able to see how different Venus/Mars pairings yield either a buzz or a challenge—that is, mutual sexual desires or incompatible ones.

Same Signs: *Sexual Magicians*

His Venus is in the same sign as your Mars, and his Mars is in the same sign as your Venus. For example, his Venus and your Mars are in Cancer; your Venus and his Mars are in Scorpio. Here, there is depth of emotion, mutual pleasure, and an intuitive awareness of the other's person physical arousal. This is a sexually explosive relationship; you'll take turns when it comes to being in control, and you'll willingly lose yourselves in this all-consuming passion.

All One Element (Different Signs): *Mutual Pleasure and Physical Desire*

When all are in the same element, there's a feeling of mutual understanding about your sexual needs. For example, his Venus is in Taurus (Earth), and your Mars is in Capricorn (Earth); his Mars is in Virgo (Earth), and your Venus is in Capricorn (Earth). Here, sensual indulgences are a perfect marriage of body and mind. Both have the stamina for long nights of steamy sex and joyfully discover new techniques, positions, or fantasy roles together.

An Out-of-Element Planet: *The Pleasure's All His*

The person whose Venus or Mars is out of element will not achieve the same degree of pleasure as the other. For example, his Venus is in Aries (Fire), and your Mars is in Leo (Fire); his Mars is in Aries (Fire), and your Venus is in Virgo (Earth). Although you share electrifying arousal and are attracted to one another by your fiery libidos, after you've spent a few passionate nights together, you'll begin to feel a little left out of the fun when he doesn't seem to understand your Virgoan need for slow buildups and gentle, sensual warmth.

An Out-of-Element Planet: *The Pleasure's All Yours*

This is the same as above, just the other way around. For instance, your Venus is in Aquarius (Air), and his Venus is in Libra (Air); your Mars is in Gemini (Air), and his Mars is in Taurus (Earth). Phone sex, reading erotica, watching X-rated films—you name it: You enjoy playing games and getting aroused through erotic thoughts or imagery. But he needs lengthy sensual rather than mental stimulation and may become frustrated by your lack of focus on pure physical indulgence.

Two-Element Balance of Planets: *Shared Pleasure*

There's a balance of pleasure for both of you. For example, his Venus is in Capricorn (Earth), and your Mars is in Taurus (Earth); his Mars is in Leo (Fire), and your Venus is in Aries (Fire). Fire and Earth can work together when you both share the very different values concerned with sensuality and spontaneous sex. You'll discover that the potent initial excitement and arousal are followed by dramatic, theatrical sex and a passionate collusion of heart-throbbing libidos.

Matching-Element Opposition: *A Charismatic Challenge*

These oppositions are arousing and vibrantly challenging as each partner attempts to physically dominate the other. For example, his Venus is in Aries (Fire), and your Mars is in Libra (Air); his Mars is in Aries, and your Venus is in Libra. You are idealists, drawn to one another's beauty and sexual charisma. And it's a powerful combination: One day you're sharing fantasies between silk sheets, and the next you're enjoying fast and furious sex in the great outdoors. Erotic conversations will lead to games to see who can arouse the other first.

Random-Element Oppositions: *Power Struggles*

Singleton oppositions are harder work, and power issues can arise. For example, his Venus is in Aquarius (Air), and your Mars is in Leo (Fire); his Mars is in Cancer (Water), and your Venus is in Capricorn (Earth). There's a battle of sexy wills, but arousal and sexual stimulation may be an intellectual exercise for him. To begin with, he will let you dominate him and lead the way, but you'll quickly tire of his lack of passion. Equally, he'll find you too demanding and controlling in the bedroom.

One of Each Element, Not in Opposition: *A Fine Balance*

There's less sexual compatibility here, so you may need to work to find different ways to please each other. For example, his Venus is in Pisces (Water), and your Mars is in Gemini (Air); his Mars is in Aries (Fire), and your Venus is in Taurus (Earth). He appears strong on the surface and has a powerful sex drive, but his Venus is likely to suffer here. He will probably side with his Mars sign; Mars in Aries is in its own sign, and he'll want to show you how he can arouse you quickly, even though your libido (Mars in Gemini) is erratic. Yet if you are changeable and playful, you may discover that he has a soft, tender, and emotional investment in sex (Venus in Pisces); he may consider sex to be a profound merger of body and soul, and your sensual Venus could weave a magical spell over him.

EROS AND EROTIC TRIGGERS IN THE AFFINITY CHART

In your chart, the asteroid Eros represents your own erotic urges as well as the powerful principle of erotic connection; that is, it describes how you connect things, people, and sensations to sexuality. Indeed, when we are "in Eros," we are enraptured, obsessed, and overcome by a highly potent, even overwhelming energy. This energy is profoundly linked to our erotic impulses; it is what connects us to our sexuality and to our deeper urge for transformation through sex as a creative life force.

Eros and the Erotic Connection

Eros was originally an ancient symbol of potent life force, and in Greek mythology was the son of Aphrodite, the goddess of love. But over the years, Eros eventually became identified as the Roman god Cupid, a babyish winged youth armed with an arrow of desire (and, usually, a flaccid penis). This compromised image has defused Eros's innate power as a phallic deity: Predating Zeus, he was one of the earliest gods of Chaos before creation began. And that just goes to show that Eros is much more than his contemporary chubby-little-cherub status would suggest.

The asteroid named after Eros is surprisingly important in your chart, too. That's because Eros reveals the thoughts or fantasies that trigger your sexual responses. Plus, Eros is about wild abandon rather than just the sexual act or the pleasure derived from it, so he can act as your escort into the realms of escapist sex, can cause hunger for excessive stimulation, and can unite you with the powerful force you may also experience through a deeper tantric or spiritual-sexual experience.

The essence of Eros is to unite opposites in a whirl of potent energy. But when his dark side comes into play, we can become chained to our fantasies or become obsessively attached to a lover and lose part of ourselves in sexual overkill. If Eros is the god who "overpowers the intelligence," as the ancient Greek poet Hesiod wrote in his poem *Theogony*, then we have no choice but to let ourselves be overcome by him and to follow where he leads.

Remember that Eros is not interested in the reality of our experience, only in aligning us to the wild, ancient life force that permeates our sexuality. So in synastry, when one person's Eros contacts the personal love planets in our charts, it can awaken fantasies, draw down obsessive desires, and set off all kinds of erotic triggers we never knew we had. Let's look at the most important of these contacts: those between Eros and Ascendant, sun, Venus, and Mars.

If Eros represents what turns us on (our erotic connection), when a partner's planet contacts your Eros, you become infatuated or hypnotized; you're struck down by physical desire and are filled with ecstatic, erotic, or obsessive joy. His planet has awoken your Erotic urge and has filled you with the desire to eroticize the other person. This works both ways—Eros is a trigger—so when your Eros contacts your partner's planet, you become obsessed with him, too. It's as if the Eros partner is holding the gun and the planet partner pulls the trigger—but either way, the erotic connection is mysteriously made, and the relationship is where the bullet hits home.

But remember, the kind of person who triggers your erotic desire in this way may not necessarily align with your Venusian values or long-term relationship needs. Being irresistibly attracted to someone through Eros contacts is about a pure, primal sexual connection and has little to do with human pleasure or romantic love. This is why Eros contacts are often fatal in drawing two people together who have nothing in common in other ways. People who already have long-term partners may suddenly find themselves cheating on their partners because of a mysterious erotic connection with another person that they feel they cannot control.

As with most contacts, same-sign conjunctions and oppositions are the most potent aspect. Three signs away can indicate a powerful attraction but can also involve friction and frustration. Same-element contacts are harmonious, but the erotic connection is not as intense as same-sign or opposite contacts. As Eros is a planet of triggers, instant experience, sudden moments, and quick reactions, instead of looking in detail at the Eros combinations in each of the elements, I'm going to provide you with a quick and easy overview of the flavors or qualities of the erotic impulse. When the planet in question is in the same sign or element as Eros, you can see which triggers can transport both partners out of themselves and into the mysterious world of eroticism.

Eros in the Fire Signs

STYLE: Exaggerated eroticism; unpredictable, spontaneous lovemaking

TURNED ON BY: Domination, excitement, danger; glamour, being the center of attention; the self

FANTASIES INCLUDE: Exhibitionist sex, dangerous locations; sex with strangers, group sex; initiation and ritualistic sex

EROTIC TRIGGERS: Mind games, power games; sex with strangers; the great outdoors; dressing up or cross-dressing; mutual masturbation

EROTIC PARTNERS:
- Eros in Aries: someone with planets in Libra
- Eros in Leo: someone with planets in Aquarius
- Eros in Sagittarius: someone with planets in Gemini

Eros in the Earth Signs

STYLE: Tactile eroticism, sensual temptations, gentle bondage; silk and lingerie

TURNED ON BY: Being in control, being out of control; ritual sex; feasting, power; furs, jewels, money

FANTASIES INCLUDE: S&M, body piercing, pornography; sexual surrogacy, whips and leather; anal sex; disciplined sex

EROTIC TRIGGERS: Submission, dominating others; bisexuality; mystery, masks, stiletto heels, glamour wear

EROTIC PARTNERS:
- Eros in Taurus: someone with planets in Scorpio
- Eros in Virgo: someone with planets in Pisces
- Eros in Capricorn: someone with planets in Cancer

Eros in the Air Signs

STYLE: The erotic power of the mind, fantasizing

TURNED ON BY: Sexual thoughts, sexy phone calls; experimentation; erotic photographs or paintings; submission

FANTASIES INCLUDE: Exhibitionism; cross-dressing; voyeurism; sexual forfeits, initiation rituals; group sex, bisexuality

EROTIC TRIGGERS: Erotic literature and movies; fiery opportunists, dangerous liaisons; beautiful women and men; watching others' perversions

- Eros in Gemini: someone with planets in Sagittarius
- Eros in Libra: someone with planets in Aries
- Eros in Aquarius: someone with planets in Leo

Eros in the Water Signs

STYLE: Escapist or fantasy sex

TURNED ON BY: Taboo subjects; clandestine affairs; sex toys; stimulants or drugs; the unknown

FANTASIES INCLUDE: Exhibitionism; sex in water; S&M, body piercing; vampirism, the macabre, leather and rubber

EROTIC TRIGGERS: Powerful people, solitary people; emotional pain; spontaneous sex; voyeurism; being touched

EROTIC PARTNERS:
- Eros in Cancer: someone with planets in Capricorn
- Eros in Scorpio: someone with planets in Taurus
- Eros in Pisces: someone with planets in Virgo

Harmonious Contacts: Same Sign or Element

If you both have Eros in the same sign or element, you're able to understand each other's erotic triggers, even if you have disparate Venus and Mars. However, if you have equally harmonious contacts between Venus and Mars, you can be assured of a highly exciting and transformative sex life. The attraction factor here is more of an unconscious one, and in my experience, people with same-sign or same-element Eros (like the outer planets) are resonating to a collective unconscious energy, and they therefore understand or intuitively know this erotic archetype that they share, which acts as a deep, powerful, and sudden draw between them.

Harmonious Contact: Eros in the Seventh House

When a person has the sun, moon, Venus, or Mars in the opposite sign to your Eros, it's likely that he or she will be one of your major turn-ons. There's also a powerful erotic connection between one partner's Eros in the seventh house of the other or vice versa.

When Eros falls in the rising-sign person's seventh house, the attraction is intense, compelling, and often compulsive. This is one of those "fated"—and even "fatal"—attractions: The rising-sign person feels obsessed with the Eros partner, desperately caught up in the erotic impulse flowing from him or her. The Eros partner may not realize that she has this effect on the rising-sign person but does somehow sense that her own sexual charisma has some kind of hold over the rising-sign person, which, in turn, makes her feel erotically empowered.

The Cancer-rising man, when approached at a party by the Eros-in-Capricorn woman, feels as if he's being drawn to the steamiest love goddess he's ever met, and he's sure he's never felt this sense of sexual eroticism before. Now, if he also had Venus, Mars, or the sun in Cancer, the erotic tension would have extra force—but even as it is, the rising sign alone acts as a lighthouse that draws Eros in Capricorn toward it, all the while emanating its own sexual light. Yes, the Eros woman gets a whiff of something about this man that triggers her own sexual eroticism, and whatever other contacts are at work in their charts, it is often this primal archetype of Eros that surges forth and overpowers our intelligence (read: our minds) and prepares us to shed our sexual inhibitions. For the Eros person, this reciprocal attraction derives from the physical impression given by the rising-sign partner. For the rising-sign person, this attraction is due to the unnerving erotic charisma Eros exudes.

This unknown erotic primal force is within all of us, but it is only activated when something or someone triggers it. So when Eros contacts the Ascendant in this way, the rising-sign person is instantly attracted to the Eros person and vice versa—but neither partner is at all sure why. That's because Eros presents as an unknown force, one that it's very hard to put your finger on.

With Eros, the affinity is always about the overwhelming or overpowering contact of the two planets involved.

Challenging Contacts: Oppositions and Three Signs Away

When Eros is in opposition or three signs away from a personal planet, then there is a powerful sense of both erotic desire and sexual challenge. The very different elemental qualities are attractive, and even though Eros usually overpowers the other planet with what seems like a foreign erotic force, this kind of unconscious provocation can create tension in a long-term relationship—depending, as usual, on other factors in the chart.

EROS AND THE PLANETS

While Eros tends to "stimulate" whatever planet it contacts because of that wave of electricity or sexual energy flow between the two people involved, the erotic force bounces back with the qualities associated with that planet. So Eros and Venus, for example, generate sensually erotic messages, which turn both on.

Eros/Sun

When Eros contacts the person with the sun in the opposite sign, both people will experience their erotic natures, but it is the sun who's really turned on by the Eros person. The solar energy of the sun is so pure that the Eros impulse picks up on this affinity and stimulates Eros's sexual desires and need for intimacy. Similarly, the sun person feels animated and vibrant around the Eros partner, as Eros puts the sun in touch with unknown or taboo desires.

Eros/Moon

The Eros person is turned on by the instinctive, natural behavior of the moon person and can sense her deeper needs and feelings. Plus, Eros is drawn to her nurturing, emotional responses. This can become a profound erotic connection when the moon, too, is turned on by Eros's passion: This can awaken the moon to her own erotic desires, and Eros, in turn, feels aroused by the moon's reactions to those desires.

Eros/Venus

This pairing is highly charged, and it's an especially compelling attraction for the Eros person. She's overwhelmed by Venus's charisma and connects instantly to his sexual pleasure principle. Venus, meanwhile, is drawn to Eros's sexual intensity and erotic nature, knowing that the two of them can strike up mind-blowing passion through mutual pleasure. And Eros's sexual arousal is explosively triggered when Venus is around. This is an irresistible, intense, magnetic bond, one that often eclipses all other relationships; it can be responsible for love triangles, betrayal, or clandestine love affairs.

Eros/Mars

When Eros meets lusty Mars, there's bound to be fireworks and electricity. This is a powerful connection for sexual compatibility, and each partner will be as sexually obsessed as the other. The Eros person finds his Mars partner to be sexually dynamic (and a huge turn-on, too, of course): Mars is also aroused by this dynamic, which stimulates her own lust and desire. Here's where trouble can arise: The Mars partner may see sex as merely sex, while Eros sees it as a compelling, erotic merger of bodies and minds. And if Mars is in a long-term relationship, that attitude can wreak havoc on it.

Eros/Uranus

This connection is electric and exciting and will keep the Eros partner on his toes. The Uranus person is sexually exciting to Eros, but she's also unpredictable and, depending on her Venus and Mars, will either be totally overwhelmed by Eros or will run for the hills out of fear. (Remember, Uranus craves space, not suffocation!) But Uranus can also initiate Eros into a brave new world of erotic triggers; and, for her part, Uranus will be inspired by Eros's erotic desires. Still, she won't be truly comfortable with Eros's sexuality unless other, more supportive sexual contacts appear in the affinity chart.

Eros/Pluto

This is an obsessive, magnetic, and often explosive merger, as Eros and Pluto seek similar fulfillment when it comes to relationships: intensity, transformation, and profound sexual intimacy. If the planets are in opposition, the attraction will be steamy, power-tripping, and sexually demanding as each partner tries to overpower or sexually control the other, which means that S&M can be a main trigger for sexual arousal. The attraction is irresistible, and drama and fireworks are *de rigueur*. Plus, it's likely that any other relationship either partner has will be laid low by this explosive, powerful erotic power struggle.

Most of the time, we step down from the exciting-yet-obsessive heights of sexual and physical lust to the reality of our relationships and realize that love is about more than just sex. But at what price? How do our relationships progress once the passion wears down to a nub or when the pretty pink lingerie wears out? Do we have the same needs, goals, and aspirations? Can we truly accept the dark, shadowy, and gloomy sides of our partners until death (or another relationship) parts us? The following chapters will show you how to spot this in the affinity chart. But first, we'll look at the significance of the other three personal planets—Saturn, Mercury, and Jupiter—in the affinity chart. Let's begin with Saturn.

13 Saturn:
Binding Love

S aturn was once considered to be a negative or malefic planet in traditional astrology, but nowadays—in psychological astrology circles, at any rate—he's thought to represent the qualities in ourselves that we find most awkward or fearsome. But what's surprising is that, as we'll see in this chapter, Saturn's influence in the affinity chart can lead to a binding, long-term relationship.

In astrology, Saturn represents our Achilles' heel, or the part of ourselves we might call our shadow. This is the weakest link in our psychological armor, and it's where we are most vulnerable. This vulnerability stems from the areas in which we feel inadequate or clumsy and is revealed around the qualities represented by Saturn's sign. Of course, we do our best to cover up this sense of lack. This "clumsy self" is usually relegated to the unconscious or is denied, repressed, and well hidden—not only from others but also from ourselves. We play tricks with ourselves in an attempt to avoid this awkward side; in fact, many of us are clever at masking this weak link by acting out the very quality that we deplore. Here's how: If Saturn in our natal charts is where we feel most inadequate and represents what we don't particularly want to show to the world (let alone to ourselves), then when someone comes along with a planet that hits your Saturn, it triggers your fear that your weakness will be revealed or unmasked. So Saturn immediately defends itself by dominating or controlling the other person, often by assuming the very qualities the other person's planet represents. That way, Saturn gets to score points over the other person and win the game—all the while continuing to cover up that scary sense of weakness or inadequacy.

This sophisticated disguise may start out as a clever cover-up, but it can also, paradoxically, lead us to master the very thing we fear. For example, we may fear committing to marriage or the "perfect relationship" (Saturn in Libra) because we feel so darned lacking, clumsy, or awkward in that sphere of our lives. So we learn to assume the role of the Perfect Partner in order to cover up our awkwardness. And eventually we become quite adept at that role and make it our own—even if, on some level, a committed relationship still makes us feel shaky or insecure. Of course, this sense of authority and mastery doesn't arrive overnight but comes after many years of painful experiences (it often begins to be felt around the first Saturn return at the age of approximately thirty), and it requires the effort of a lifetime. So Saturn is about the qualities that we feel we lack in order to make something "real" of ourselves, so to speak, and often rides in tandem with our evolving sun's urge to unfold itself and with the M.C.'s drive for recognition.

SATURN: THE MYTH

In order to better understand Saturn's vulnerability, let's look at the myth of Cronus (or Saturn, his Latin name) and Ouranos, the god of the heavens. Ouranos was not pleased with the hundreds of ugly giants he had for offspring, so he hid them deep within Gaia, the earth. This angered Gaia, who asked for help from her son, Cronus. Cronus agreed to castrate Ouranos on her behalf so she could be in peace at last. After he'd castrated Ouranos with a sickle, Cronus became ruler of the Titans, the first gods born to Gaia, but was warned that he would be overthrown by one of his own children. So every time his consort, Rhea, gave birth, he swallowed the child whole. When Cronus's son, Zeus, was born, Rhea secretly gave the child to Gaia. She wrapped a stone in swaddling clothes, which Cronus swallowed, believing it to be Zeus. Eventually Cronus was overthrown by Zeus as predicted.

So our oh-so-friendly Saturn not only castrates his father, but, in fear of losing his power, also devours all his children. This myth can help us understand how Saturn operates in the affinity chart. If our weakest link feels threatened, we defend ourselves, either by "castrating" the very thing that we fear in the other person (usually by slowly undermining him or her through coldness, distance, blame, and so on) or by filling ourselves up with it—swallowing it whole or engorging it, as Cronus tried to swallow Zeus, until we're expressing the quality of the other person's planet and sign even more thoroughly than he or she is.

If we feel we have been denied something, then when we meet someone who seems to have what we don't have, we crave it. It makes sense, right? So the four most important key words for Saturn in the affinity chart are *mastery*, *craving*, *fear*, and *control*.

SATURN IN RELATIONSHIP

Saturn appears to be one of the most subtle-yet-frustrating, binding-yet-tormenting, enduring-yet-exhausting energies in the affinity chart. Often it doesn't raise any issues until you've gotten to know your partner very well—that is, when you've moved beyond the first stages of dating or new love. That's because Saturn is concerned not only with your own personal growth through the relationship, but your acceptance (or not) of your partner's personal growth, too.

As a master of disguise, Saturn is actually more wily than you might think. He can, more or less, cloak himself with the qualities of any sign or planet that feels like a threat to him—without, of course, realizing that this is the very quality he must master within himself. If the Saturn person is honest enough to support her partner's planet and can admire and help shape those qualities instead of resenting them, then she may be able to draw her hidden inadequacies out into the light of day and to work with them to accept and even cherish them.

For instance, the chart for Jennifer Aniston and Justin Theroux reveals a powerful contact between Jennifer's seventh-house Saturn and Justin's moon in Aries, not to mention Jennifer's moon in Sagittarius opposing Justin's Saturn in Gemini. There's a mutual sense of vulnerability, yet there's a powerful and binding draw or connection between the two.

What we've seen so far in this book is that what we love about others is usually what we need to love or recognize within ourselves; but now we can also see that what we fear or resent about others is usually the same thing that's lying at the bottom of our psychological basements. It's a lurking shadow within us, too. Saturn may loathe someone because he or she has pushed the "fear" button—but more often than not, Saturn overcompensates for that fear and is driven to conquer the other person, usually "in the name of love." When someone steps on your shadow in this way, you sense it through your Saturn, and nothing can stop you from "castrating" or "engorging" the other's person's power in some way; after all, it's threatening that vulnerable Achilles' heel.

Saturn contacts are often thought to be fated or karmic in some way. And yes, the two people involved do experience a compelling energy, especially when they first meet. This is a trigger that can draw two people together in more than just a passionate embrace, and there's usually something deeply binding here. Saturn has a tendency to bind yet torment, to enrapture but confine, and this often leads to a long-term internal tension within the couple. But with honesty and effort, the Saturn person can become true to his own self-mastery, and the other person can become more aware of the gifts of her planetary quality, too.

Although Jennifer finds love risky, Justin's moon in Aries "gets" who she is and understands her vulnerable side. Jennifer's Saturn is in her seventh house, so she fears getting too close to someone and then being abandoned. (Saturn says, "it's easier to put up the barriers and pretend there's no one home"). Then along comes Justin (his Saturn in Gemini), who knows how hard it is to laugh, play, and act a part, and he sees Jennifer (moon in fun-loving Sagittarius) playing the role of comedian "naturally." Her moon provokes his Saturn to see that life isn't about being serious all the time, and his moon feeds her Saturn with "it's OK to be independent, but also to love someone too." If each can learn to accept that their greatest fear or inadequacy is standing before them, and that they have a chance to master that fear, then they could become the perfect couple that maybe deep down inside both long to be together.

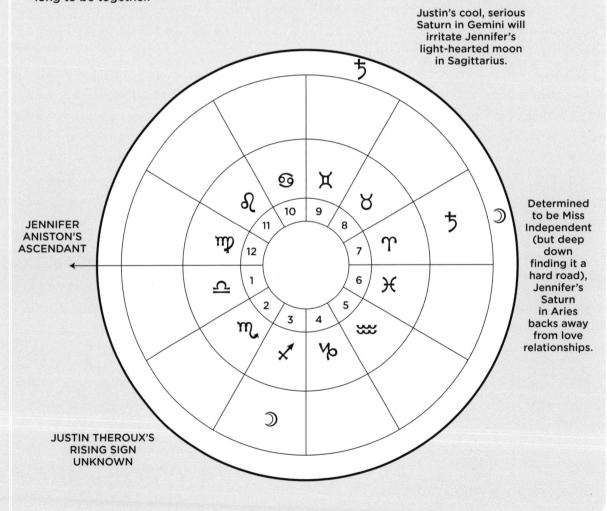

Justin's cool, serious Saturn in Gemini will irritate Jennifer's light-hearted moon in Sagittarius.

JENNIFER ANISTON'S ASCENDANT

Determined to be Miss Independent (but deep down finding it a hard road), Jennifer's Saturn in Aries backs away from love relationships.

JUSTIN THEROUX'S RISING SIGN UNKNOWN

I believe that all Saturn contacts—whether conjunctions, oppositions, trines, or squares—have the same effect and can lead to the same outcome. If the two people involved are aware of how Saturn is working within their relationship, then it can be a positive journey for both of them. So although I have included harmonious contacts for the sun and Venus in this chapter, the power of Saturn is always challenging (just like Pluto) and should never be taken lightly.

We've already seen how Saturn operates with the sun, moon, Venus, and Mars, so let's take a look at how he operates when threatened by the other planets. As all contacts between Saturn and the remaining planets are challenging, we'll find out what it is that challenges Saturn and how Saturn uses its defenses—like castration, inertia, or disguise—to control the other person.

SATURN/MERCURY CONTACTS

If Saturn is the planet of restriction, then when it contacts Mercury, the Saturn person will find himself restricted and/or restricting the other person in all forms of verbal expression. This can manifest as a teacher/pupil relationship, in which Mercury will feel he constantly has to provide the "right" answers. The Saturn person will find it hard to communicate the truth but will play the part of Mercury as a great trader of ideas quite well.

For example, let's say that his Saturn is in Aries, and her Mercury is in Aries. She talks nonstop; she's quite ferocious in the way she asks questions; and she wants quick answers, is impatient, and get into disputes quickly. Equally, she holds few grudges and, once the fiery outcry is over, is back to normal, ready for the next challenge. At the outset, he'll be just as argumentative: quick to take offense, quick to say his piece, and ready to win the war of words. (He's a master of disguise, remember?) But he'll soon grow tired of the battle and, feeling deeply inadequate around issues of communication, will turn the tables and attempt to limit her verbal expression by either ignoring or constantly criticizing her. This can be a strong tie between two minds but is rarely a bonding contact. The Mercury person may feel all her mental energy—and her natural style of communication—is being suffocated and may resort to finding another partner who's more willing to listen.

SATURN/JUPITER CONTACTS

We now move from the realms of the personal planets (we've already seen Saturn in action in earlier chapters with the sun, moon, Venus, and Mars) to Jupiter, who, like Saturn, sits on the boundary between the conscious and unconscious worlds. Jupiter is about excess, risk-taking, and confidence-building: Saturn fears risk, is overcautious, and is often pessimistic about life rather than filled with optimism for it (Jupiter). Yet Saturn can build, structure, and create boundaries for a relationship. So when these two energies come face-to-face, their apparently opposing, and therefore incompatible, qualities are actually far more promising than they seem at first sight.

When a woman with Jupiter, say, in Cancer, and a man with Saturn in Cancer meet, the Jupiter woman's kind, caring, compassionate nature may well have a beneficial influence on the Saturn man. This isn't a very romantic contact, nor is it anything particularly physical, but it can be enlightening and illuminating in a more material sense. But both people involved must have the guts to be honest about what they believe in (Jupiter) and what they really fear (Saturn).

The Saturn-in-Cancer man may well find himself awakened to the fact that feelings aren't actually such a bad thing if you try to understand them, while the Jupiter-in-Cancer woman may begin to realize that she could do something practical with her belief in caring for the world and using her intuition if she shapes those talents according to the structure that Saturn provides. This contact works best in same signs or same elements. While in opposite signs or three signs apart, Jupiter's ideals don't always gel easily with Saturn's conventions.

SATURN/SATURN CONTACTS

When Saturn is in the same sign in the affinity chart, then either the couple are approximately the same age or there's an age gap of about twenty-eight years between them. Now, if they're in the same sign, you'd think they'd get along well because they'd share an unconscious understanding that they have mutual vulnerabilities, fears, and inhibitions. Well, there's an unsaid acceptance to begin with, but on the whole, when Saturn's in the same sign, it tends to bring out both partners' insecurities in a subtly controlling way. After all, no one wants to see her own inadequacies reflected in another person.

So resentment builds up. Important things are left unsaid (unless there are plenty of other contacts to compensate for this). Each partner is afraid to come clean or make the first move; each is afraid to own up to their Achilles' heels, each resents the other person, and so often they both lie or deceive or feel misunderstood and unloved. This is a very difficult contact unless both people make a conscious effort to heal their mutual wounds. If the couple's Saturns are in opposition or three signs away, their defenses will be very different from one another, and although there will be the usual Saturn "issues," they may be able to work through their differences if they can accept one another's fears and vulnerability. Again, if other, more harmonious contacts in the affinity chart are present, they can help to balance out the defensiveness of one partner or the other.

SATURN/URANUS CONTACTS

If Uranus is about disrupting the status quo, then Saturn is about maintaining it; if Uranus is about invoking or bringing about change, then Saturn is about resisting it. These two very different qualities can cause even the most compatible chart to have contradictory energies that affect both individuals in very defensive ways.

Initially, the Saturn person will demonstrate respect for the Uranian person's mind. Maybe he'll listen intently to Uranus's radical ideas and, on some level, may be willing to accept that he wants this relationship to change for the better. In fact, when the Uranian archetype of the rebel is triggered, it feels hugely life-changing to the Uranus partner—and it can feel dazzling to the Saturn person, too, so playing the role is worth it for him. But unless they can both put that possibility of change into practice without feeling threatened by it, harmony won't come easily here, even if Saturn is in a supportive aspect to Uranus.

BEAR WITH ME

For example, say a Uranus-in-Sagittarius man inherits $10,000 (lucky guy!) and decides to use it to spend the winter filming polar bears in the Arctic Circle. His Saturn-in-Virgo lover enthusiastically joins him in celebrating his idea (Saturn here plays the Uranian role to a T), but a few weeks later, she suggests he might be wasting his money: Wouldn't it be better spent on something more "useful"? Our Saturn-in-Virgo lady begins to get defensive because his Arctic trip is a mighty threat to her need to be in control of him. But if the Saturn woman faces her fear and consciously avoids stifling her Uranian partner's vision, then perhaps she too can share in it. And as for Uranus, maybe he needs to reflect on whether his partner might have a point: Is it really a good idea to blow all that money in one go?

SATURN/NEPTUNE CONTACTS

Neptune, as we'll see in the following chapter, is also a transpersonal planet like Uranus, and as such it has no boundaries. Where Neptune is in our own natal charts is where we are caught up in the collective longings of our generation. Neptune is compassionate, but it does not discriminate in its compassion; it is elusive, numinous, and nonexclusive. Someone who is really "in" his or her Neptune has few boundaries and therefore has no real sense of identity. Yes, the Neptune person can say, "I love you and accept all your vulnerabilities," but she can also say, "I love the whole world too; you're not the only one in it."

And that's a problem since the walled-up Saturn person demands exclusive love for "me and me alone." So when Saturn comes across the boundlessness of Neptune, Saturn unconsciously goes on the defensive, sensing some kind of dissolution, loss, or even betrayal (for if Neptune can love all the world, how can she have an exclusive relationship?).

Remember that Saturn takes on the disguise of the other planet in order to conquer it when it's triggered by the other person's planet. In this case, the Saturn person is capable of being just as deceptive

and elusive as the Neptune person. But because it is almost impossible for either partner to truly understand what it means to be "in Neptune" or "in Saturn," this dynamic can also get played out in betrayal,
martyrdom, or sacrifice.

LOST IN ILLUSIONS

Here's an example of this deeply chaotic yet compelling relationship. He has Neptune in
Sagittarius; she has Saturn in Sagittarius. To begin with, she'll play the Sagittarian game
of promising much and delivering reluctantly; she'll show him how independent she is and
how she doesn't like (or need) commitment. She is being seduced by the lure of Neptune,
who, as a planetary archetype or god, pulls his prey into the deep waters of desire like a
siren who draws sailors to their watery deaths. Neptune is surprisingly powerful: After all,
this ocean god caused tidal waves and storms as he stirred the churning waters with his
trident and was just as promiscuous as his brother, Zeus. Yet as our Saturn lady plays the
game, the man with Neptune in Sagittarius finds himself overwhelmed by the Neptunian
side of himself, which may not have found expression before. But now he is "in" his
Neptune: He longs to enrapture Saturn and to take her out of herself—yet this is both of
their undoing. Neptune casts a net of illusions around love to such an extent that both
are lost in the very relationship they are trying to find.

Like any other contacts in the affinity chart, it's important to see where more conscious harmonies
occur before judging this contact, but still, it's a tough aspect to deal with. Saturn will always realize
that he can't have exclusive rights to Neptune's oceanic, all-encompassing longings, while Neptune will
be tantalized by, yet wary of, Saturn's equally deceptive game-playing. This is nothing less than double
deception and a contest to see who's better at the game.

SATURN/PLUTO CONTACTS

To put it simply: When these two control freaks meet, a power struggle inevitably ensues.

Let me explain. Saturn is all about controlling the environment to protect himself from outside threats.
Meanwhile, Pluto, the god of the underworld, controls his inner world; he knows he is eternal, possesses
ultimate power, and seeks to regenerate himself through cycles of beginnings and endings. When Pluto is
activated by another person's planetary contact, he walks invisibly within the relationship. An archetype

of ultimate power arising from the collective unconscious, the Pluto person mysteriously (and unknowingly) provokes a power struggle—and it can certainly become a theatrical and passionate one.

If both partners are totally unaware of the problems that can arise from this contact—such as anger, jealousy, resentment, and even physical violence, depending on other factors in the affinity chart—the Saturn person will intuit that this is a fight for survival. Saturn, when threatened by such a destructive archetypal quality, is both fascinated and fearful, craving the greater power of Pluto but simultaneously resisting it by erecting psychological barriers and boundaries left, right, and center. The Pluto partner will experience a sense of confrontation at a very deep level and will rise to the bait in the most subtle—and often subversive—ways and will eventually take control of the relationship. Why? Because Pluto always wins.

SATURN/RISING SIGN CONTACTS

If Saturn points to where we feel most inadequate, and the rising sign is where we light up the world like a beacon, it's hardly surprising that when the Saturn person meets the rising-sign person, she comes face-to-face with the very qualities she appears to lack (and, therefore, crave). Here's a perfect model of what I haven't got, thinks Saturn. Unconsciously fearing she can never be good enough when she's in the rising-sign person's presence, she may either run and hide—or take control. The rising-sign man will be attracted to Saturn if she does take control: Saturn, as a mistress of disguise, will replicate his beacon of light, and the rising-sign man feels comfortable and welcome in her presence as a result.

For example, let's take a woman with Saturn in Taurus and a man with Taurus rising. He's physically aware of his body; he has a keen eye for beauty, likes to show he's got good taste, and has a materialistic approach to life. The Saturn-in-Taurus woman is likely to be fearful of her own lack of taste, lack of money, apparent lack of sensuality, and so on—but she may have already begun to (unconsciously) master the art of doing exactly what she believes she lacks. So when this man pushes her psychological buttons, she rises to the occasion, spurred on by craving and fear, intent on becoming more sensual than any other woman, more beautiful than he could ever imagine, and possessed of a compulsion to conquer him. He, meanwhile, is probably totally unaware of her hidden despair but likes the fact that she's so Taurus—in fact, even more Taurus than he's aspiring to be. Whether or not this will be a long-term relationship depends on what's going on in the rest of the rising-sign person's chart and whether there are other supportive contacts in the affinity chart.

Now let's move on to one of the most important components of any relationship: communication. That's where Mercury comes in. Contacts to Mercury in the affinity chart indicate whether two people are on the same proverbial wavelength, and chapter 14 will show you how to spot them.

14 Mercury:
Meeting of Minds

n the natal chart, Mercury is about the way we use our minds, and in this chapter, we'll see what happens when two minds meet within the affinity chart, whether in dispute or agreement. What's more, since Mercury represents the way in which we trade ideas, it also describes our negotiation tactics—an important aspect of any relationship.

The placement of Mercury in your natal chart describes the way you interact with others—how you listen, comprehend, learn, and give and receive information. But there's a subtler side to Mercury, too. When we're "in Mercury," we offer our opinions freely; we can be eloquent—or not—depending on aspects in our own natal charts, and we can reveal our wisdom, genius, wit, and imagination to the world. And if we agree that action follows thought, it makes sense that our thoughts about another person color our perceptions of her or him before we've even really had a chance to connect. In this way, then, Mercury is an important part of establishing and living out a relationship—after all, Mercury is all about how you communicate your desires. If, for instance, you had Mercury in Virgo, you would communicate with wit and style; you'd long to know the truth about everything; and you'd want a smart, articulate partner who could offer significant observations and cultivated ideas rather than basic chitchat.

MERCURY: THE MYTH

Here's Mercury's backstory. In Greek mythology, Hermes (the Greek name for Mercury) was a smart, precocious child right from the start. When he wasn't even a day old, he'd already made himself a lyre (a stringed instrument) and had taught himself to play music on it. Then, when he stole his half-brother Apollo's herd of cows, he disguised his tracks by driving the cows backward and crossing sand-covered land so that no footprints would be left behind. When their father, the great god Zeus, intervened, Hermes agreed to trade his golden lyre for Apollo's cattle, which is how Apollo became the god of music. As for Hermes himself, he became known as the god of prophecy, theft, and trading and was also the messenger of the gods. In this capacity, not only did he act as a go-between in the dramas that took place among the gods themselves, he also acted as a guide for lost (human) travelers. Finally, as a psychopomp, he was responsible for escorting the souls of the deceased to the underworld.

MERCURY IN RELATIONSHIP

Mercury is a messenger in astrology, too, and is highly useful when it comes to understanding the development of a couple's day-to-day communication. The most important contacts are to the other person's own Mercury, or his or her sun or moon, and they're the first things to look for. Mercury-to-rising-sign harmonies promote beneficial communication at the outset of a relationship, while Mercury-to-rising-sign clashes can signal mutual disagreement or endless disputes. However, Mercury contacts can also help us to understand our own thought and communication patterns and can help us figure out whether our opinions are truly our own or not. (This is especially true when your Mercury is in contact to another person's outer planets—Uranus, Neptune, and Pluto.)

Take, for instance, the affinity chart of Tom Cruise and Katie Holmes, which reveals a Mercury/Mercury opposition creating lively but spicy debates and contradictory thinking.

MERCURY/MERCURY CONTACTS

Mercury-to-Mercury contacts (as well as Mercury-to-sun contacts; see chapter 7) are the most important contacts in the chart when it comes to how well—or how poorly—communication flows within a romantic relationship.

Harmonious Contacts: Same Sign and Element

When two Mercuries are in the same sign or element, both partners will be able to communicate with ease: They'll be able to say what's on their minds without upsetting one another. Let's take a couple with their Mercuries in Gemini, for instance. They flit around their social scene together like a couple of kids, having fun and making jokes, and not really taking life seriously at all. Their conversations are light-hearted but analytical and logical, and when it comes to curiosity, they leave no stone unturned. Their

The energetic exchange of information between two mutable signs (in this case, opposites between Gemini and Sagittarius) can create lively disputes, all-night debates, changing plans, and provocative rows. Mercury (which rules Gemini and Virgo) is sly, wily, and tricky and often plays games just for the sake of playing—not for winning. Tom's Mercury in Gemini is certainly carefree, but when riled by the wider perspective of Katie's Mercury and sun in Sagittarius, he simply gets competitive and plays the game to win. However, Gemini is a known "trader" of ideas while Sagittarius likes to put their foot down and say, "this is how it is and that's that," so it's likely that Katie's audacious and sometimes tactless thinking can provoke the less fun side of Tom's Mercury, which reacts with flippancy and sarcasm. Similarly, batting the proverbial ball back into Tom's court, she will be irritated by his impertinence and presumptions. This exchange is stimulating and challenging enough to keep them both on their toes.

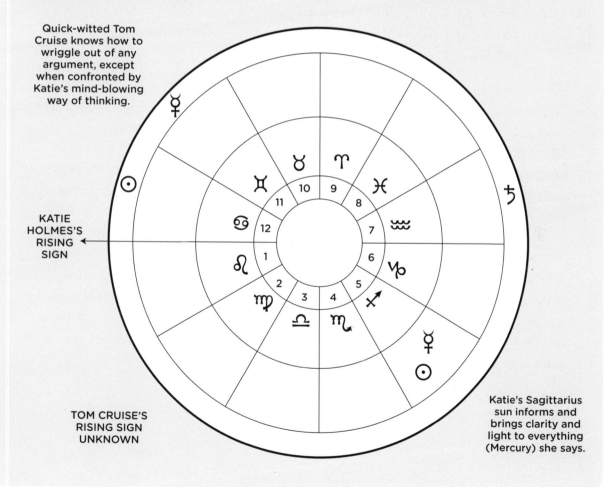

Quick-witted Tom Cruise knows how to wriggle out of any argument, except when confronted by Katie's mind-blowing way of thinking.

KATIE HOLMES'S RISING SIGN

TOM CRUISE'S RISING SIGN UNKNOWN

Katie's Sagittarius sun informs and brings clarity and light to everything (Mercury) she says.

powers of reason and logic are in sync, and each has a spontaneous, fluid understanding of what the other means—even if one partner is talking a mile a minute or explaining something very complex. This rapport really helps facilitate smooth communication in all long-term relationships.

Challenging Contacts: Oppositions and Three Signs Away

It's true that communicative and intellectual differences can add spice to some relationships—but the problems that can arise here are not for the fainthearted. Let me explain.

Fire sign Mercury is the only one who can stand the heat from the disputes that may arise between an earthy Mercury (Taurus), who takes forever to reach a conclusion, and an impatient-for-answers Mercury (Leo, Aries, Sagittarius). Although they're three signs away, Gemini and Virgo are pretty cool about keeping debates rational and sane because they are both Mercury-ruled. In this case, there's a balance between the glibness of Gemini and the seriousness of Virgo; in fact, the partners often trade these qualities back and forth between one another just because they're equally fascinated by contradictory thinking. However, both may have trouble with the slipperiness of Mercury in Pisces and the preachy attitude of Mercury in Sagittarius.

When two Mercuries are in opposition, both are thinking or conceptualizing in totally different ways. And that means a great deal of misunderstanding and misinterpretation.

CUTS LIKE A KNIFE

Let's say we have a man with Mercury in Aries and a woman with Mercury in Libra. The Mercury-in-Aries man is tactless and can even come across as hostile. He says the most cutting, unkind things without thinking (in fact, he often doesn't even realize he's said them); then, ten minutes later, he wonders what all the fuss is about, anyway. By which time the Mercury-in-Libra woman has, of course, taken it all in, digested it, recalled every line, and has become convinced that Mercury in Aries is a brutish thug. She will mentally prepare herself for revenge—or, at the very least, will strive to restore her intellectual dignity. Then again, maybe she'll be able to teach him how to communicate in a less brash and impatient way? Perhaps. She'll be willing to compromise, but her peace-loving ideas and gentle words may be like the proverbial water off a duck's back to the Mercury-in-Aries man.

MERCURY/JUPITER CONTACTS

Great minds think alike, as the saying goes, and when Mercury and Jupiter meet in the same sign or element, it's especially true. Look at the analytical Mercury partner, understanding exactly what the Jupiter person is *really* saying! Mercury's ability to communicate seems to be increased tenfold by the presence of Jupiter, whose beliefs, ideals, and bountiful desires fuse nicely with the Mercury person's mind-set. When differences of opinion arise in oppositions and three signs away, acceptance and honesty can help to generate mutual progress and to manifest communal dreams.

Harmonious Contacts: Same Sign and Element

Here, both people are able to share all kinds of ideas about future progress and personal dreams. This isn't a particularly bonding contact, but the good conversation it promotes sure does lighten up the relationship. The Jupiter person will find it easy to persuade the Mercury partner to follow her lead, while the Mercury partner will enjoy playing a few mind games. They'll share an outrageous sense of humor, and together, they'll generate an enthusiastic, spirited approach to love and life.

Challenging Contacts: Oppositions and Three Signs Away

What the Jupiter person considers meaningful will seem of little significance to the Mercury person, so arguments can arise when Jupiter feels put down. The Jupiter partner may come across as self-righteous or a know-it-all, and then the Mercury person feels insecure about his own lighthearted approach to the same subject. Views will certainly clash, and although this can yield some stimulating, spicy altercations, it doesn't help cement a long-term commitment. For example, when Jupiter in Aries lays down the law about how important personal achievement is, Mercury in Cancer won't find it easy to express his thoughts about how family and a sense of belonging are important, too.

MERCURY/URANUS CONTACTS

Here, the day-to-day communication of Mercury meets the higher mind of Uranus. That doesn't mean that the Uranus person has greater knowledge or that she's is in touch with the gods: It's just that when these two planets meet, the Mercury person is awakened to his own Mercury and is aware of how easy (or not) it is to interact with the other person, while the Uranus person has to rationalize her own ideals and come to terms with her unconscious dreams of reform and rebellion.

Harmonious Contacts: Same Sign or Element

When Mercury and Uranus are in either the same sign or the same element, it's far easier for both partners to wake up to what they need to know. The Mercury person will listen avidly to the Uranian person's vision for a perfect future, and he'll click into her desire to change her life or change the world. Meanwhile, the Uranus person will take Mercury's easy chitchat as a welcoming, positive sign that the two of them can communicate on an intellectual level. This is a useful contact for long-term relationships.

Challenging Contacts: Oppositions and Three Signs Away

When Mercury is three signs away or in opposition to Uranus, clashes are inevitable, and the bad times might outweigh the good—unless the Mercury person happens to have the same Uranus sign. However, if other contacts are positive, this can lend a necessary heat to the relationship and can bring both people to a deeper understanding of their life's focus; the Mercury person may realize that what he says, hears, and thinks isn't necessarily the only way to act, while the Uranus person finally concludes that she can't change the world until she changes herself.

MERCURY/NEPTUNE CONTACTS

Here, intellectual and rational Mercury meets Neptune's dreams and illusions. With harmonious contacts, there's a chance that each will find delight in the other's lighthearted side—but with challenging contacts, Mercury may find himself deceived by his own thoughts.

Harmonious Contacts: Same Sign or Element

Of course, the Mercury partner will be fascinated by the romantic side of the Neptune person and by her imagination and dreams; Mercury may even be surprised to discover that he seems to have the same spiritual longings as Neptune (especially if he has Neptune in a different sign). For example, Mercury in the Fire signs will sense Neptune in Fire's visionary side; spontaneous, intuitive, and inquisitive, Mercury will be able to offer strength of self-conviction and belief in action to Neptune, bringing her back to earth from cloud nine.

Challenging Contacts: Oppositions and Three Signs Away

As with all difficult Mercury contacts, dreams (Neptune) will clash with rational thinking (Mercury), and it's likely that the Mercury person will quickly tire of being led astray by Neptune's romantic notions. Unless other bonding or powerful contacts are in the affinity chart, this contact doesn't encourage the pair to form a lifetime bond. The Mercury partner will always be running in circles around the Neptunian fog of self-deception and illusion and will start to get sick of it, too, unless the Neptune person's Mercury is in a beneficial contact in the chart.

MERCURY/PLUTO CONTACTS

We've already seen how Pluto destroys the personal planet it contacts—without consciously raising a finger or a voice. So when Mercury meets Pluto in the affinity chart, unless there are very beneficial contacts elsewhere between sun and moon, Venus and Mars, and so on, then the Pluto person will have total control over the Mercury person's mind. Because there is no such thing as a harmonious contact when Pluto is involved—even in the same sign or element—Mercury will sense that he's under threat from Pluto and that whatever he does or says is "wrong." The result is that Mercury will only say things he thinks Pluto might want to hear. The Pluto person, of course, is blithely unaware that this unconscious archetype is working its stealthy way into the relationship, but will find herself in a position of dialectic power eventually nonetheless.

MERCURY/RISING SIGN CONTACTS

On a less insidious note, Mercury-to-rising-sign contacts are generally one of two things: They're either hugely favorable when it comes to early romance and dating or they invoke instant contradiction and differences of opinion.

Harmonious Contacts: Same Sign or Element

Mercury and the rising sign find that they can view the world from the same perspective, simply because Mercury can rationalize the impression given by the rising-sign person, and, in turn, the rising-sign person feels good about himself since his opinions are being confirmed. Of course, you'll need to look at both Mercuries and both rising signs to establish other supporting contacts, but at least both partners are off to a good, romantic start, thanks to easy conversation and a stimulating exchange of ideas.

Challenging Contacts: Oppositions and Three Signs Away

As with all rising-sign oppositions and three signs away, two very different outlooks are at work here. Looking across to her seventh house, the rising-sign partner sees a person whose approach seems to be at cross-purposes with her own, and she finds this threatening (unless she happens to have Mercury in her own seventh house, creating a positive Mercury/Mercury contact!). This means that the rising-sign person will quickly close all windows of opportunity; that way, Mercury's chitchat can't get to her. Meanwhile, the Mercury partner won't be able to read between the lines when faced with the rising-sign person and may move rapidly into a more welcoming pair of arms.

Let's turn now from Mercury to Jupiter, the planet that represents our most profound values and ideals.

15 Jupiter:
Great Expectations

oving on from Mercury's mind games, we'll now explore a deeper level of connection or understanding that can exist between two people. This connection, represented by Jupiter, is about whether we can share and accept one another's personal beliefs, values, and romantic ideals.

Jupiter is about exaggerated, fiery energy and like Mars—as we've seen when it's contacted by Venus—is often an indicator of powerful attraction. But it's not quite that straightforward: Jupiter (again, like Mars) has the power to stir up the stormiest love affairs imaginable.

Jupiter is the planet of inflation and expansion, wisdom, purpose, and, most of all, meaning in life and love. Jupiter describes both good and bad luck, opportunity, and our sense of greed, desire, and wealth (whether we have it or not). But it also tells us how we travel in order to arrive at our destinations, and that includes the kind of journey on which we embark in hopes of finding true love, or the ideal of love we all search for. Take care, though: Jupiter can exaggerate the expression of the planets it contacts—either for better or for worse.

JUPITER: THE MYTH

In Greek mythology, Zeus (or Jupiter, in Latin) was the god of the heavens. He was highly promiscuous and totally irresponsible. He hurled thunderbolts and lightning from his seat on top of Mount Olympus and seemed to be engaged in his own private mission to seduce every goddess, nymph, or mortal woman he could find. Fathering hundreds of half-mortals and divine offspring, Zeus is renowned throughout Greek mythology for his seductive skills. In one story, Semele, a priestess of Zeus, fell in love with him. Riddled with jealousy, Zeus's consort, Hera, disguised herself as an old hag and persuaded Semele that the only way the nymph could be sure her beloved was the great god himself was to ask him to reveal himself in all his divine glory. (He usually disguised himself as a mortal when visiting earth.) Zeus agreed reluctantly, and when he visited her the following night, his lightning bolts incinerated her into a ball of flames as they made love. Semele was pregnant with Dionysus—the god of wine, wild abandon, and religious ecstasy—at the time, so Zeus rescued the child and sewed him into his thigh. (Later, Semele was rescued from the depths of Hades by Dionysus.) This story is a great analogy for the exaggerated effect of Jupiter in the affinity chart, which sometimes makes us feel as if we are being burned alive by the Jupiter person's potent influence or as if we're passion personified—just like Jupiter himself.

WORKING WITH JUPITER IN THE AFFINITY CHART

In the affinity chart, Jupiter describes our ideals when it comes to love, but it also tells us how conditional or unconditional we are toward love and sex. Jupiter to rising sign or Venus contacts (unless other subduing or highly negative contacts are present in the affinity chart) are about the flourishing, blossoming romance of the relationship and the sense of liberty it seems to bestow on both partners. "It's great to be so carefree and in love," these contacts seem to say. "Who cares about the rest of the world?"

When we see harmonious Jupiter contacts to the other person's dynamic planets (the rising sign, sun, Mars, Venus, and Jupiter), we can be pretty sure that the Jupiter person will get a boost to her own Jupiter experience: She'll discover some new signpost that indicates she's on the right track in her search for love. Meanwhile, the other person will be influenced by Jupiter's power and will feel abundant, bountiful, and damned lucky. In fact, the rising sign, sun, Venus, Mars, or a fellow Jupiter person brings out the best in the Jupiter person in more ways than one. Jupiter also reveals the way in which we present or show off the best of ourselves, so when the Jupiter person meets another Jupiter who's showing off in the same way, it's not surprising that he'll want to join in.

Jupiter brings a powerful light to the affinity chart, but the light can be both passionate and destructive when it's aligned with certain planets and challenging aspects. For example, when plotting your own Jupiter, first see what aspects it makes in your own chart. Is it subdued by other planets, like the moon or Saturn, or are its dynamic qualities reinforced by aspects to Mars, Venus, and the sun? When you're looking at your partner's chart, first observe his chart separately, too. If either or both of you have a dominant Jupiter in your own natal charts, you'll begin to see that if they meet in the affinity chart, they're going to result in rivalry or challenge. However harmonious they are, Jupiter contacts are certainly going to bring you both a sense of bountiful love and passionate excitement.

JUPITER/JUPITER CONTACTS

When two Jupiters collide, two worlds collide. Our beliefs are discovered and uncovered; our meaning in life is revealed (or we begin to realize that we must imbue life with some kind of meaning); and it is often through the other person that this happens. In harmonious contacts, we feel joyous, as if we're touched by a kindred spirit; we're animated and grandiose. In challenging contacts, we rise to the bait, enjoy wrangles and disputes, and aim our fiery lightning bolts of passion into the other person's heart, burning them up in our flames of desire.

Harmonious Contacts: Same Sign and Element

Both people have the same ideals and beliefs, and, if in the same sign, there's even more optimism, lightheartedness, and romance when the two are together. Both partners can freely discuss their ideas, goals, and desires without getting emotionally involved. This is a great contact when it comes to enjoying the good things in life and developing joint interests and future objectives. It doesn't necessarily seal a relationship, but it does give both people a generosity of spirit and a genuine sense of freedom from all responsibility.

Take, for instance, the affinity chart for Edward VIII and Wallis Simpson. Both have Aquarius rising signs (representing the same unconventional viewpoint about life), and Wallis Simpson's stellium in fun-loving Gemini and Edward's dynamic Jupiter conjunct her Venus/Neptune adds excitement and daring to their lifestyle and dreams for the future.

If one of the most glamorous men of Wallis Simpson's era, Edward VIII, was allured by Wallis' charismatic personality (Gemini and Leo planets), then she was equally besotted with the idea of living out the ultimate romance to become a princess, or even a queen. Yet, Edward gave up his kingship for the woman he loved, an irony meaning that for the rest of her life Wallis didn't quite live out the idealistic expectations she had (Jupiter in Leo). In their affinity chart, we can see how Edward's Jupiter stirred all her childhood dreams (Gemini) to life. How her own Jupiter opposing his rising sign (and her own) lured him into the Zeuslike heavens of make-believe romance, giving up all that he was meant to do for the sake of love.

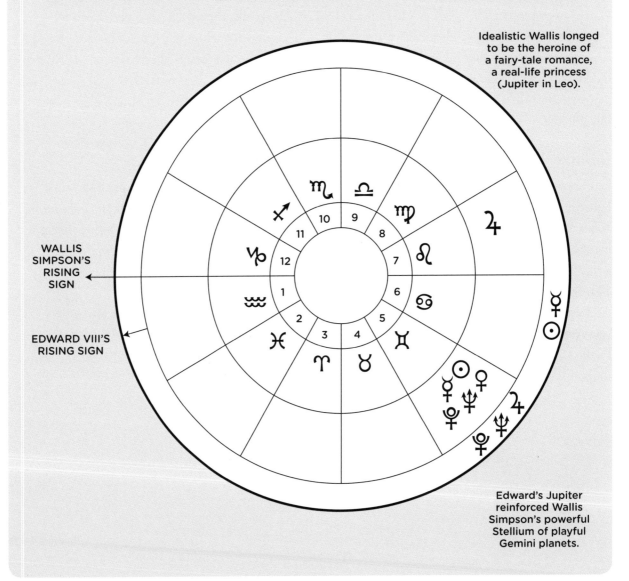

Idealistic Wallis longed to be the heroine of a fairy-tale romance, a real-life princess (Jupiter in Leo).

WALLIS SIMPSON'S RISING SIGN

EDWARD VIII'S RISING SIGN

Edward's Jupiter reinforced Wallis Simpson's powerful Stellium of playful Gemini planets.

Challenging Contacts: Oppositions and Three Signs Away

Because they have very different views on life and love, the lovers may spend more time and energy fighting for their own beliefs than in accepting their differences. In fact, any physical attraction between them will become less important than the value they place on their own opinions. This is a difficult contact for long-term love because each person is battling with the other's very different philosophy of life. What gives one Jupiter person joy and optimism seems to be bleak or untenable to the other, so they're always trying to persuade each other that one is right and the other is wrong. Still, check for more stabilizing and balancing contacts before concluding that this is the end of a good relationship since sometimes the very challenge inherent in this contact can, with acceptance and tolerance, add a lively, exciting energy to the relationship.

JUPITER/URANUS CONTACTS

Contacts between Jupiter and Uranus can be sparkling, vitalizing, and sexy, and even challenging contacts can bring illumination and progress to the relationship.

Harmonious Contacts: Same Sign and Element

This is a freewheeling, adventurous relationship, in which both people are willing to try just about anything new. They find each other physically exciting and are highly original in thought, action, and sexual experimentation. When they first meet, there's a sense that they've known each other in some other life, and the Jupiter person feels liberated from all inhibitions, allowing her to express all kinds of things she never dared express before. An inventive and tireless energy flow, if other contacts in the chart are good, can make for an unusual and passionate relationship.

Challenging Contacts: Oppositions and Three Signs Away

Here, the Jupiter person's beliefs, talents, and sense of meaning in life will be put to the test by the clash with Uranus. In fact, the Jupiter person will probably struggle to defend himself, creating the kind of fireworks that end in disagreements rather than discussions. The Uranian person becomes more spontaneous and unpredictable; however, it is possible that her dissident energy will encourage Jupiter to fight for his cause. But if they can learn to live with each other's crusading attitudes, they can form an impregnable bond that's based on intellectual friendship and physical attraction and supported by creative sex and wide-ranging interests.

JUPITER/NEPTUNE CONTACTS

When Jupiter contacts Neptune, there's a wild exaggeration of the energy between the two people since Jupiter expands and boosts the spellbinding, seductive effect of Neptune in the other person. Like Pluto, Neptune is always a challenging contact, although on the surface it may seem as if romance and dreams can become reality. But here, there's really no difference between harmonious and challenging contacts because Jupiter simply inflates the Neptunian energy out of all proportion. To see how this works, let's take a dramatic example of Jupiter in Sagittarius (the ruler of Sagittarius) and Neptune in Sagittarius.

SEDUCTION'S PULL

At a party, the Jupiter man is laughing with a gang of pals about his recent escapades when backpacking around Europe. Of course, he didn't have time to stop off in Paris to have dinner with the French president—and he did miss all his celebrity friends back in LA, but hey, isn't traveling what life is all about? His eyes roam the room looking for romance, for a woman who might be up for a one-night stand, and he spots the Neptune-in-Sagittarius woman holding court at the center of a pack of admiring academics. Out of the corner of her eye, she spots the Jupiter man, too: What fun they could have! What she's best at is seduction (when her Neptune is armed), so she drops the intellectual conversation with the group of academics, sidles up to the Jupiter man as if she's known him all her life, and says quietly, "Hey, fancy meeting you here. Let's go get a drink and catch up on old times." He laughs, smiles, kisses her cheek: It's a game, but it's the type of game he really likes to play, and there's something in her face that tells him this is going to be the sexiest night he's had in a long time. But once they get a bit further down the line, the question is, will this Neptunian seduction stand up to the light of reality?

This is how Neptune operates when faced with something desirable. When this Neptunian *je ne sais quoi* is dissolved into the elixir of love, it can lead both partners to a deep awareness of the universe within them—but usually at some cost to one or the other. (For more information on Neptune, see page 198.)

JUPITER/PLUTO CONTACTS

Although the Jupiter person seeks joy, when she comes across a blatant, in-your-face Pluto, chances are she'd rather run a mile than lock swords with the underworld threat, particularly if Pluto is conjunct or in opposition to her Jupiter. Why? Just think about how Zeus ruled the heavens and how his somber brother, Hades, ruled the underworld. In mythology, both were hostile, vengeful, wrathful, and threatening. Yet Zeus was the god who stormed around ravishing nymphs and mortals, taking delight in the light of the heavens; Hades (or Pluto), for his part, remained alone in the underworld, only rising from the darkness to steal a maiden, Persephone, who changed his life—but only for six months of the year. (See chapter 10 for more on the myth of Hades and Persephone.) So when these two gods or planetary archetypes come face-to-face in the affinity chart, there's little love between them. They're both greedy, and when they meet, they exaggerate the worst and best qualities of both energies. The Jupiter person becomes more despotic, yet longing for passionate release; the Pluto person becomes more subversive, more controlling, and more indulgent in his own power.

Whether in harmonious contact or not, this pairing does create extraordinary challenges surrounding sexual and other power games for the two people involved. Yet with openness and self-awareness, this contact can make for an empowering twosome who could rule the world together.

JUPITER/RISING SIGN CONTACTS

When the Jupiter person meets the same-sign rising-sign person, he immediately feels a sense of romantic carelessness, as if all the joy in the world stems from being with the rising-sign person whose presence embodies all of Jupiter's principles about love, romance, and how good he feels about himself, too. The rising-sign person immediately gets a kick out of the same quality, suddenly aware of the grand impression she is making, of being as large as life as the Jupiter person. When Jupiter is in a tense aspect to the other person's rising sign, you can be pretty sure Jupiter's antics will irritate the rising-sign person enough to ignore—or, at the very least, attempt to defend—her beliefs about love and life.

Harmonious Contacts: Same Sign and Element

Jupiter and the rising sign boost each other's qualities when in the same sign or element. In Earth, Jupiter finds meaning in love through the senses. So when, for example, an Earth-rising person encounters a Jupiter-in-Earth person, she is suddenly transformed into the best articulation of her rising sign: All her senses are illuminated to such an extent that she feels and experiences her own sexual power, and her sense of loving and being loved is amplified. So, too, are the Jupiter person's own qualities. This means that both grow in self-awareness: It's okay to be vain; it's okay to want to spend hours in indulgent lovemaking; and it's okay to be obsessed and possessed. Like any ideal, when the romance fades or when the rest of the affinity chart shows the harder evidence, they may begin to find their exaggerated self-indulgences are simply that, and nothing more. But this can be a mighty connection if they have other supporting contacts in their chart.

Jupiter in Air is bubbling with ideas, is enthusiastic about love and romance, and wants to plan his love life every second of the day. He loves to demonstrate his fascination with everything around him and becomes even more charismatic, while the rising-sign person can't seem to make herself stop talking. Depending on the rest of the chart, this is a fun-loving, lighthearted, youthful approach to life and love and can be hugely rewarding.

In Water, Jupiter exaggerates both emotions and the depth and intensity of the other person's love and strength of commitment. Hugely sensitive to other people's moods and feelings, when Jupiter meets another Water rising sign, there's an instant attraction based on an intuitive response. The Water-rising person comes alive in Jupiter's presence, as if all she has ever felt, longed for, needed, or believed in can finally come true. It's as if the Water Jupiter person is a magician, waving a glistening wand of pure happiness over them both. Awash in love and romance, this couple will go everywhere together, never leaving the other's side, and they'll believe they are genuine soul mates. Depending on the rest of the affinity chart, this can lead to a lifelong bond.

Challenging Contacts: Oppositions and Three Signs Away

All that glistens isn't gold, as the saying goes, and when Jupiter is involved in any clash or challenging contact, feelings, ideas, beliefs, desires, and meaning in life can become distorted and ugly rather than illuminating and beautiful. Things can become especially challenging—in both good and bad ways—when Jupiter opposes the person's rising sign. Jupiter takes great delight in stirring up the rising-sign person's viewpoints, while the rising-sign person peers out from behind her blinkers and sees these challenging ideals as both a threat and a (possible) treat.

All of this depends on other factors in the chart, so here's a brief look at some of the zodiac oppositions to see how we're uplifted yet niggled, inspired but mistrustful, and desperately in love but still dissatisfied when we meet someone who has Jupiter in our seventh house (unless we have Jupiter in our seventh house, too).

When the Jupiter Air man meets the glamorous, self-absorbed Fire-rising woman, he immediately wants to shock her with his original ideas and need for space and freedom. In fact, when he is confronted by this fiery starlet, he's driven to express his wildest ideas about sex just to wind her up and get a reaction out of her—any reaction. Unless she has Jupiter or Venus in her seventh house herself, she'll probably enter into a fiery dispute about independence and who dominates whom in the bedroom and will quickly put an end to his self-importance.

Jupiter-in-Water people go to emotional extremes. They are ultra-romantic yet deeply sensitive, so when they're faced with the sensually savvy Earth rising signs, their belief in another plane of existence, an afterlife, or a romantic escape route to paradise becomes highly tenable, and they may resort to evasive tactics to cover up for their vulnerability. Earth rising sees this brooding, sultry passion as both highly desirable and disdainful; after all, how can anyone be so unrealistic about love and life?

There is little doubt that, when Jupiter is in Fire, it burns with a vivid flame, and so when the Air-rising person sees an inferno of exaggerated theatrics out there in her seventh house, it's hardly surprising that she either becomes totally intent on reintroducing this irrational person to the world of logic or enters the flames to find out what the fuss is all about. (Of course, again, this depends on other contacts in the chart.)

Not only are Jupiter-in-Earth folks indulgent (Taurus in comfort, Virgo in criticism, and Capricorn in ambition), they're also excessively sure that they know what's best in all areas of sex, love, luxury, and money. Coveting their material know-how, Water rising is either infatuated or feels inferior, and Water will either retreat or move closer at this point (if it's the latter, Water is in for a luxe experience of pure indulgence).

CROSSING THE CHASM OF LOVE

We've fallen in love (rising sign to Venus/Mars); we've experienced great sexual chemistry (Venus/Mars/Jupiter/Eros); and we've discussed our joint goals (sun/Mercury). Now we're ready to settle down (Saturn)—maybe. Up until now, we've played games, maybe pretended to be something we're not to claim our catch; maybe we've tried to be what our partners want us to be or have found ourselves living out the ideal they've projected on us. But as we get to know our partners better, all of this starts to wear thin, and our boring old habits (the moon) and our defenses (Saturn) begin to rise up in revolt against this perfect picture of ourselves. Why does this this romantic self-portrait lack depth? Because deep down we know that it's not an accurate reflection of who we are.

Enter the outer planets: Uranus, Neptune, and Pluto. Let's turn to them in detail now because as part of the archetypal nature of the universe, they are the planets that can cause the most drama, crisis, and sexual havoc when they're in contact with your partner's personal planets. As you've seen in the preceding chapters, Uranus, Neptune, and Pluto seem to take over the affinity chart when they contact personal planets. The next chapter will help you understand the key archetypal energies represented by these three planets, giving you insight into the unconscious dynamics at work within your relationship.

16 The Outer Planets:
A Twist of Fate, Illusion, and the Dark Side

The slow-moving outer planets—Uranus, Neptune, and Pluto—can create a mysterious, fated quality in the affinity chart when they're in contact with your personal planets. This chapter will explain why that is, and it'll show you why falling in love so often feels like falling into a deep well or like stumbling into an alternate universe in which you and your partner are no longer yourselves: All you can be certain of is that the two of you were simply destined to find one another.

Uranus, Neptune, and Pluto connect us to higher planes of consciousness and to the deeper workings of the universe. On another level, they represent generational influences rather than individual character since they act as powerful archetypal energies. If these planets are in powerful aspect to a personal planet or are prominent in some other way in an individual's affinity chart, then the individual is often designated as a conduit or message-bringer—an oracle of the gods, if you like—for the archetypal energies of that generation, and it's as if he or she is somehow driven to bring them to public attention.

This is known as a transpersonal influence because it extends beyond the personal. It is usually unconscious, and it creates tremendous clashes, magnetic attractions, and deeper challenges in a relationship when in aspect to another's personal planets. If either you or your partner has any outer planets in completely different signs from each other, this can signify an attractive difference in ages, too: Often this person represents archetypal figures such as the father figure, an eternal youth, a mother figure, or the virgin-whore.

THE OUTER PLANETS IN THE AFFINITY CHART

When it comes to contacts between your outer planets and his personal planets or vice versa, a very strange thing happens. The result is an experience that's often compared to the sense of fate we've talked about throughout this book. In it, we feel as if we were meant or destined to meet this person for some unknown reason. And this often results in a life-changing experience, even though the relationship itself may not last long. In the aftermath of relationships like these, we may recall how "fate threw us together" or how "we'll never forget the effect we had on each other," even though it may have only been a brief encounter or a holiday romance. In fact, most of these "fateful" encounters show up in affinity charts when the outer planets—particularly Pluto—make powerful contacts to the other person's personal planets, such as the moon.

Outer-planet contacts to personal planets do, however, prove to be (strangely) more magnetic and transformative than links between personal planets. They "move you" to change your life because they push you to see that you need to grow, evolve, or "realize yourself," as psychotherapist Carl Jung might put it, through this relationship, whether it lasts forever or for a single day. They put you in touch with the archetypal or universal energy that's inherent in everything, including our psyches. Often these kinds of fated relationships don't last, simply because once one of you grows into an awareness of an evolving sense of self, you are no longer bound by the chains of human vulnerability—or, we could say, innocence.

If you have the same outer-planet sign placement as your partner (a generational influence), then the energy will feel less intense—but, as always, this depends on other factors in the affinity chart. Because these planets are slow-moving, there won't be much difference between two charts apart from generational similarities or differences. So we won't waste time looking at Uranus-to-Neptune or Pluto contacts, and so on. The most crucial contacts are those to our personal planets.

URANUS

Uranus is also known as "The Liberator" and is personified by Ouranos, the god of the heavens, who likes to upset, shake up, and disorganize the world in order to create progress. In the birth chart, Uranus reveals through sign and house the areas in your life in which things seem to be at their most unstable, chaotic, or disruptive. It's about shock, awakening, and challenge: In love relationships, it's what I call the "wake up, break up, or make up" planet.

But Uranus also describes the ideals and visions of an entire generation. It reveals what the generation has to realize or wake up to, and individuals who are spurred on to express this transpersonal energy can be shocking or upsetting to earlier or later generations. And Uranus also points toward the areas of our lives in which we most fear the loss of freedom. So the generation in Cancer, for example, unconsciously fears that family will stifle their freedom of expression; as a result, they break free from traditional familial values and obligations so that they can progress toward complete autonomy. In the affinity chart, Uranus contacts can awaken both individuals to the possibility of change and are also indicators of breakups or of alterations to conventional relationships.

Uranian vision is awakened in each of us when someone else's personal planets touch our natal Uranus; or we discover the radical nature of someone else's Uranus when we feel compelled to change our lives because of meeting them, or we split up or change our relationships dramatically. The great psychologist Carl Jung and his long-term associate, friend, and lover Toni Woolff inspired one another and created some of the most radical intellectual ideas and theories of their time. They were bound together for a lifetime, not only shown by the classic combination of Toni's Saturn in Leo rising opposite Jung's Aquarius rising, but also in Jung's sun and Uranus conjuncting Toni's Saturn/rising sign.

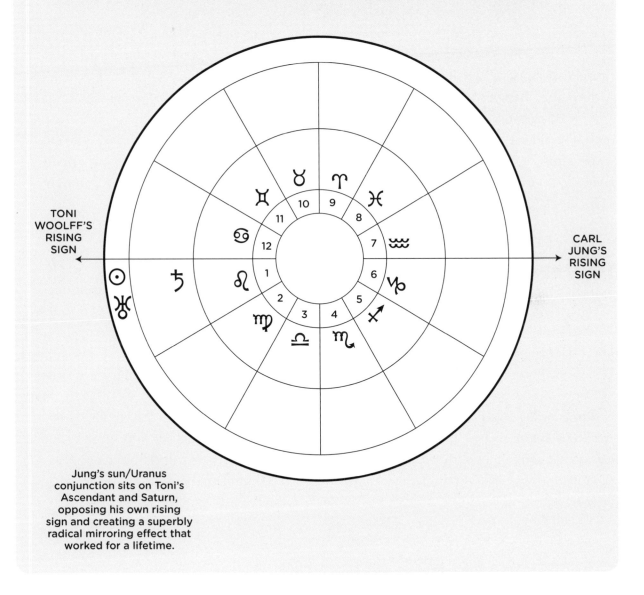

TONI WOOLFF'S RISING SIGN

CARL JUNG'S RISING SIGN

Jung's sun/Uranus conjunction sits on Toni's Ascendant and Saturn, opposing his own rising sign and creating a superbly radical mirroring effect that worked for a lifetime.

If you both have Uranus in the same sign, then you'll be able to deal with this energy a little more easily. But if you have it in different signs, then your generational ideals will be very different, which can often be a magnetic attraction in itself. Uranus by its very nature is unstable, but it can wake both you and your partner up to who you truly are: The Uranian person will become aware of his or her generational influence, while the personal-planet partner becomes conscious of untapped potential in his or her own character.

NEPTUNE

This cruel shape-shifter of a god worms his way into our perceived reality and also fools us into thinking that all of it is for real. When you look at your Neptune contacts, be sure you're not deceiving yourself about what this devious god brings to your planetary party.

We've already encountered Neptune in previous chapters, so you already know that this is a planet of dreams, fantasies, longings, compassion for all, and idealistic love. Neptune's realm is also boundless, undiscriminating, and dissolving. The planet's dark side, however, is that it invokes deception and sacrifice, glamorization and seduction. Make no mistake about it: This is a hugely complex outer planet. When we're emotionally knocked to the ground by Pluto, we can usually rise like a phoenix to live and love again, and Uranus can shock, reform, or radically change us—but Neptune's influence is far more elusive and deceptive. So when your Neptune contacts someone else's personal planets, some pretty confusing—and often chaotic—interactions can result. Here are some examples of how Neptune operates in the affinity chart.

Neptune: The Myth

Neptune, known as Poseidon in Greek mythology, was the god of the ocean. He churned the seas into great tidal waves and storms but also created heavy sea mists and fogs that put sailors and their ships off-course, leading them into dangerous waters: Unable to see the stars, they lost all sense of direction. Deluded and confused, they were soon overcome with desire for Neptune's deceitful water nymphs, the Sirens, who sang the most beautiful love songs and lured them into the still, calm ocean—only to drown them. Similarly, we can say that Neptune lures us to drown in love because it has a seductive, bewitching nature: In relationships, when Neptune is activated by someone else's planet, it casts a spell around us, dissolving the truth of the situation. Yet it can also power the imagination, so that our love affairs are filled with make-believe and games. But when the other "gods" (or an outside force, like a transiting planet) issue a wake-up call, the spell begins to lose its power. Then it is usually the Neptune person who suffers a sense of loss or disillusionment when the ideals he projected onto his beloved fall apart in the wash.

Neptune and Longing

When your Neptune contacts one of your partner's personal planets, then your own collective "longings," as described by Neptune, will either be in harmony with or will challenge his individual sense of identity. For instance, let's say you have Neptune in Libra a few degrees within orb of his Libra moon. And let's also say that his Neptune is in Scorpio (therefore making him younger than you), bang on your Mars in Scorpio. In this case, all your generational longings for a perfect relationship, for harmony and ideal love, gel very nicely with his moon, which feels supported by a Neptunian romantic ideal. His collective yearning for something all-consuming and deeply binding, as described by his Scorpio Neptune, is stimulated by the intense sexual power-tripping of your Scorpio Mars. Yet there's more to this than meets the eye. It all sounds harmonious on the surface, but Neptune doesn't care much for the individual's needs or feelings; in fact, Neptune leads the wandering romantic astray—and down a very dangerous road indeed—as we'll soon see.

If Neptune's doing the seducing, we'd think it'd be the personal-planet partner who gets lost in the murky waters of Neptune's world. But from my experience, the Neptune person—especially if she has a chart with very little grounding earth energy—deceives herself as much as she deceives her partner.

To help you understand the influence of Neptune in your own chart, remember that he weaves a spell around you; he seduces you into believing that the perfect lover is out there or that the ideal relationship exists. He weaves a fairy tale around you that resonates (cleverly!) with your Neptune sign and house placement and with any configurations to Neptune in your natal chart. But these are, ironically, aligned to your soul's purpose. This is so that one day you'll understand the true message concealed within the fairy tale you're attempting to live out through your love relationships—and Neptune's underlying message is always "Dissolve, and be at one with the universe."

Neptune's Objective

Remember that Neptune is, ultimately, about freeing us from our apparent realities and the chains of the material world through our love relationships. Neptune is often associated with escapism (found both in love and in mind-altering drugs), simply because both allow us to surpass our boundaries to a place that knows no limits, where we discover our desire to return to the stars.

The good news is that if we can see beyond the mists of this deceptive fairy tale, Neptune can allow us to truly know and accept one another. This is the ultimate form of trust—not just in each other, but also in the universe itself. Yes, Neptune makes us aware of the beauty of our partners, but it's really the beauty of the divine that reaches out to us through the other person's grace. Thus, Neptune encourages us to surrender to that universal power, so that both self and other are at one with the universe itself. In this sense, then, Neptune teaches us that whatever affects us as individuals or affects us as a couple, affects All.

DORA MAAR AND PABLO PICASSO'S AFFINITY CHART

Neptune operates in a mysterious way but also manifests as the muse or model in many artists' lives. Dora Maar was one such muse and was the well-known subject of Picasso's aptly titled, The Weeping Woman. Picasso's relationship with his lover, photographer Dora Maar, was fraught with deceptions, emotional turmoil, and passionate games. Dora's Neptune conjuncts Picasso's Mars, (obsessive and seductive hooks both ways) and her sun also opposes his Neptune (idealization of him by her). But with both Dora and Picasso's sun in Scorpio, the dark sexual power games they played were likely overlaid with the addictive and spellbinding power of Neptunian longing and desire. Both became crutches for the other person's obsessions and depressions—another spell cast by Neptune's powerful influence in their individual natal charts too.

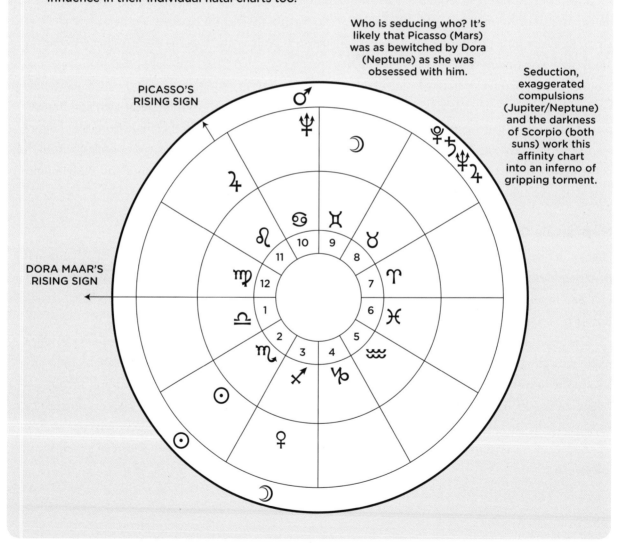

Who is seducing who? It's likely that Picasso (Mars) was as bewitched by Dora (Neptune) as she was obsessed with him.

Seduction, exaggerated compulsions (Jupiter/Neptune) and the darkness of Scorpio (both suns) work this affinity chart into an inferno of gripping torment.

PICASSO'S RISING SIGN

DORA MAAR'S RISING SIGN

PLUTO

Are you fascinated by torrid love affairs, power trips, and love triangles? Welcome to the world of Pluto and "th' equivocation of the fiend, who lies like truth," as Shakespeare wrote in *Macbeth*. This, the shadowy underworld of love, is Pluto's realm.

You've already met Pluto before in earlier chapters in this book, so let's get right down to the hard facts about his influence in the horoscope. In Greek and Latin mythology, this god ruled not only the underworld but also the storehouse of the earth's treasures. That includes crystal vaults and gold mines as well as the earth's dangerous, rumbling inner core that's sometimes responsible for deadly earthquakes. So we need to respect Hades (Greek for Pluto), and we can only ignore at our own peril.

Unlike Neptune's elusive, subtle, deceptive influence in the affinity chart, when Pluto contacts his partner's personal planet, both people usually know all about it—and they feel, experience, and act it out in the most dramatic, theatrical way. If Neptune is a trickster god disguised as a knight in shining armor, then Pluto is truly a bat out of hell—snatching, raping, and pillaging like a fiend. Pluto wields the upper hand in all contacts simply because he can never be overpowered—and what's more, he knows it. So when your Pluto is triggered by another person's planet, this unconscious archetypal urge will overpower the rest of your lovely chart and will rule indiscriminately within the relationship, draining each other's energy and beating you both to an emotional pulp.

So whatever happens, when one person's personal planet meets another person's Pluto, she'll be awakened to both the planet's potential and her own planet's dark side. This is why Pluto contacts are often about love triangles and clandestine affairs. Pluto's methods work best under the cover of intrigue, jealous imaginings, betrayal, and secrets, so he can keep hold on the reins of power. In a love triangle, it's often the Pluto person who's either the instrument of betrayal or the one who betrays. (Unfortunately, the betrayed partner gets very little out of this complicated geometry.)

In this way, then, the personal planet's potential is burned up in Pluto's inferno or is left to rot in the underworld until someone else comes along and saves her—or until she's able to return the light of the world and restore her own sense of power by herself. However it happens, whenever someone's personal planets are touched by Pluto, she'll never be the same again. Pluto's energy lies beyond the bounds of one's conscious ego—it is mythical and archetypal in the most profound sense. When it contacts other planets in your own birth chart, it not only intensifies the qualities of that planet, but it also—and more importantly—intends to "bury" or even "rape" the other planet of its own qualities.

THE NATAL CHART AND PLUTO OBSESSION

Before you get all worked up because you've spotted a Venus/Pluto contact in your affinity chart, try looking at your own natal chart and see if you can work objectively with any Pluto contacts there. That way, you'll be able to be more objective about what you find in the affinity chart. If, for example, you had Pluto square Mercury in your natal chart, you'd be intensely curious and determined to find out the truth about something. Obsessed with knowledge, you'd find yourself thinking such dark, gloomy, and even evil thoughts that it feels like all sense of light or illumination is blocked. In this way, Mercury's lightness of thought, swift thinking, and quick reflexes are buried beneath Pluto's heaviness. People with natal Mercury square Pluto are often prone to negative thoughts, but there is always a positive side to all planetary contacts, too. This Mercury and Pluto combination means that the individual has incredible powers of research and concentration and never gives up on her quest for the truth.

The Myth: Persephone

The myth of Persephone is a good analogy for this experience. In it, Hades (or Pluto) abducted Persephone, the daughter of Zeus and Demeter, the goddess of the harvest, while she was picking wild-flowers and took her to the underworld to be his queen. As Demeter wept at the loss of her daughter, she also withheld earth's fertility in retribution: Plants withered and no crops grew. Finally, the gods decided to arrange for Persephone to return to her mother for six months of each year so that the world could burst into bloom again. Just as Pluto violated or abducted Persephone, so the planet Pluto violates or undermines the qualities or expression of the planets it contacts.

It's not difficult to see that in synastry, Pluto isn't about light, love-dovey, custard-and-cream romance; instead, it's a dark, transformative, rich elixir comprised of the unknown. The planet is also about secrecy, forbidden fruits, taboos, and survival. It is often unfathomable in its darkness because it evokes the raw principles of sex and power: When, for example, Pluto and Venus are in contact between two people, physical desire and sex will be compelling yet obsessive; it'll be all-consuming yet violating; secretive yet volcanic; and taboo yet complete.

Conclusion: What Next?

We've come full circle, from the first inklings of potential love via our rising signs to the deeper relationship cycles represented by Pluto. Somewhere in between is every relationship you'll ever have, and it's up to you to use the information in your affinity chart to make each relationship the best it can possibly be—and to be the best version of yourself, too.

Now you have a sense of the affinity chart, but you've probably got other questions, too. You might wonder about the future of your relationship, and, perhaps, whether you'll stay with your partner; will you be able to weather the storms of a difficult Pluto contact or to see through the veil of a Neptunian romance? More importantly, do you want to? Questions like these will encourage you to understand both yourself and your current (or chosen) partner. They will also help to reinforce a sense of mutual acceptance and understanding because once we can understand the other person's "bad" Saturn or "cruel" Pluto, we may be able to help both them and ourselves. That's not to say that you should ever remain in a painful, abusive relationship; it's simply to suggest that this kind of acceptance can be a beneficial source of relationship-enhancing compassion. Far from being an excuse to remain stuck in a destructive relationship pattern, astrology (and synastry in particular) can help us to free ourselves from our own illusions and to move toward healthy, stable, mutually fulfilling partnerships.

We all have ideals when it comes to relationships. Maybe yours is a trip down the aisle followed by happily ever after; maybe it's a sexy, passion-filled union or a satisfying friendship. All of these are wonderful goals. But theory and practice can be very different, and it's never desirable to neglect your individual selfhood in favor of ideals like these. That's why it's important to remember that synastry is about accepting one another and learning from each other and developing both as individuals and as part of a relationship. I hope you'll continue on that journey—it's such a fascinating one.

KNOW THYSELF

It's also worthwhile to contemplate what you're seeking from your relationships. What are they about? Maybe they're there to unlock your solar potential. Maybe they exist in order to teach you karmic lessons or to teach you something about who you really are. At the end of the day, each one of us is a spark that fell from the stars, and one day, you'll return to the stars from which you came. Your inner spark—your sacred solar center—guides and guards you throughout life, however difficult or treacherous the journey may be. Like the sacred oracles of Apollo at Delphi, we get glimpses of this divinity from time to time through our inner temples—and slowly we come to befriend it. Eventually, we become able to tune in to that place in the constellations where our soul-sparks were once guided by Apollo's chariots of fire—when we were at One with the Cosmos. And sometimes meeting a new partner can help us on this journey since it's often when we meet someone new that our inner oracles begin to speak, as if for the very first time.

But maybe you don't really believe in all that—and that's completely okay. Still, it's only when you begin to "know thyself"—the inscription above Apollo's oracle at Delphi—that you can begin to love and to "bear" yourself, too. After that, you're more and more able to love, "bear," and, therefore, relate to other people in ways that are right for you. Every relationship is another step toward understanding yourself and accepting yourself for who you truly are. That's what synastry truly teaches us: to see our relationships as maps of human kindness, desire, needs, goals, and failings—and to see all of this as perfectly human and perfectly lovable and acceptable. Whatever happens to each of us as individuals within our relationships, synastry encourages us to walk on—or out, as the case may be—and to be proud of who we are.

Blessings, and let the light of the universe shine through you every day.

Appendix: Eros Tables

In the following tables, you can look up your year and date of birth to find out where Eros was on that day. For example, if you were born on March 20, 1973, you can see that Eros was in Taurus between February 22 and March 28 of that year. If you were born, however, on the day that Eros changed sign, it is possible that your Eros was in the following or previous sign given. If this is the case, the best approach is to read both the given sign and the adjacent one to determine which one you think is most like you.

Alternatively, if you know your time of birth, you can get Eros's exact degree calculated for you online. Go to www.astro.com and once you have got your natal chart calculated, select "Extended Chart Selection." For "Chart drawing style," choose "Astrodienst w. asteroids." Then select "Click here to show the chart." This chart includes all the main asteroids, and you can see Eros clearly shown as "eros" with its degree marked on the chart.

1940	
Jan. 1–Jan. 31	Scorpio
Feb. 1–Mar. 25	Sagittarius
Mar. 26–June 5	Capricorn
June 6–Sept. 28	Sagittarius
Sept. 29–Nov. 29	Capricorn
Nov. 30–Dec. 31	Aquarius
1941	
Jan. 1–Jan. 20	Aquarius
Jan. 21–Mar. 7	Pisces
Mar. 8–Apr. 17	Aries
Apr. 18–May 24	Taurus
May 25–June 28	Gemini
June 29–July 31	Cancer
Aug. 1–Sept. 1	Leo
Sept. 2–Oct. 5	Virgo
Oct. 6–Nov. 10	Libra
Nov. 11–Dec. 19	Scorpio
Dec. 20–Dec. 31	Sagittarius
1942	
Jan. 1–Feb. 2	Sagittarius
Feb. 3–Mar. 26	Capricorn
Mar. 27–Dec. 10	Aquarius
Dec. 11–Dec. 31	Pisces

1943	
Jan. 1–Jan. 27	Pisces
Jan. 28–Mar. 7	Aries
Mar. 8–Apr. 11	Taurus
Apr. 12–May 14	Gemini
May 15–June 16	Cancer
June 17–July 19	Leo
July 20–Aug. 23	Virgo
Aug. 24–Sept. 30	Libra
Oct. 1–Nov. 11	Scorpio
Nov. 12–Dec. 27	Sagittarius
Dec. 28–Dec. 31	Capricorn
1944	
Jan. 1–Feb. 15	Capricorn
Feb. 16–Apr. 8	Aquarius
Apr. 9–June 4	Pisces
June 5–Aug. 8	Aries
Aug. 9–Nov. 6	Taurus
Nov. 7–Dec. 31	Aries
1945	
Jan. 1	Aries
Jan. 2–Feb. 14	Taurus
Feb. 15–Mar. 19	Gemini
Mar. 20–Apr. 20	Cancer

Apr. 21–May 25	Leo
May 26–July 2	Virgo
July 3–Aug. 15	Libra
Aug. 16–Oct. 2	Scorpio
Oct. 3–Nov. 21	Sagittarius
Nov. 22–Dec. 31	Capricorn
1946	
Jan. 1–Jan. 11	Capricorn
Jan. 12–Mar. 2	Aquarius
Mar. 3–Apr. 20	Pisces
Apr. 21–June 4	Aries
June 5–July 15	Taurus
July 16–Aug. 21	Gemini
Aug. 22–Sept. 24	Cancer
Sept. 25–Oct. 26	Leo
Oct. 27–Nov. 27	Virgo
Nov. 28–Dec. 31	Libra
1947	
Jan. 1–Feb. 10	Scorpio
Feb. 11–Oct. 9	Sagittarius
Oct. 10–Dec. 7	Capricorn
Dec. 8–Dec. 31	Aquarius
1948	
Jan. 1–Jan. 27	Aquarius

Jan. 28–Mar. 13	Pisces
Mar. 14–Apr. 23	Aries
Apr. 24–May 31	Taurus
June 1–July 5	Gemini
July 6–Aug. 7	Cancer
Aug. 8–Sept. 9	Leo
Sept. 10–Oct. 12	Virgo
Oct. 13–Nov. 16	Libra
Nov. 17–Dec. 25	Scorpio
Dec. 26–Dec. 31	Sagittarius
1949	
Jan. 1–Feb. 8	Sagittarius
Feb. 9–Apr. 4	Capricorn
Apr. 5–Aug. 24	Aquarius
Aug. 25–Oct. 9	Capricorn
Oct. 10–Dec. 18	Aquarius
Dec. 19–Dec. 31	Pisces
1950	
Jan. 1–Feb. 2	Pisces
Feb. 3–Mar. 14	Aries
Mar. 15–Apr. 19	Taurus
Apr. 20–May 22	Gemini
May 23–June 24	Cancer
June 25–July 27	Leo
July 28–Aug. 31	Virgo
Sept. 1–Oct. 7	Libra
Oct. 8–Nov. 18	Scorpio
Nov. 19–Dec. 31	Sagittarius
1951	
Jan. 1–Jan. 2	Sagittarius
Jan. 3–Feb. 21	Capricorn
Feb. 22–Apr. 16	Aquarius
Apr. 17–June 17	Pisces
June 18–Nov. 12	Aries
Nov. 13–Nov. 20	Pisces
Nov. 21–Dec. 31	Aries
1952	
Jan. 1–Jan. 24	Aries
Jan. 25–Feb. 29	Taurus
Mar. 1–Apr. 2	Gemini

Apr. 3–May 4	Cancer
May 5–June 6	Leo
June 7–July 13	Virgo
July 14–Aug. 24	Libra
Aug. 25–Oct. 10	Scorpio
Oct. 11–Nov. 28	Sagittarius
Nov. 29–Dec. 31	Capricorn
1953	
Jan. 1–Jan. 17	Capricorn
Jan. 18–Mar. 8	Aquarius
Mar. 9–Apr. 27	Pisces
Apr. 28–June 12	Aries
June 13–July 25	Taurus
July 26–Aug. 31	Gemini
Sept. 1–Oct. 4	Cancer
Oct. 5–Nov. 5	Leo
Nov. 6–Dec. 7	Virgo
Dec. 8–Dec. 31	Libra
1954	
Jan. 1–Jan. 11	Libra
Jan. 12–Feb. 25	Scorpio
Feb. 26–May 16	Sagittarius
May 17–Aug. 12	Scorpio
Aug. 13–Oct. 19	Sagittarius
Oct. 20–Dec. 13	Capricorn
Dec. 14–Dec. 31	Aquarius
1955	
Jan. 1–Feb. 2	Aquarius
Feb. 3–Mar. 20	Pisces
Mar. 21–May 1	Aries
May 2–June 9	Taurus
June 10–July 14	Gemini
July 15–Aug. 16	Cancer
Aug. 17–Sept. 18	Leo
Sept. 19–Oct. 21	Virgo
Oct. 22–Nov. 25	Libra
Nov. 26–Dec. 31	Scorpio
1956	
Jan. 1–Jan. 2	Scorpio
Jan. 3–Feb. 16	Sagittarius

Feb. 17–Apr. 15	Capricorn
Apr. 16–July 21	Aquarius
July 22–Oct. 27	Capricorn
Oct. 28–Dec. 25	Aquarius
Dec. 26–Dec. 31	Pisces
1957	
Jan. 1–Feb. 10	Pisces
Feb. 11–Mar. 21	Aries
Mar. 22–Apr. 27	Taurus
Apr. 28–May 30	Gemini
May 31–July 2	Cancer
July 3–Aug. 4	Leo
Aug. 5–Sept. 7	Virgo
Sept. 8–Oct. 15	Libra
Oct. 16–Nov. 24	Scorpio
Nov. 25–Dec. 31	Sagittarius
1958	
Jan. 1–Jan. 9	Sagittarius
Jan. 10–Feb. 27	Capricorn
Feb. 28–Apr. 24	Aquarius
Apr. 25–July 5	Pisces
July 6–Sept. 12	Aries
Sept. 13–Dec. 22	Pisces
Dec. 23–Dec. 31	Aries
1959	
Jan. 1–Feb. 4	Aries
Feb. 5–Mar. 12	Taurus
Mar. 13–Apr. 13	Gemini
Apr. 14–May 15	Cancer
May 16–June 18	Leo
June 19–July 24	Virgo
July 25–Sept. 3	Libra
Sept. 4–Oct. 18	Scorpio
Oct. 19–Dec. 5	Sagittarius
Dec. 6–Dec. 31	Capricorn
1960	
Jan. 1–Jan. 24	Capricorn
Jan. 25–Mar. 15	Aquarius
Mar. 16–May 4	Pisces
May 5–June 21	Aries

June 22–Aug. 4	Taurus
Aug. 5–Sept. 12	Gemini
Sept. 13–Oct. 16	Cancer
Oct. 17–Nov. 17	Leo
Nov. 18–Dec. 20	Virgo
Dec. 21–Dec. 31	Libra
1961	
Jan. 1–Jan. 26	Libra
Jan. 27–Aug. 28	Scorpio
Aug. 29–Oct. 27	Sagittarius
Oct. 28–Dec. 20	Capricorn
Dec. 21–Dec. 31	Aquarius
1962	
Jan. 1–Feb. 8	Aquarius
Feb. 9–Mar. 27	Pisces
Mar. 28–May 8	Aries
May 9–June 16	Taurus
June 17–July 22	Gemini
July 23–Aug. 24	Cancer
Aug. 25–Sept. 26	Leo
Sept. 27–Oct. 28	Virgo
Oct. 29–Dec. 2	Libra
Dec. 3–Dec. 31	Scorpio
1963	
Jan. 1–Jan. 10	Scorpio
Jan. 11–Feb. 24	Sagittarius
Feb. 25–May 4	Capricorn
May 5–June 17	Aquarius
June 18–Nov. 8	Capricorn
Nov. 9–Dec. 31	Aquarius
1964	
Jan. 1–Jan. 3	Aquarius
Jan. 4–Feb. 17	Pisces
Feb. 18–Mar. 29	Aries
Mar. 30–May 4	Taurus
May 5–June 7	Gemini
June 8–July 10	Cancer
July 11–Aug. 12	Leo
Aug. 13–Sept. 15	Virgo
Sept. 16–Oct. 22	Libra

Oct. 23–Dec. 1	Scorpio
Dec. 2–Dec. 31	Sagittarius
1965	
Jan. 1–Jan. 15	Sagittarius
Jan. 16–Mar. 6	Capricorn
Mar. 7–May 3	Aquarius
May 4–Dec. 31	Pisces
1966	
Jan. 1–Jan. 4	Pisces
Jan. 5–Feb. 14	Aries
Feb. 15–Mar. 21	Taurus
Mar. 22–Apr. 22	Gemini
Apr. 23–May 25	Cancer
May 26–June 27	Leo
June 28–Aug. 2	Virgo
Aug. 3–Sept. 11	Libra
Sept. 12–Oct. 25	Scorpio
Oct. 26–Dec. 11	Sagittarius
Dec. 12–Dec. 31	Capricorn
1967	
Jan. 1–Jan. 30	Capricorn
Jan. 31–Mar. 22	Aquarius
Mar. 23–May 13	Pisces
May 14–July 2	Aries
July 3–Aug. 18	Taurus
Aug. 19–Sept. 28	Gemini
Sept. 29–Nov. 4	Cancer
Nov. 5–Dec. 8	Leo
Dec. 9–Dec. 31	Virgo
1968	
Jan. 1–Jan. 14	Virgo
Jan. 15–July 12	Libra
July 13–Sept. 9	Scorpio
Sept. 10–Nov. 3	Sagittarius
Nov. 4–Dec. 26	Capricorn
Dec. 27–Dec. 31	Aquarius
1969	
Jan. 1–Feb. 14	Aquarius
Feb. 15–Apr. 2	Pisces
Apr. 3–May 15	Aries

May 16–June 24	Taurus
June 25–July 30	Gemini
July 31–Sept. 1	Cancer
Sept. 2–Oct. 4	Leo
Oct. 5–Nov. 5	Virgo
Nov. 6–Dec. 10	Libra
Dec. 11–Dec. 31	Scorpio
1970	
Jan. 1–Jan. 17	Scorpio
Jan. 18–Mar. 5	Sagittarius
Mar. 6–Nov. 17	Capricorn
Nov. 18–Dec. 31	Aquarius
1971	
Jan. 1–Jan. 9	Aquarius
Jan. 10–Feb. 24	Pisces
Feb. 25–Apr. 5	Aries
Apr. 6–May 12	Taurus
May 13–June 15	Gemini
June 16–July 18	Cancer
July 19–Aug. 20	Leo
Aug. 21–Sept. 23	Virgo
Sept. 24–Oct. 29	Libra
Oct. 30–Dec. 8	Scorpio
Dec. 9–Dec. 31	Sagittarius
1972	
Jan. 1–Jan. 22	Sagittarius
Jan. 23–Mar. 12	Capricorn
Mar. 13–May 14	Aquarius
May 15–Sept. 2	Pisces
Sept. 3–Nov. 19	Aquarius
Nov. 20–Dec. 31	Pisces
1973	
Jan. 1–Jan. 13	Pisces
Jan. 14–Feb. 22	Aries
Feb. 23–Mar. 29	Taurus
Mar. 30–May 1	Gemini
May 2–June 2	Cancer
June 3–July 5	Leo
July 6–Aug. 10	Virgo
Aug. 11–Sept. 18	Libra

Sept. 19–Oct. 31	Scorpio
Nov. 1–Dec. 17	Sagittarius
Dec. 18–Dec. 31	Capricorn
1974	
Jan. 1–Feb. 4	Capricorn
Feb. 5–Mar. 28	Aquarius
Mar. 29–May 20	Pisces
May 21–July 12	Aries
July 13–Sept. 3	Taurus
Sept. 4–Oct. 26	Gemini
Oct. 27–Dec. 31	Cancer
1975	
Jan. 1–Feb. 24	Cancer
Feb. 25–Apr. 20	Leo
Apr. 21–June 8	Virgo
June 9–July 28	Libra
July 29–Sept. 19	Scorpio
Sept. 20–Nov. 11	Sagittarius
Nov. 12–Dec. 31	Capricorn
1976	
Jan. 1	Capricorn
Jan. 2–Feb. 21	Aquarius
Feb. 22–Apr. 8	Pisces
Apr. 9–May 22	Aries
May 23–July 1	Taurus
July 2–Aug. 7	Gemini
Aug. 8–Sept. 9	Cancer
Sept. 10–Oct. 11	Leo
Oct. 12–Nov. 13	Virgo
Nov. 14–Dec. 17	Libra
Dec. 18–Dec. 31	Scorpio
1977	
Jan. 1–Jan. 25	Scorpio
Jan. 26–Mar. 16	Sagittarius
Mar. 17–June 25	Capricorn
June 26–Sept. 18	Sagittarius
Sept. 19–Nov. 24	Capricorn
Nov. 25–Dec. 31	Aquarius
1978	
Jan. 1–Jan. 15	Aquarius

Jan. 16–Mar. 2	Pisces
Mar. 3–Apr. 12	Aries
Apr. 13–May 19	Taurus
May 20–June 23	Gemini
June 24–July 26	Cancer
July 27–Aug. 28	Leo
Aug. 29–Sept. 30	Virgo
Oct. 1–Nov. 5	Libra
Nov. 6–Dec. 15	Scorpio
Dec. 16–Dec. 31	Sagittarius
1979	
Jan. 1–Jan. 28	Sagittarius
Jan. 29–Mar. 20	Capricorn
Mar. 21–May 31	Aquarius
June 1–July 31	Pisces
Aug. 1–Dec. 3	Aquarius
Dec. 4–Dec. 31	Pisces
1980	
Jan. 1–Jan. 22	Pisces
Jan. 23–Mar. 1	Aries
Mar. 2–Apr. 6	Taurus
Apr. 7–May 9	Gemini
May 10–June 10	Cancer
June 11–July 14	Leo
July 15–Aug. 18	Virgo
Aug. 19–Sept. 25	Libra
Sept. 26–Nov. 6	Scorpio
Nov. 7–Dec. 23	Sagittarius
Dec. 24–Dec. 31	Capricorn
1981	
Jan. 1–Feb. 10	Capricorn
Feb. 11–Apr. 3	Aquarius
Apr. 4–May 29	Pisces
May 30–July 27	Aries
July 28–Dec. 31	Taurus
1982	
Jan. 1–Jan. 31	Taurus
Feb. 1–Mar. 8	Gemini
Mar. 9–Apr. 11	Cancer
Apr. 12–May 16	Leo

May 17–June 25	Virgo
June 26–Aug. 9	Libra
Aug. 10–Sept. 27	Scorpio
Sept. 28–Nov. 17	Sagittarius
Nov. 18–Dec. 31	Capricorn
1983	
Jan. 1–Jan. 7	Capricorn
Jan. 8–Feb. 26	Aquarius
Feb. 27–Apr. 16	Pisces
Apr. 17–May 31	Aries
June 1–July 11	Taurus
July 12–Aug. 16	Gemini
Aug. 17–Sept. 19	Cancer
Sept. 20–Oct. 21	Leo
Oct. 22–Nov. 22	Virgo
Nov. 23–Dec. 27	Libra
Dec. 28–Dec. 31	Scorpio
1984	
Jan. 1–Feb. 4	Scorpio
Feb. 5–Apr. 2	Sagittarius
Apr. 3–May 18	Capricorn
May 19–Oct. 2	Sagittarius
Oct. 3–Dec. 1	Capricorn
Dec. 2–Dec. 31	Aquarius
1985	
Jan. 1–Jan. 22	Aquarius
Jan. 23–Mar. 9	Pisces
Mar. 10–Apr. 19	Aries
Apr. 20–May 27	Taurus
May 28–July 1	Gemini
July 2–Aug. 3	Cancer
Aug. 4–Sept. 4	Leo
Sept. 5–Oct. 8	Virgo
Oct. 9–Nov. 12	Libra
Nov. 13–Dec. 21	Scorpio
Dec. 22–Dec. 31	Sagittarius
1986	
Jan. 1–Feb. 4	Sagittarius
Feb. 5–Mar. 29	Capricorn
Mar. 30–Dec. 12	Aquarius

Dec. 13-Dec. 31	Pisces

1987	
Jan. 1-Jan. 29	Pisces
Jan. 30-Mar. 10	Aries
Mar. 11-Apr. 14	Taurus
Apr. 15-May 18	Gemini
May 19-June 19	Cancer
June 20-July 22	Leo
July 23-Aug. 26	Virgo
Aug. 27-Oct. 3	Libra
Oct. 4-Nov. 14	Scorpio
Nov. 15-Dec. 30	Sagittarius
Dec. 31	Capricorn

1988	
Jan. 1-Feb. 17	Capricorn
Feb. 18-Apr. 10	Aquarius
Apr. 11-June 8	Pisces
June 9-Aug. 27	Aries
Aug. 28-Sept. 26	Taurus
Sept. 27-Dec. 31	Aries

1989	
Jan. 1-Jan. 14	Aries
Jan. 15-Feb. 21	Taurus
Feb. 22-Mar. 26	Gemini
Mar. 27-Apr. 27	Cancer
Apr. 28-May 30	Leo
June 1-July 7	Virgo
July 8-Aug. 19	Libra
Aug. 20-Oct. 5	Scorpio
Oct. 6-Nov. 24	Sagittarius
Nov. 25-Dec. 31	Capricorn

1990	
Jan. 1-Jan. 13	Capricorn
Jan. 14-March 5	Aquarius
March 6-April 23	Pisces
April 24-June 8	Aries
June 9-July 20	Taurus
July 21-Aug. 26	Gemini
Aug. 27-Sept. 29	Cancer
Sept 30-Oct. 31	Leo

Nov. 1-Dec. 2	Virgo
Dec. 3-Dec. 31	Libra

1991	
Jan. 1-Jan. 5	Libra
Jan. 6-Feb. 14	Scorpio
Feb. 15-June 17	Sagittarius
June 18-July 25	Scorpio
July 26-Oct. 12	Sagittarius
Oct. 13-Dec. 8	Capricorn
Dec. 9-Dec. 31	Aquarius

1992	
Jan. 1-Jan. 28	Aquarius
Jan. 29-Mar. 14	Pisces
Mar. 15-Apr. 24	Aries
Apr. 25-June 3	Taurus
June 4-July 8	Gemini
July 9-Aug. 10	Cancer
Aug. 11-Sept. 12	Leo
Sept. 13-Oct. 15	Virgo
Oct. 16-Nov. 19	Libra
Nov. 20-Dec. 28	Scorpio
Dec. 29-Dec. 31	Sagittarius

1993	
Jan. 1-Feb. 10	Sagittarius
Feb. 11-Apr. 7	Capricorn
Apr. 8-Aug. 9	Aquarius
Aug. 10-Oct. 17	Capricorn
Oct. 18-Dec. 20	Aquarius
Dec. 20-Jan. 31	Pisces

1994	
Jan. 1-Feb. 5	Pisces
Feb. 6-Mar. 17	Aries
Mar. 18-Apr. 22	Taurus
Apr. 23-May 25	Gemini
May 26-June 27	Cancer
June 28-July 30	Leo
July 31-Sept. 2	Virgo
Sept. 3-Oct. 10	Libra
Oct. 11-Nov. 20	Scorpio
Nov. 21-Dec. 31	Sagittarius

1995	
Jan. 1-Jan. 5	Sagittarius
Jan. 6-Feb. 23	Capricorn
Feb. 24-Apr. 19	Aquarius
Apr. 20-June 23	Pisces
June 24-Oct. 8	Aries
Oct. 9-Dec. 12	Pisces
Dec. 13-Dec. 31	Aries

1996	
Jan. 1-Jan. 29	Aries
Jan. 30-Mar. 5	Taurus
Mar. 6-Apr. 7	Gemini
Apr. 8-May 9	Cancer
May 10-June 11	Leo
June 12-July 18	Virgo
July 19-Aug. 28	Libra
Aug. 29-Oct. 12	Scorpio
Oct. 13-Nov. 30	Sagittarius
Dec. 1-Dec. 31	Capricorn

1997	
Jan. 1-Jan. 19	Capricorn
Jan. 20-Mar. 11	Aquarius
Mar. 12-Apr. 29	Pisces
Apr. 30-June 16	Aries
June 17-July 29	Taurus
July 30-Sept. 5	Gemini
Sept. 6-Oct. 10	Cancer
Oct. 11-Nov. 10	Leo
Nov. 11-Dec. 12	Virgo
Dec. 13-Dec. 31	Libra

1998	
Jan. 1-Jan. 17	Libra
Jan. 18-Mar. 10	Scorpio
Mar. 11-Apr. 18	Sagittarius
Apr. 19-Aug. 20	Scorpio
Aug. 21-Oct. 22	Sagittarius
Oct. 23-Dec. 15	Capricorn
Dec. 16-Dec. 31	Aquarius

Acknowledgments

Many thanks to everyone at Fair Winds Press for all your dedication and time spent on this book. Blessings particularly to Jill Alexander, Megan Buckley, and Jennifer Kushnier for their gentle and patient guidance. I would also like to thank my family and friends for being astrological love guinea pigs here and there!

About the Author

Sarah Bartlett is the author of many spiritual and occult books, including the best-selling *Tarot Bible* and *The Essential Guide to Psychic Powers*. An astrologer for women's magazines such as *Cosmopolitan (UK)*, *She*, *Spirit and Destiny*, and the *London Evening Standard*, Sarah currently contributes to BBC Radio 2 show, *Steve Wright in the Afternoon*, as well as to www.theastrologyroom.com, of which she is a founding member. She is the author of *Spellcraft* and *Secrets of the Universe in 100 Symbols*, *Supernatural Places*, and *The Afterlife Bible*. Dividing her time between London and the south of France, Sarah teaches and practices astrology, tarot, Wicca, and other occult arts.

Index

Illustrations are indicated by page numbers in *italics*.

Hephaetus, 115
Hera, 186
Heraclitus, 13
Hermes (Mercury), 178
Hesiod (Greek writer), 139, 160
Holmes, Katie, 178, *179*
Homer, 139
houses, 22, 33, 50, 71, 196, 199. *See also* first house;
    seventh house

I

I.C., *23*
idealization, 13
Iliad (Homer), 139
imagination, 74, 90
imbalances, *39*
Immum Coeli, 23
"The Importance of the Order of the Planets in This
    Book," 15
inspiration, 75
"Intense Sexual Attraction," 163
inter-aspects. *See* planetary contacts

J

Jolie, Angelina, 100, 101
Jung, Carl, *197*
Jupiter
    in affinity charts, *36*, 38, 43, 186–187, *188*
    Eros and, 165
    Jupiter and, 187, 189
    Mars and, 146, 154
    Mercury and, 181
    moon and, 95, 102, 111–112
    Neptune and, 190
    as personal planet, 41
    Pluto and, 191
    rising sign in, 191–193
    Saturn and, 171–172
    sun and, 80, 85–86, 111–112
    Uranus and, 189
    Venus and, 115, 123–126
Jupiter (Zeus), 125, 139, 168, 174, 178, 186, 202

L

Leo
    Eros and, 161, 162
    in Fire, 19, 20, 60, 62
    Mercury and, 180
    rising sign in, 59, 60, 62, 66
    in seventh house, 54
    sun and, 75, 76, 77, 79, 85
    Venus and, 97, 117, 120, 125–126, 156
Letizia, Queen of Spain, 67, *68*
"The Liberator" (Uranus), 198
libido, 83, 123, 139–141, 143–146, 149–150, 156,
    158–159. *See also* sex/sexuality
Libra
    in affinity charts, *36*, 37–38, *37*, 43
    in Air, 19, 21, 61, 63
    Eros and, 161–162
    Mars and, 141, 143, 148, 156, 158
    Mercury and, 180
    moon and, 111–112
    Neptune and, 199
    rising sign in, 59, 61, 63, 64–65
    Saturn and, 168
    sun and, 75, 76–78, 91, 111
    Venus and, 117–119, 125–126, 129, 133, 156, 158
Lord of the Underworld (Pluto), 133
"Lost in Illusions," 174
love. *See also* erotic connection
    in astrology, 18, 19, 23
    mirrors of, 51, 53–54
    mystery of, 11–14
    synastry and, *32*

M

Maar, Dora, *200*
Macbeth (Shakespeare), 201
"Mapping Your Birth Chart," 17
Mars
    in affinity charts, 41, *44*, 140–141, 142–144, *142*,
        154, *155*, 156–159
    in elements, 140–141
    Eros and, 164
    Jupiter and, 123, 146, 185–187
    Mars and, 140–141, 143–144

N

U

Uranus
    in affinity charts, 196, *197*, 198
    Eros and, 164
    Jupiter and, 189
    Mars and, 147
    Mercury and, 178, 181–182
    moon and, 102
    as outer planet, 41, 195
    in same sign, 196, 198
    Saturn and, 172–173
    sun and, 86–87
    Venus and, 127–129
Uranus (Ouranos), 115, 127, 168, 196

V

Venus
    in affinity charts, *132*, 154, 156–159
    on the cusp, 29
    Eros and, 160, 162–164
    Jupiter and, 123–126, 185, 186–187, 192–193
    Mars and, 140, 141, 144, 145, 147, 149, 150, 154–159
    Mercury and, 122–123, 183
    moon and, 93, 94, 95–97
    Neptune and, 129–130
    Pluto and, 131, 133–135, 202
    in relationships, 115
    rising sign in, 65, 135–137
    Saturn and, 121–122, 171
    sun and, 72, 80, 82, 86
    Uranus and, 127–129
Venus (Aphrodite), 115, 127, 134, 159
Virgo
    in affinity charts, 43
    in Earth, 19, 21, 61, 62
    Eros and, 161, 162
    Jupiter and, 193
    Mars and, 141, 144, 145, 147, 151, 156, 157–158
    Mercury and, 177, 180
    moon and, 102, 108
    rising sign in, 59, 61, 62, 67
    Saturn in, 173
    sun and, 73, 75, 76–77, 79–80, 85, 89, 108, 111
    Venus and, 117, 118, 120, 126

W

Water
    as element, 19, 20, 22, 38–39
    with Eros, 162
    with Jupiter, 192–193
    with Mars, 141, 146, 156–157, 158
    with moon, 95, 105, 111
    with rising sign, 59–60, 63
    with sun, 75–76, 90, 111
    with Venus, 116, 122, 125, 126, 128, 135–136, 156–157, 158
"we," 64–65, 78
websites, 17–18
"Who Really Is Who?" 80
"Wildly Civilized," 141
"The Wit Factor," 85
Woolff, Toni, *197*

X

X, Ms., 53, 54

Y

Y, Mr., 53, 54
yin/yang, *49*

Z

Zeus (Jupiter), 125, 139, 168, 174, 178, 186, 202
zodiac, 22, 24, 28, 64, 80, 148, 192
zodiac signs, 13, 35, 50. *See also names of individual signs*

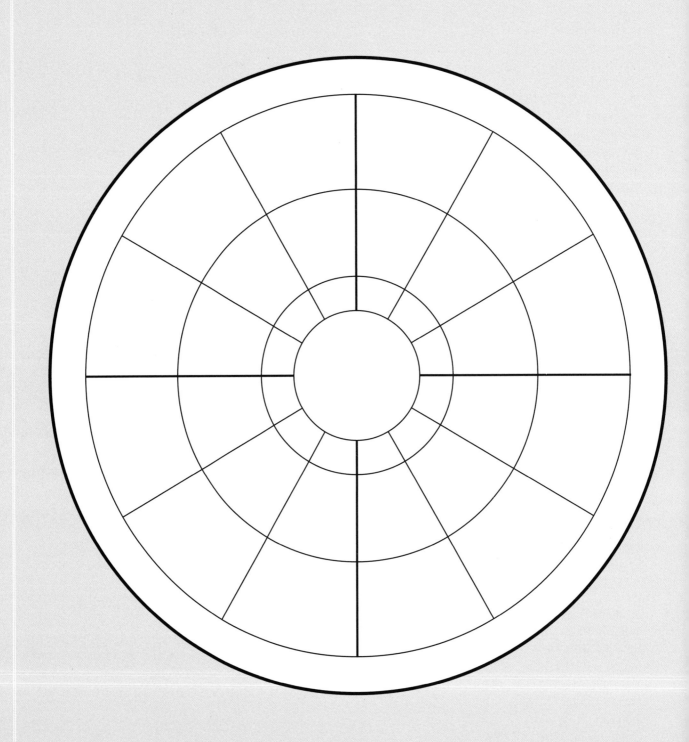

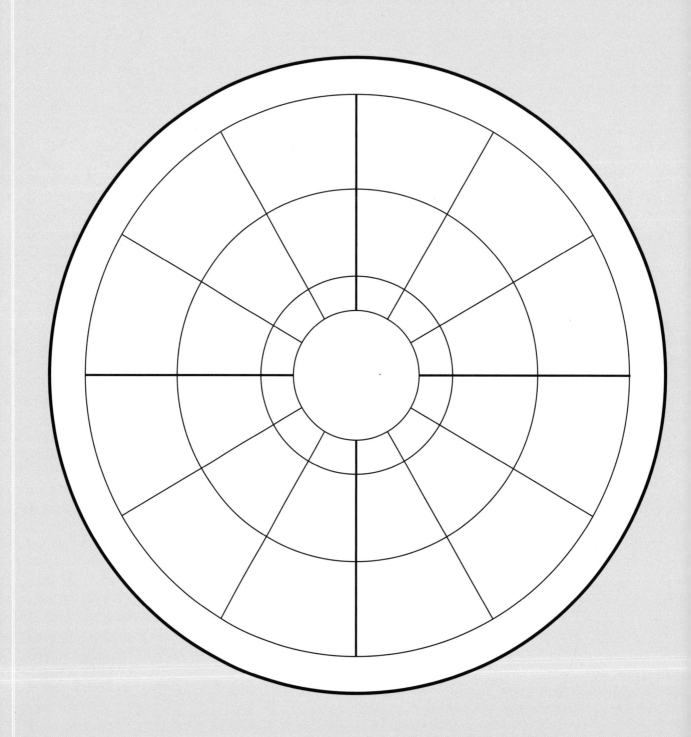

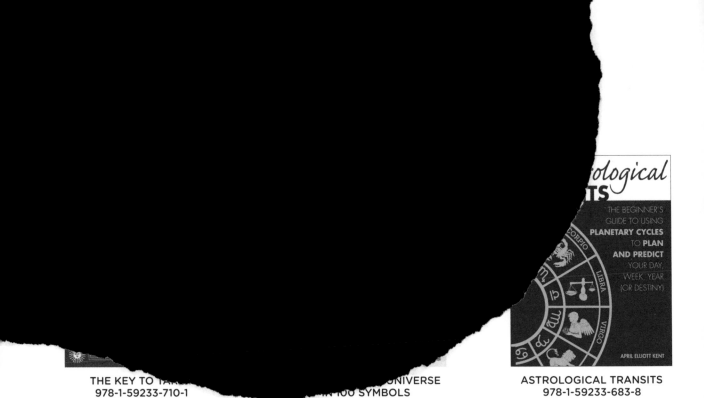

THE KEY TO TAR...
978-1-59233-710-1

...UNIVERSE
...N 100 SYMBOLS
978-1-59233-676-0

ASTROLOGICAL TRANSITS
978-1-59233-683-8

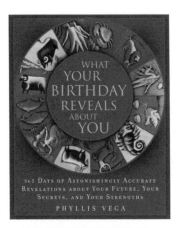

WHAT YOUR BIRTHDAY
REVEALS ABOUT YOU
978-1-59233-170-3

LOVESTROLOGY
978-1-59233-235-9

THE ULTIMATE GUIDE
TO TAROT
978-1-59233-657-9